D1536686

"Psychologist, internationally known actor, human rights activist. Any of these vocations could be a life's work but Hector Aristizábal's life's work encompasses all three. Here is an intimate view of his coming of age in the complex and violent society of Medellín, Colombia, and how his experiences gave him insight and compassion faced with the complex and violent society he found as an immigrant to the U.S. I have witnessed just a small part of his work: bringing hope and healing to those who—like him—are survivors of torture. This book now offers his dramatic story along with his powerful ideas of healing, art, and advocacy to a wider audience." —**José Quiroga, M.D.**, founder and medical director, Program for Torture Victims

"A must read. Hector personifies the suffering of the Colombian people. But his biophilic love of life overcomes the necrophilic love of death and power, as the victims of torture, the victims of crass and brutal violence, elevate their suffering by seeing the world through eyes that have not yet been born." —**Blase Bonpane**, Director, Office of the Americas

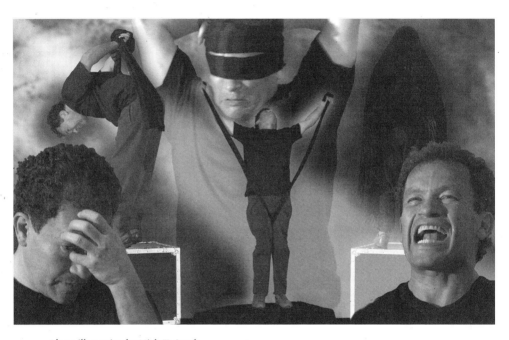

Photo illustration by Nick T. Spark

The
BLESSING
next to the
WOUND

A STORY OF ART, ACTIVISM, AND TRANSFORMATION

Hector Aristizábal and Diane Lefer

LANTERN BOOKS • NEW YORK
A Division of Booklight Inc.

2010
LANTERN BOOKS
128 Second Place
Brooklyn, NY 11231
www.lanternbooks.com

Copyright © 2010 Hector Aristizábal and Diane Lefer

Cover design by J Lops
Cover photo by Nick T. Spark

All rights reserved. No part of this book may be reproduced,
stored in a retrieval system, or transmitted in any form or by
any means, electronic, mechanical, photocopying, recording,
or otherwise, without the written permission of Lantern Books.

Printed in the United States of America

LIBRARY OF CONGRESS CATALOGING-IN-PUBLICATION DATA

Aristizabal, Hector.
 The blessing next to the wound : a story of art, activism, and
transformation / Hector Aristizabal and Diane Lefer.
     p. cm.
 ISBN-13: 978-1-59056-171-3 (alk. paper)
 ISBN-10: 1-59056-171-6
 1. Violence—Colombia—History—20th century.
 2. Colombia—Social conditions—20th century.
 I. Lefer, Diane. II. Title.
 HN307.A37 2010
 303.6'2092—dc22
 [B]
                        2010004078

*Dear Lois
and friends at
East Side Institute*

To the memory of Hernán Darío and Juan Fernando
and to the future of Camilla and Gabo

*Thanks for your commitment to
Social Justice and healing

With my deepest admiration*

Contents

Introduction

FOUR A.M. A LOW-INCOME housing project on the outskirts of Medellín, Colombia. The whole neighborhood shook as military trucks rumbled into the barrio on the hunt for subversives. It was 1982; I was twenty-two years old. We were living under the Estatuto de Seguridad, a repressive law that looked on almost any opposition to the government as Communist-inspired. It was dangerous to talk politics. Sometimes even more dangerous to create art. Friends of mine from the university had been seized and disappeared only to reappear as cadavers found in a ditch, bodies covered with cuts and burns, toes and fingers broken, tongues missing, eyes gouged out.

It could happen to me. With my theater company, I performed plays that encouraged dissent by poking merciless fun at the military and the rich, at presidents and priests. I'd participated in protests and human rights demonstrations and had organized cultural events where we sang the protest songs of Victor Jara and Mercedes Sosa and showed our revolutionary sympathies by watching Cuban films.

It could happen to my younger brother. It might have already happened. Juan Fernando had left the house two days before to go camping with three other kids. Then my family got word he'd been arrested. My father and I went searching for him and were told he'd been turned over to the army, but we hadn't been able to learn his whereabouts or anything about his case. I'd spent a restless night, my sleep troubled by fear for my brother.

Now I was instantly alert. I pulled on a T-shirt and warm-up pants and ran to look out through the blinds. One of the trucks stopped in front of our house directly beneath my window. Should I try to escape? A cold mist made everything indistinct but by the light of the streetlamp, I could see Juan Fernando surrounded by soldiers in the open back of the truck. So at least he was alive. But there was no running for it now. I couldn't try to save myself if the army had my brother.

"Open the door! This is a raid!" A platoon of ten soldiers and a sergeant burst in, pointing their weapons at my terrified parents. My father grabbed our little dog, his beloved Chihuahua, trying to keep her still. "All of you! Sit there!" There was my teenage sister Estela, scared and embarrassed to be seen in the old nightclothes she slept in. There were my brothers—Hernán Darío who was fighting demons of his own that had nothing to do with politics, and Ignacio, the steady, reliable one who worked as a delivery boy to help support the family.

"You!" One of the soldiers pointed his rifle at me. "What's up there?"

"It's where the boys sleep. Me and my brothers."

I led them up the stairs. They overturned furniture, threw clothes and papers everywhere, tossed my mattress as they ransacked my room. I started to calm down as I watched them search. This meant they weren't after me for anything I'd done. They expected to find something and I knew they wouldn't. I always cleaned the house when a government crackdown was expected. Pamphlets that criticized the president, leaflets demanding social justice, anything that mentioned trade unions or socialism—including books assigned at school—I'd gotten rid of everything. That's what I thought, and I was wrong.

When I was fourteen years old, I'd written a letter to Radio Havana

Cuba asking for books and magazines about the Revolution. I was so proud of that letter, I'd kept a copy for myself. I'd forgotten all about it. Now it was in the hands of the soldiers. And worse. Among my school papers, they found a booklet from the ELN, the Ejército de Liberación Nacional, the second largest guerrilla group in the country. This little pamphlet could mean a death sentence. It had to be Juan Fernando's. No one else in the family had any interest in the ELN. Was he hiding it? Or had he left it for me to find, a follow-up to our recent disagreement? Then they picked up the photos. As a psychology student, I'd been documenting the degrading treatment of mental patients at the charity hospital. According to the sergeant, these wretched looking human beings were hostages held by the guerrillas.

My mother cried and begged the soldiers to let me go, but I was handcuffed and pushed out to the street where a cold gray dawn was breaking. All the world's colors seemed washed out, gone. And it was quiet, abnormally quiet. No shouts, no street vendors, no radios. But hundreds of neighbors had come out of their houses to see what was happening. They watched in silence and I remember thinking, *Witnesses*, hoping that would make a difference, that the army would not be able to just disappear us when so many people had seen us detained.

I was put in the back of the truck with my brother.

"Mono!" I called him by his nickname. Soldiers kicked us and struck us with their rifle butts and told us to shut up, but I had to talk to him. If we couldn't explain away that ELN booklet, one or both of us might die. "I'm going to say you've been in the mental hospital, okay?" We could admit yeah, he might have picked up some guerrilla propaganda, but he wasn't capable of understanding what it meant. My brother said nothing, but his eyes were full of pain.

We were driven to Batallón Bomboná, an army post in another part of town. We entered the compound followed by three more trucks, each carrying one of the boys who'd gone camping with Mono. Soldiers ordered us out and stood us facing a wall. It was cold as hell out there in the yard. I shivered until the sun came up at last, throwing shadows against the whitewashed adobe. I can still remember the brief touches of warmth, now on my shoulders, now my back.

Comunistas! Subversivos! Soldiers ran by in formation, hollering insults: *Hijueputas!* The firing squad stopped and aimed their rifles. Someone shouted: *The one with the red shirt!* Bang! *The one with the long hair!* My heart exploded in my throat. *Long hair* meant me. Bullets slammed into the wall again and again just above our heads, but didn't hit us.

What were they going to do to us? We stood under guard for hours at that wall. The morning went on and on and I waited.

"Don't look!" But I looked, and saw a short fat man lead my brother's friends away, one by one. They were so young, just kids. What would happen to them? At last the soldiers brought them back. "Don't look!" But I saw the boys were soaking wet and trembling. "Shut up! Don't talk!" But there were whispers. *We were tortured. They were tortured. They were tortured.*

The man took Juan Fernando. Minutes went by. Hours. He didn't bring my brother back. Images roared through my mind: mutilated bodies, my brother's face. Torture. When the man came back, he was alone.

The man came for me.

He led me up a hill to a cell at the end of a long, one-story building. He blindfolded me. He demanded information. "Where are you keeping the hostages?" He beat me. He kicked me. He forced my head underwater again and again, bringing me to the verge of drowning.

"Your brother has told us everything," he said. "So have his little friends. We know you're an urban guerrilla commander. You're the one who's training those kids."

The son-of-a-bitch had to be lying. Juan Fernando would never have said such a thing.

"He's crazy," I said. "My brother has been hospitalized." The worst pain was imagining what they might do to him. "Please don't hurt him."

I thought of Mono's growing sympathy for the guerrilla movement. It was what we argued about. Maybe he was more involved than I'd realized or had wanted to know. So what? He was my brother and I would do what I could to protect him.

"He's not responsible. He has mental problems."

Soldiers attached electrodes to my testicles and sent jolts of electricity tearing through every nerve. They twisted my arms up behind my back and left me hanging until the pain and helplessness became so great, I was blown right out of my body and mind. Soldiers drove me around in a small jeep. One forced the barrel of his rifle into my mouth. "You're going to die now," he said. "Just like your brother."

Instead, they forced me into an underground passage where I found Mono, alive, and his friends, all of us hidden from view while—as we later learned—a human rights delegation searched for us somewhere above our heads. The ceiling of our dungeon was so low we had to crawl. The air was hot, thick, and the stench unbearable from human waste and from the festering wounds of a black man from Chocó we found chained and shackled there, bleeding to death in the dark. He told us he had no idea why he'd been arrested and tortured. "Worse than a street animal," he said. Nothing we could do could help him or ease his pain till it turned out another prisoner had bribed a guard for marijuana. "Here, brother." The dying man filled his lungs and began to laugh and the smoke filled the dark and filthy crawlspace. We all filled our lungs and laughed and I believe I'll hear our laughter echoing in that cave and in my nightmares for the rest of my life.

IT MUST HAVE BEEN the witnesses and the human rights delegation that saved us. We could have been executed in secret. Instead we were brought before a judge. Our mental hospital story worked. The ELN booklet was deemed harmless, but my brother and the other boys went to prison for carrying a subversive weapon—a machete. Mono went in an idealistic young man. He came out a committed revolutionary, convinced no alternative existed to the armed struggle.

As for me, ten days after my arrest, the army let me go, but the ordeal marked me. It marks me still.

I'm marked as well by my self-inflicted wounds. Years later, in California, my life was a shambles. My marriage had collapsed and the identity I'd so painstakingly constructed in exile had shattered. I was overwhelmed by my history of loss: I'd lost my country and my language and so many people I loved to violent death. Then the photographs from Abu Ghraib seared themselves into the nation's consciousness and I was galvanized back into action. I was asked to participate in an anti-torture event. When I improvised a few scenes about my experience, I saw immediately that I'd brought home to the audience the human reality of torture in a way no newspaper account or news broadcast could do. The pain I'd suffered was now a source of power—the blessing next to the wound. To carry the message further I asked my friends Diane Lefer, BJ Dodge, and Enzo Fina—a writer, a director, and a musician—to collaborate with me. We created the play *Nightwind*, which I've now performed all over the United States and around the world.

This work helped me heal from torture, but offstage I was still a mess. Some days, I felt myself disintegrating, plunging into the void, but I always knew for the sake of my two young children I had to regain my footing.

When I worked as a therapist, I often asked clients to tell me the story of their lives. I would then offer them narratives in which they could recognize not just themselves, but their strengths. I would invite them to discover what they'd learned and could make use of from the most difficult experiences. And so I began to tell Diane my story—all of it—and I asked her to write it.

Chapter 1

Origins

I came of age in Medellín, Colombia, at the time considered the most dangerous city in the world. In the barrio where we lived, few jobs and little opportunity for education existed and so it was prime recruiting ground for Colombia's four armies: the government military, the right wing death squads, the revolutionary guerrilla groups, and the cocaine mafia. I buried most of the kids I played soccer with and I assumed that my life, too, would be short, and my death a violent one.

My generation was not the first to be plagued by violence and early death.

My father's family were peasants, driven out of the mountains by the civil war that raged between the country's Liberal and Conservative parties. In those days, the late 1940s, just as today, ideology wasn't the only, or even primary motive for the killings. Armed factions sowed terror in order to take possession of fertile lands and wherever natural resources could be found to be exploited. And so the Aristizábals arrived in the city. My father, Pedro, a teenager without formal education, found work at Fabricato, the huge textile mill in the town of Bello, which made him one of those fortunate enough to be employed.

My parents met when my mother, Nidia, was taking a stroll—*un paseo*—with her married sisters. In Latin America, the *paseo* was a highly respectable form of cruising, a way for single people to meet. My parents liked each other right away, but their courtship lasted three years as my father couldn't afford to marry. He was supporting his entire family and was committed to putting his younger brother through school. My Uncle Marcos had his arm blown off as a child when he picked up a stick of dynamite that had been left near a gold mine. His stump limited his capacity for manual labor but also opened up an opportunity. Thanks to my father's hard work, he had the chance to become a teacher. I looked up to him as the one educated member of the family while I failed, as a child, to appreciate my father's generous sacrifice. My father has always shown his deepest feelings through his actions rather than his words. When we kids were growing up, he never raised a hand or an angry voice to us, but it's taken me many years to recognize his tenderness and the nonverbal language he uses to express love.

My mother's family was more solidly working class: slightly, though significantly more prosperous. My mother was twenty-seven when she married, considered way past a woman's prime for that time and place, and she was entirely ignorant of the facts of life. As far as she knew, babies came when a woman secluded herself in a room with her knitting and waited for the Virgin Mary to bring the newborn. Nidia was only nine when her mother bled to death behind such a closed door, miscarrying what would have been her twelfth child. Her father remarried, and her stepmother also died soon in childbirth, but these events remained mysterious and unexplained to Nidia. As she prepared for her wedding, no one—not even the married sisters who'd chaperoned her first meetings with Pedro—told her anything of the intimacies of married life. When my father tried to consummate the marriage, she was horrified. How could her respectful, gentle suitor even consider such a thing?!

For all her strict religious belief and clinging to respectability, my mother never seemed to accept the notion of sin. She retained an innocence that made her see everyone as God's children, and she only saw the good in people. When a neighborhood man and reputed murderer, nicknamed Peligro, which means Danger, tried to befriend my youngest brother, my mother was moved by his kindly friendliness. My mother always blamed herself for what she learned years later about their relationship. As a teenager, I was cruel to my mother, dismissing her values in ways that tore at her heart. I demanded that she see life as it really was, or as I, at that time, believed it to be.

When Pedro and Nidia did marry at last, they had help from my mother's father who let them live at nominal rent in the big house he owned behind his workshop. So that's where I was born in 1960, in that big old house in Bello, and spent my early years fascinated by Grandpa Carlos and his skill at repairing cars and doing all sorts of things with hammers, drills, torches, and soldering irons.

On the other side of the garden wall, the neighbor's mango tree held the sweetest fruit in the world, a constant temptation to my brothers and me. We would climb to the top of our own tree and then step onto the crumbling wall that divided our yards and brave the three vicious dogs that guarded the mangoes as though they were golden apples of the gods. An abandoned chicken coop became our submarine, our space ship, even the lamp from which a genie appeared to grant our every wish. We had never seen an actual computer, but we knew the power of computers from *Star Trek*, and when our games reached crisis point, we often asked our imaginary computer what to do.

I was the oldest: the instigator and clown. My mother says even in the cradle I made *muecas*—funny faces—to get her attention. Next came Ignacio, lover of almanacs. When we submerged, à la Jules Verne, to the bottom of the sea, he told us that Lake Titicaca lies 3,810 meters above sea level, covers 8,300 square kilometers, and reaches its greatest recorded depth at 280 meters. Juan Fernando, nicknamed Mono—

Colombian slang for *blond*—came next. He was the biggest and tallest and most likely strongest of us all, but he never used his strength to intimidate. Mono never spoke much. He rarely invented our games, but quietly took every heroic action. I admired his self-containment, which I saw even as a child as nobility of soul.

We didn't always want to play with our youngest brother, Hernán Darío. He cried easily. He was afraid of falling, of getting hit when the games got rough, of getting hurt. When we needed someone, though, to play the poor widow woman who needed rescue, we chose Hernán Darío. We teased him and called him names: "pío pío," the *cheep cheep* of a baby chick; "Nidio," a play on my mother's name as a way to call him "mama's boy," and other words—ugly words like "maricón," or "faggot," syllables that today taste like poison on my lips. The real girl in the family, Estela, was a baby, too young to join us. She was born sickly and spent her early months in an incubator and even required a full transfusion of blood. Estela was different from the rest of us, with a hot temper, quick to anger, something we attributed to the transfusion, saying, "Who knows whose blood she inherited?"

In those early days, I wanted to grow up to be a fireman or else a scientist. I had no idea what a scientist was or what one did, but I'd heard people speak with admiration about Albert Einstein and, since he was a scientist, I figured I would be one, too. I was even more excited when I heard he had invented a "theory"—whatever *that* was—even though he hadn't done well in school.

One day my Uncle Marcos told me my name meant "entertainer" and my middle name, Augusto, meant "intelligent." In Spanish, we don't pronounce the "h" so "Hector" does sound very much like "actor." But if you look me up in a dictionary of names, you'll find that Hector means no such thing, but is the Latin version of the Greek for *steadfast*—very different from my own impulsive self. My uncle's translation of Augusto wasn't accurate either, but I liked being called *intelligent* and took his words very much to heart. I excelled in school and grew up to be an actor.

WHEN I WAS TEN, Grandpa Carlos sold his property and my father was confronted with the challenge of paying real rent. In Medellín, the government was trying something new, building a whole neighborhood intended for low-income workers. For a lower mortgage than you could find anywhere else, a family could move into an unfinished adobe structure and then, with savings, bit by bit turn it into a completed house. During the nineteen years we lived there, we never had a spare penny for improvements and the building remained forever in a state of incompleteness and disrepair. When you showered, you had to be careful not to step in the hole in the bathroom floor. I used to say we lived in a house with leprosy, because the adobe was crumbling, chunks constantly falling from the walls. And it's where our family itself began falling to pieces.

Life in the barrio was noisy, crowded, overflowing—the street vendors calling out their wares: *plátanos, bananos, verduras,* or offering to repair irons or sharpen knives. Voices carried from the houses nearby—arguments, sometimes violent ones. Early each morning, my mother would wake my brothers and me. The four of us slept on the second floor in what we called our rooms though they lacked doors. Music would erupt joyfully from the homes of the Afro-Colombians who'd fled the violence in Chocó. Cars honked on the narrow streets and on the nearby highway, and the trains whistled as they pulled into the station and then picked up speed along the dangerous tracks where we were forbidden to play and always did. Lalo was killed trying to jump onto a moving train. Beto lost both legs. The danger didn't stop me. The chance to see the world, or at least ride to the next town, was irresistible, and good practice for the life-and-death challenge of going to high school. Though buses passed on the highway nearby, they were always full by the time they got to the barrio at rush hour. The only way to ride was to grab onto the outside of a window and try to hang on while the driver turned the bus into a bucking bronco.

Our house had electricity, but no hot water. To this day, I shower in cold water, not understanding how a person can feel clean after immersion in something the temperature of piss. We argued in the morning over who would get to shower first and use our shared towel while it was still dry. I was often the one sent off to the bakery to buy sweet rolls for breakfast, the fresh bread we dunked in hot chocolate. Going to the bakery wasn't bad—the baker usually gave me an extra treat— but sometimes I would find something terribly important to do, something that absolutely couldn't wait, and fight with my brothers until one of them agreed (or was compelled) to go.

The baker was a neighbor who put an extra large oven in his kitchen. Everybody had a sideline. Even with full-time wages, it was impossible to make ends meet. The unfinished houses all remained just that way until some kids started dealing drugs or working as mafia hitmen and suddenly, their houses got done. Three doors down from us, Claudia's mother sold socks and underwear out of the living room. I was at the age where I fell in love with almost every girl I saw, but Claudia, two years older than I, was special. I loved her from afar and imagined her initiating me into the mysteries of sex. In a way, that's what would happen, but not how anyone would have wished.

Our family had sidelines, too. My father sold cheap perfumes on the street. At night, after his day job, he managed a bar. For a while, we tried selling ice cream. This meant investing in a freezer and traveling by bus to the distributor of Helados Alpina to bring the product home. But the vanilla covered in chocolate topping was so delicious, we kids ate up all the profits, and after a couple of years, my parents took the Alpina sign out of our window.

I missed the ice cream business. Too many meals consisted of salted water with a bit of potato floating in it, creating in me an eternal aversion to soup. We drank *agua panela*—water with brown sugar—the energy drink common to the army, the guerrillas, and the poor. Sometimes we took the bus back to Bello, to the cooperative store where we could buy staples like rice, beans, and soap in bulk at discount prices. The problem was, at the co-op you had to pay in cash which is something my father rarely had. So like everyone else in the barrio, we bought on credit from the local store and paid when we could. The store was the sideline of a retired policeman and he routinely cheated his customers, adding all sorts of charges for things we didn't buy. It enraged me that my father knew he was being cheated but never challenged the man, as if to say beggars can't be choosers.

For years I looked down on Pedro, my father, and considered him a peasant. I hated the sight of him at the dinner table sucking the marrow from a bone as a substitute for meat, little dreaming that one day I would be a prisoner, and grateful to the soldier who gave me a bone from his own meager rations.

IN THE BARRIO, I became street smart. Some streets were paved, some weren't. Most of the streetlights were out; breaking them with rocks was a favorite pastime. We were all obsessed with soccer, playing for hours with balls made of crumpled newspaper tied up with twine. Some of us had shoes, some didn't. Mafia guys scouted our games. Who was most aggressive? Who bullied the other kids? Who looked the most hungry? By the age of twelve, some of my friends had already been recruited into crime, but I'd discovered books. I preferred to sit up on the second-floor balcony, looking out over the games and arguments going on below, the air heavy with fumes from the chemical plant nearby. I'd read while holding my little transistor radio to my ear, the sound so faint it could hardly be heard over the noisy life happening around me. In those days, my greatest dream was to have a giant sound system with which I could flood the world with the magnificent music of Mozart and Pink Floyd.

LIKE MOST COLOMBIAN CHILDREN, I was initiated early into the beliefs and rites of the Catholic Church. Though I have rejected much of what I was taught, I carry the imprint of mythic scenes of sacrifice and resurrection or rebirth. More problematic for me was what seemed the absolute split between good and evil, and the split between body and soul. There seemed no way to reconcile my carnal desires with the strictures of the Church, and the local priest bored me with his monotonous drone. Yes, the Latin American bishops met in Medellín in 1968 to affirm their commitment to Liberation Theology and to the poor, but I saw no evidence of this commitment around me. I harangued my devout relatives with speeches about the evils of the Inquisition, the extermination of the pre-Columbian peoples, and the wealth of the Vatican compared to the poverty of the faithful.

At the same time, I wanted to sacrifice myself to something larger, become larger through expansion of the soul, and so I began a spiritual search. Mormon missionaries came to the barrio and I was briefly intrigued by rumors of multiple wives. I rejected the Hari Krishnas. Long hair was my sign of rebellion, and I wasn't about to shave my head for any god.

At that time, I didn't think to explore traditional cultures. I'd grown up with folklore: Madre Monte, the huge woman who represented Nature; La Llorona who roamed through the dark, wailing and seeking children to abduct and who we thought of when we heard cats yowling in the night; the maleficent El Patatarro with his rotting leg; and El Sincabeza, the decapitated peasant who rode his horse through the countryside looking for people to behead.

Instead I turned to other ancient traditions and immersed myself in mysticism: Gnosis and Rosicrucianism, cabalistic knowledge, Egyptian and Greek mysteries about the Inner Order and the Outer Order. I devoured all the books on esoteric knowledge that I could find—Alpha and Omega, The Golden Dawn, Eastern philosophies, the seven chakras—finding magical theories that explained all the mysteries of life and death. I dreamed that some day I would be able to read and understand the Emerald Tablet of Hermes, or find access to the cabalistic Tree of Life and transform myself into a wizard of white magic. My task in life was to raise myself up to the highest possible state of consciousness, above plants, animals, and my less evolved fellow humans.

Some of our neighbors turned their rooms at night into centers for Gnostic meetings. It took me a while to see that my fellow believers were poor, uneducated people who had known nothing but misery. They fantasized about magical powers since they saw no other way to gain power in this world over their own lives. One day, an old lady suggested to me that I could become the "kalki avatara" of the Aquarius era, just as Jesus had been the "kalki avatara" of the Pisces era. Even given my moments of grandiosity, I don't think I believed her, but instead of setting her straight, I swore her to secrecy.

In spite of my spiritual search, my blossoming sexual desires never stopped sabotaging my metaphysical efforts. I remember trying to transmute my sexual energy into fuel for my astral trips so I could travel in my dreams to any place in the world. En route to the ancient pyramids, my astral itinerary took detours in the hopes I'd get to see people having sex or, at the very least, watch the most attractive female neighbors I knew taking off their clothes. I tried esoteric breathing to gain longevity like Samael Aun Weor, the Gnostic writer, who was supposedly 230 years old. I used to meditate upside down like a bat until I hyperventilated. Then, my body shaking, I would come downstairs, convinced my family could see me levitating. My biggest spiritual struggles took place in the bathroom, the only place I could be totally alone to do my higher practice. As illustrated in the Gnostic books, I used my right hand to hold my nose while chanting a mantra and imagining my semen traveling like a snake from my sexual chakra, up my spinal cord, and into my third eye. In the meantime, however, I could not stop my left hand from playing with my penis. About ninety-nine percent of the time it was my left hand that won the battle, and my supreme energy ended up against the bathroom walls.

FROM MY PERCH ABOVE the street, I read—no, *devoured*—books, sometimes two a day: Cervantes, Dostoevsky, García Márquez, Shakespeare, and any other author I could get my hands on. In the printed word, I sought social and spiritual truth, seeking the life models that were not to be seen in the physical world around me.

I read Marx and Engels and the booklets I received about the Cuban Revolution from Radio Havana. Now I could really be a pain-in-the-ass militant around my relatives, not only criticizing their beloved Church, but asserting the supreme scientific truth of dialectical materialism. Utopia was possible here and now if I could only convince them to participate in the insurrection needed to overthrow the government. All that happened was that my grandfather called me the Antichrist and threw me out of his house.

My grandfather surely thought my book-knowledge had ruined me. In truth, it may have made me obnoxious, but it also stimulated my mind and saved me, kept me from joining street gangs or guerrilla armies. I went into battle with words and ideas, with passionate beliefs, many of which I would repudiate as I grew.

When I discovered Wilhelm Reich, his work became my main inspiration. I was attracted to him as an eternal rebel. He'd been expelled from both the German Communist Party and from the Psychoanalytic International and his fate confirmed my worst suspicions about the United States, as he died incarcerated in this country. Reich explained that sexual repression of the people, especially the youth, was what allowed those in power to oppress the masses. What could be better? Through Reich we could have our revolution and orgasm, too.

At first, this was nothing but theory.

Chapter 2

The Womb as Tomb

A guttural wail tore through the air. I was fifteen, just dressed and ready to leave for school and this awful sound was coming from Claudia's house, three doors down. She was the girl I loved and dreamed about, and so I ran as fast as I could to be by her side. I found her father trying to calm his wife who shrieked, distraught, while Claudia's brother punched the wall, grunting like a wounded animal.

The door to her bedroom was open, the bedroom I'd entered so many times in my adolescent fantasies. Now, no one stopped me. Claudia lay in bed, her pretty brown face drained pale, her body floating in a pool of blood, her eyes fixed somewhere in eternity. She had bled to death after aborting a fetus that later that morning was found clogging the toilet.

She was seventeen years old.

WHEN *I* WAS SEVENTEEN, I met Julia. It was, in what would prove to be my usual way, love at first sight. Sometimes I think Julia saved me, focusing all my urgency and violent energy into tenderness and passion. Certainly, she gave me what I now look back on as some of the happiest, most ecstatic days of my life. Julia was generous and patient and while she didn't always understand me, she understood how to be with me. I was different from the boys she was used to. If a film moved me, I didn't want to talk about it. Words would break the spell, when all I wanted was to stay inside its magic. We'd leave the theater in silence. I'd close my eyes to block out the real world around us and Julia would take my arm and lead me safely home. I used to compare her to a flower growing in the middle of a train track, fresh and unspoiled no matter how much social garbage passed over her. Together, we explored and experienced all the joys of young, new sexuality.

Of course, we had no place to go. Even when it was possible for me to obtain condoms, somehow I never had them just at the rare moments when we had a chance to be alone. So we stole what intimacy we could, passionate and desperate for each other and usually unprepared. We took risks. There was too much bliss in giving ourselves to one another with everything we had. Being together, joining our bodies—*that*, not the possible consequences, was a matter of life and death.

When Julia became pregnant, we were terrified. We were alone with our secret in a country where abortion is illegal, even when medically necessary to save a woman's life. Somehow, I managed to find a doctor and, though we had no money, I convinced him to help us. That's how we dealt with it. The first time.

I HAD MORE REASON than ever to escape into a world of passion with Julia as life wasn't happy at home. My childish idea had been that my family would always be together. Since high school, I'd been writing and acting and I'd had the chance to visit other towns and cities to perform. Theater was starting to open up the wider world to me and I wanted my brothers to have the same chances. I believed Hernán Darío had more talent than I did, so I decided we would start a theater company together. Or maybe we would found an important publishing house. Whatever we did, it would be creative and wonderful and we'd all live together in a huge house with wives and girlfriends and lots of children. I led my younger brothers to see films at the Goethe Institute where people stared to see children in attendance, children obviously from the barrio. I wanted the boys to be stunned, as I was, by Werner Herzog's *Aguirre, the Wrath of God*. I'd gone to a public college-prep high school, probably the best secondary education in Medellín, and I wanted them to do the same. But first Ignacio and then Juan Fernando—Mono—dropped out of school.

My dream wasn't working out, though my mother said the boys followed in my footsteps all the same. "You brought all the plagues to this house!" she accused me. "Drugs! Sex! Communism! Atheism!"

Mono spent most of his time hanging out in the street. Hernán Darío sneaked out the window at night. Ignacio, always the serious one, went to work, came home, and kept his head down and his thoughts to himself. I used to think he was the most intelligent of us all, but now he retreated from the turmoil at home and in the barrio into an unreflective life of survival. And almost from the time we'd left Bello, there had been problems in my parents' marriage. Estela, *la niña*, now shared a bed with our mother and drowned every night in Nidia's helplessness and tears while struggling with problems of her own that remained unspoken.

My father worked all day at the textile mill, mostly as a *gomador*, spending long shifts in a room filled with heavy steam as he operated the machinery that sprayed huge bobbins of filling yarn with the conditioner that set it and got out the kinks. He also worked weekends and nights to make ends meet or maybe to get away from an old-fashioned wife and five rowdy kids. Besides the venture of our short-lived ice cream business, he sold wicker chairs. He managed a series of bars, including *Las Brisas*, where he became involved with the waitress.

Hernán Darío took our mother's side. Once, blocking the door, he told my father to go away and stay away. This was the only time I ever saw Juan Fernando get violent, as he grabbed our youngest brother, slammed him against the wall and told him he needed to respect our father, no matter what. Estela, sadly, as she too often did, just blocked out everything happening around her and remained silent.

As far as I was concerned, if my father wanted to live with someone else, that was his choice and I said as much, a naïve know-it-all. After all, thanks to a purely ideological understanding of life, I'd rejected any notion of monogamy and marriage. I adored Julia, and we would remain together for years, but once I entered the university, my world expanded and she didn't grow along with me. I met lots of women who excited me and I seduced as many as I could. Julia was always generous with me and I was deeply grateful but I failed to see that sincere gratitude in the heart is no substitute for reciprocity.

I was essentially clueless about how complicated relationships, especially marriage, can be and Reich and Marx were not much help. I lost patience when Dad kept telling me what a wonderful woman my mother was: "the best." I didn't need to hear that while I watched "the best" become a river of sorrow. My mother made me her confidante. Instead of comforting her, I confronted her with her sexual hang-ups, and flaunted my own liberated sexuality.

Sex was delicious. Sex was great, while the evidence was all around me: sex was also danger.

JULIA WAS PREGNANT AGAIN. She tried douching with detergent. She swallowed down all sorts of concoctions made of traditional herbs, but she was still pregnant and I was too ashamed and indebted to approach the doctor again. Instead, I found a nurse.

The nurse wanted to help, but she didn't want to risk prison. So she agreed to let us use her apartment. She'd leave the instruments there, waiting for us, and she agreed to tell me what to do. "But I won't be there. I have nothing to do with this if anything goes wrong."

I knew very well what could go wrong. I'd seen how Claudia paid with her life, but I shut off those memories. I was terrified enough as Julia and I entered the nurse's unfamiliar room.

"Julia, are you all right?"

Yes, she was ready to go through with it. I still ask myself why: because she trusted me, because she was desperate, because we were young and unable to recognize consequences? And me? I knew her body, I'd seen and loved every inch of it; but the way I was seeing it now was different.

The nurse had kept her word. There was the metal tool, the speculum. That's what I had to put into her vagina so I could see inside. Then, at hand, the nurse had left me the tweezers and the *sonda*, the probe, just as she had promised.

"Julia, are you all right?"

She was so scared, her voice hardly came out, but she said she was.

Use the tweezers to insert the probe in the cervix. It looks just like the behind of a chicken.

"Are you all right, Julia?"

"It's okay." She was crying in pain, but she said, "Keep going."

I slowly pushed the probe up to the cervix and then stopped. I couldn't do this. I stood there frozen until Julia said again, "Keep going." Holding my breath, I pushed the probe through the cervix and into her uterus. Gone.

"Now what?"

Now we had to wait for her uterus to expel the foreign object, along with the fetus.

This is the hardest story for me to tell.

The next day we were with a group of friends when Julia began to have painful contractions. She jumped up from her chair and rushed away. I followed. We found a bathroom and I stood with her as blood and mucus came pouring out. "Are you all right?" I kept asking, but she was in too much pain to answer. Then I saw the probe pushing its way out of her body. I reached for it and pulled it and as I did, a fetus came pumping out from the lips of her vagina and into my hands. "Don't look!"

Neither one of us had known what to expect, and I wasn't prepared for this. I found a plastic bag in the trash and placed the fetus inside. I made Julia sit down and held her a moment, asking again if she were all right. I was desperate to know she was okay but also desperate to take the bag and be gone before she could see what it held.

"Don't look!" But I looked and saw the small chest inflate in what was probably its last breath in this world. That's when I understood what we had done. "Are you all right?" I asked once more and when Julia said *yes*, I left her just long enough to carry the bag outside in the dark and hide it in the bushes. I imagined eyes watching me, condemning me, and I imagined wild animals feeding off the small mass of flesh that could have become our own baby.

We were lucky. My probing didn't puncture Julia's womb. And the nurse had left pills for her to take to prevent infection.

I wish it had not happened. I believe I will never get over it. But if I had my life to live over again, I would make the same choice. It seemed like the only choice we had.

THERE WAS ANOTHER NURSE in Medellín. Her name was Carmen and she was estranged from her respectable family because they knew of her secret life. Carmen was not just an advocate for change; she risked prison every day by performing safe but illegal abortions. I became the go-between, putting desperate students from the university in touch with her.

For me, attending Antioquia University was like winning the lottery, as 3,500 students applied and there were places for only 250. Though it was a public institution and the fees were low, they were impossibly high for my family and so I took out loans and worked a variety of part-time jobs which taught me as much as school did.

There were several entrances to campus where guards checked student IDs before letting you pass the wrought-iron gates. I always came onto the grounds from Avenida Barranquilla, which put the science, mathematics, and engineering buildings to the right, humanities and social sciences quite appropriately on the left. The intellectual discourse of the 1970s and 80s melded Marxism with psychoanalysis and so you couldn't study psychology or literature or theater in those days without being exposed to leftist ideology.

France was the country we all dreamed of as we read Julia Kristeva and Jacques Lacan. We studied culture through the lens of structuralism and post-structuralism, building on the theories of linguist Ferdinand de Saussure and anthropologist Claude Lévi-Strauss. For all the radical activity on campus, no graffiti was painted on the buildings; we had too much love and respect for the places where we attended class. But slogans covered every other bare surface of concrete wall: *¡Venceremos! ¡Muerte al Imperialismo Yanqui! ¡Patria o Muerte!* and the initials of the whole alphabet of leftist groups: *FARC, ELN, EPL, PCMLN, MOIR, M-19.* I spent a lot of my time in the theater department but my official course of study was psychology. The subject matter fascinated me, and I was also driven to seek help for my increasingly troubled family, especially for Hernán Darío, whose drug use had clearly progressed beyond experimentation to addiction.

The campus had shade trees and flowers—Hernán Darío would have known all their names. The buildings, dating back to 1803, had cantilevered red-tile roofs and, built of beautifully weathered brick rather than adobe, already seemed to promise initiation to a world far beyond the barrio. There was an athletic center with a swimming pool and running track and, perhaps of more interest, "the airport," the adjoining secluded grove where students went to smoke marijuana and to make love, accounting for much of Carmen's business.

The phone would ring at home. Another girl asking for me. My mother knew I had other girlfriends besides Julia, but so many?

"I have a problem and I heard that you could help."

"Who told you that?"

"Antonia." Good. I'd helped Antonia a month earlier. It was less risky for Carmen when the referral came from someone who had herself violated the law.

"Okay. Can we meet? Tomorrow in the cafeteria at 10:00? I'm a skinny guy with long curly hair," I told her. "I'll be carrying a copy of *Las formaciones del inconsciente*." In fact, I recognized *her*. I had experience at this game now, and pregnant girls were often easy to spot. It was the glazed look in Tita's eyes and the stiff way she walked. Like so many others, from the moment she learned she was pregnant, she must have girdled her stomach tightly, terrified that anything would show.

In the cafeteria, I got her a cup of coffee. In those days, I was always broke and living on Coca-Cola (so much for my anti-imperialist rhetoric!) and guava-cheese pastry, but the girls were always scared and I felt it was my responsibility to treat them to at least some little thing. We found a small table in a corner.

I usually heard explanations like this:

"If my father finds out, he'll kill me."

"If I don't end the pregnancy, my boyfriend will leave me."

"My parents will blame the university. They always said higher education isn't for girls."

But what Tita said made me identify with her right away. She was desperate to finish school, receive a degree, and start to earn money. Her family, like mine, was counting on her to lift them out of poverty.

I explained the procedure and asked if she had a place. It was too risky for Carmen to let any patient know her name or address and she didn't dare do the work in her home.

"I live with my parents," Tita said.

Of course: How would she have the money for a place of her own?

There was a place I sometimes had access to and that's where we went.

If Tita's boyfriend was still in the picture, he had decided not to be involved, and so while Carmen worked, I was the one who held Tita's hand.

While Carmen cleaned up, I tried to talk to Tita about what we'd just done, but she kept her eyes closed and as soon as she felt well enough to leave, she was gone.

Every time I made an introduction, a fetus was aspirated away, but I told myself I was saving someone from Claudia's fate. I kept reliving my own experience without ever facing it, at least not directly or consciously. But there I was, again and again, because I had something to learn even though I told myself I was there with something to teach. I imagined I could use my developing skills as a therapist and counselor to listen to the girls, talk with them about the experience. A wound won't heal when it's hidden, and no matter how necessary an abortion may be, no matter how right the decision, the mind and soul may need help coming to terms with the womb that is also a tomb.

Though I was incapable of recognizing these truths in my own life, I looked at these young women and knew that as long as they denied and ignored the consequences of their actions, they would remain caught up in behavior that would return them again and again to their wound. But most of the young women I brought to Carmen didn't want to talk. The fear and shame were too great. As soon as the procedure was over, they wanted to be invisible, anonymous, gone. They resumed their daily lives with the pretense that nothing at all had happened.

I could not presume to know what went on in the hearts of the young women I brought to Carmen, but I knew the conflict inside of me. If Julia and I were to have a baby, the only word I could think of for the situation was *disaster*. Abortion? Of course. But at the same time, I longed to be a father. I'd always wanted to bring life into the world, to raise children. Having a baby was out of the question. It was also what I wanted from very deep places in my soul. But we never talked about this. We remained trapped in our cycle of bliss and terror. So did the young couples on campus.

And so the phone would ring.

"Hi, it's Tita. I need your help."

"You have a friend?"

"No. It's for me."

Again.

YEARS LATER IN THE U.S., I faced young pregnant girls again and again. With my Masters degree in psychology earned in Medellín along with a Masters in marriage and family therapy earned in California, I offered my services as a therapist and counselor for pregnant teens and with kids coping with the powerful drives of sexuality. I wasn't there to tell them what to do but rather, I hoped, to help them make sense of their lives. Most likely, I was trying to make sense of my own.

In California, I've met incarcerated girls who've given birth as many as three times without ever experiencing motherhood. The way the system works here, if a girl gives birth in a Youth Authority facility, she's allowed only two days with the baby. If no relative is willing to take the child, it goes up for adoption right away.

This shocks me. When I led workshops in a women's prison in Pune, India, children were everywhere, allowed to live with their mothers until age five. After that time, they could return to visit, but the moment of separation was of course a very difficult and traumatic one. Together, we designed a letting-go ritual for the mothers and children to acknowledge that rupture in their lives.

Two weeks after I returned to California from India, I met Jackie. She wasn't a criminal, just a kid who became affiliated with a gang at age thirteen. Her parents weren't looking out for her, gang activity was the norm in her neighborhood, and no one on earth seemed cooler than the gang member she fell in love with. He briefly made her feel cherished, like someone who mattered. Next thing she knew, she was pregnant, and locked up. Jackie never even saw the life she gave birth to. There was no time for attachment, or mourning, or even consciousness. She ended up feeling she'd never even had a baby.

Jackie got out on parole and almost immediately got pregnant again. Once again, she served just as a body. The baby came out and then the baby was gone.

For three years, I worked with students at the Los Angeles opportunity school that pregnant girls as young as twelve can choose to attend. These are kids who've been "abandoned" by parents who work all the time to keep a roof over their heads. They've grown up in the streets, educated by the influence of the media and then pressured into sexuality at a very early age. They end up getting pregnant in the first or second experience of having a penis inside of them. I was amazed to learn most of these girls did not know what a clitoris was. They'd never heard that females could experience orgasm. Even those who did have information about condoms and other ways of avoiding pregnancy didn't think it could happen at age twelve or thirteen. They were children who had bodies capable of reproducing life though their minds and souls didn't yet know much about what life really is.

We live in a culture where kids are constantly sexualized: by rap music, television commercials, porn sites on the Internet, mainstream fashion and more. Yet the honest discussion is silenced. It seems nothing is as taboo in our society as sex.

When I facilitate groups, there's a theater game I play in which I invite people to create a machine. One person begins making a mechanical, repetitive motion. Someone joins in onstage adding another action; someone joins and adds a third movement until an entire machine is working away before our eyes. I say "The machine is sad," and everyone continues moving, but dejectedly now, and with sighs. "The machine is happy," and the rhythm turns bouncy and fast. I turn the machine into a serial killer and people go along with it, vicious and menacing. But almost every time, especially if I'm working with adults, when I say, "the machine is horny," everyone stops, embarrassed.

For some girls at the opportunity school, pregnancy made their whole world collapse. Others were thrilled to be having a baby to love, something to hold onto from the boyfriend who dumped them, or might be in prison, or might be dead tomorrow in gang violence or in Iraq or maybe was already dead.

Most of the students were immigrants or else the first generation born in the U.S. Some didn't know abortion was legal here. Most were Catholic and were raised to see abortion as a sin. I know if my daughter were to become pregnant in middle school or high school, I hope she would choose abortion. But for young women who can't, won't, or don't make that choice, this school offers a wonderful program that tries to keep teenage mothers on track so they can raise (or give up) their babies without foreclosing other possibilities in their lives. The curriculum includes parenting classes and support services. After the babies are born, nursing breaks are built right into the school schedule. This special treatment doesn't make education easy for the girls, but does make it possible without changing the reality they face, that one child out of every four in LA County lives below the federal poverty line.

Poet Fernando Castro has encouraged the students to write poems and tell the stories of their lives. I got them to recite and perform their poetry, not necessarily to turn them into spoken-word artists, but to give them the experience of asserting themselves with dignity in front of an audience and experiencing the respect of being seen and being heard.

Not every person is an artist, but everyone can benefit from the experience of making art. These girls learned they were capable of reaching inside themselves to make something beautiful—and not just a baby.

I also work with boys, many of whom have fathered several children while still in their teens. It's a strange experience to hear a gang member who has killed people say abortion is murder. But maybe we put the highest value on the unborn, and therefore "innocent," when we ourselves feel guilty.

People ask how I teach sexual responsibility to boys like these. I don't. We put behavior in categories all the time—responsible/irresponsible—and these labels don't seem to me very useful. I'd rather talk to kids about what they *can* do instead of what they shouldn't. I tell boys to refuse violence, not sex. Say *yes* to pleasure, *no* to disrespect. We talk about touching, mutual masturbation, and oral sex, and I present this as playful, pleasurable, affectionate, loving, and less risky, but every bit as "real" as penetration.

With Gisela Burquet, I co-lead a family group that brings together mothers, fathers, boys, and girls. She and I can offer female and male perspectives as we speak openly about the physical and emotional changes of puberty and beyond. To my surprise, many of the girls and women say they didn't know it was possible for females to masturbate. Embarrassed and intrigued, they ask how. Girls who know they can masturbate achieve a certain degree of self-sufficiency in the expression of sexuality and its satisfaction. They may still choose to be a willing partner to a boy but won't be as quick to get into risky situations. Parents and children begin to have conversations about the body with knowledge, understanding, and without shame.

One day recently, a young man was being particularly disruptive and kept announcing he had a boner. I told him to go to the bathroom and take care of it. Kids aren't used to hearing an adult say that openly, but what I saw was he needed to take care of himself and calm down. Then he could rejoin the group. To me, this approach is not so much permissive as pragmatic. Kids are lectured at and scolded all the time, to very little effect.

I love the story I've heard that among the Babemba people of Zambia, when a person is accused of irresponsible behavior, he's made to sit in the center of the village, alone. Everyone gathers around him and each person speaks, not to cast blame, but to recall everything good the person has ever done. Mistakes are an opportunity for teaching, and the Babemba teach by reweaving the person back into their cultural values. He listens and hears about all his strengths, every act of kindness. Every positive incident the community can remember has to be told, even if the ceremony goes on for days.

Is this true? I don't know, but I recognize the truth in the lesson. When I work with kids, I don't offer blind praise for anything a kid does, but I do express sincere appreciation. I also try to help them recognize qualities inherent in behavior that's been labeled as bad. Have they been punished or judged for masturbating in public or for touching a girl? I invite them to see and understand the awakening of sexuality. Shoplifting? I point out that stealing may show a capacity for survival. I invite them to see that these particular expressions of sexuality or survival skills can get you arrested and so we look at how these natural expressions can be channeled in a different way. I can help kids work out new values, but I can't take a punitive or harshly judgmental stance. You can't reach young people by humiliating them or by pretending you never did any of these things yourself when you were young.

AN UNPLANNED PREGNANCY is a crisis in a young woman's life whether abortion is legal or illegal, and whether the woman lives in the barrio or in the suburbs. One of the most moving stories I've heard comes from Cheryl on the Philadelphia Mainline, and she agreed to let me share it.

Just like the girls in Medellín, Cheryl was silenced by her shame and her fear until she went through drug and alcohol rehab. At AA meetings, Cheryl began to speak up: *I have had three abortions.* She was surprised that many men responded, saying how upset they had been over an abortion and how they had never been able to talk about it, while women came up to her privately to say thank you.

She recalls her first abortion, the one where the decision was "obvious," but still deeply troubling. She had always talked about being pro-choice, but assumed she would never herself terminate a pregnancy.

"I thought it would never happen to me. When reality came and I instantly thought 'end it,' I felt like a failure as a person." Cheryl never had the opportunity to process her decision and see that the act, though it felt out of character, did not mean the ruin of her character.

She remembers protesters screaming at her as she made her way to the front door of the clinic. She ignored them. "In the room I was put up on a table after removing the bottom half of my clothing. I lay down after noticing what looked like an industrial vacuum cleaner in the corner. The nurse was kind, patient with me. The doctor wouldn't look at me. The machine was turned on after a tube was inserted and I cried out. Nobody had prepared me for how much it was going to hurt."

Cheryl cried into the tissue paper that covered the table, sobbing as the doctor walked out.

She still can't quite figure out when she started to hate herself and her life or why. Maybe as far back as high school or even earlier. "Mostly growing pains," she says. "Too typical for words." After falling in love and getting badly hurt, she decided sex was best without deep emotional ties. "I used sex to feel worthwhile, then felt worthless for having meaningless sex." The abortion added to "the pile of shame." To dull the pain, she turned to alcohol.

"Alcohol led me to do things I might not have normally done. Alcohol led me to dangerous situations in which I was sexually assaulted. Alcohol led me to three abortions."

With each negative experience, her self-loathing grew.

For the second abortion she went to another clinic and asked for full anesthesia. The third time, she felt she couldn't go through it again and decided to have the child, but her boyfriend had his say. "He reminded me of how worthless I was as a person: Who did I think I was that I could manage a baby?" She agreed to the abortion. "It was further along than the previous times, but still within the limits. I refused to be put to sleep for this; this would be my punishment. I was given Valium and a snide, cruel doctor. This was what I deserved."

The boyfriend moved out, but not before introducing Cheryl to heroin. "It was the perfect thing to dull the pain I felt from being alive."

When he showed up one night, she thought she could win him back. That night, she became pregnant. Then he told her it was over.

"After he left, anything I could put into a needle I tried . . . heroin, cocaine, Valium, ketamine. It didn't matter. The needle quickly became my only friend. I was ready to die.

"One night my boyfriend climbed over the back wall and got inside the house. He shoved me and hit me in the stomach. I spent all my time in the bars crying over him, then. I spent all my time in my bedroom crying over him. I spent the rest of the time injecting pain management into my veins. Soon after, I called out to whatever God might be listening, 'Take this decision from me!' I remember one brief moment of clarity then: I thought if I miscarried due to the drugs, then it would somehow not be my fault (insane thinking, obviously), but that if the baby stayed, if the baby kept growing, then my life would be forced to change.

"That last night I spent walking from one ATM to another in the pouring rain, trying to get cash advances of any amount of money I could. I managed to get $30. I needed $50 to get the coke from my dealer. I gave him the money with promises and assurances that I'd have the rest the next day. In my room, I melted it down in the spoon, pulling up the liquid into the needle ever so slowly. I tied the tourniquet around my bicep and began my ritual. I shot it all that night, praying for an overdose."

She didn't have enough.

The next day she phoned her mother. "I need you to come get me."

"I'll be right there."

In the emergency room, the doctor took her hands, stretching her forearms out into view so everyone could see the track marks. "There was no ultrasound machine and so they measured what was there of my stomach to try and give an estimate. They were far, far off the mark. I was six months pregnant. You could not tell by looking at me, because the way I was living had shed pounds from my body. I was a good twenty pounds underweight, my face a skeleton with bluish-grey skin stretched across it.

"We went to a clinic to find out about an abortion. The technician was like a robot; devoid of feelings of sympathy. He scoffed at me when he did the ultrasound and discovered how far along I was, telling me I had no option. A small part of me hoped and wondered that if the baby inside me continued to grow, perhaps my life would finally change."

Cheryl went into rehab. The baby's father visited several times, once to tell her he was going to bring a razor blade so she could kill herself.

In the past, Cheryl had lived through critical events without finding her identity in the crisis. She'd doped her emerging spirit, dulling it along with the pain as she clung to an identity that always felt wrong, one that she actually hated. Now she'd hit bottom. Like the initiate in a tribal ceremony, she was naked and vulnerable, removed to an unfamiliar place and unsure of the outcome. Cheryl had wanted to die. Now, instead, she was ready to have parts of herself undergo a symbolic death so that a new self, along with the baby, could be born.

"My daughter arrived in this world at 12:40 A.M. on December 16th, 1995 at 7lbs, 11oz." The baby was healthy and drug-free. Cheryl was twenty-seven years old. Today, she is married, running a business with her husband in the home where they are raising her child and his dogs. She says, "Getting pregnant with my daughter quite literally saved my life."

Every pregnant girl—at age fourteen or twenty-seven, in the barrio or in the suburbs—must know that she has choices. She must understand that having an abortion doesn't make her a bad or immoral person. She must understand that having a baby doesn't mean her life is ruined.

Cheryl shows what is possible, though it's unlikely she could have succeeded in changing her life all on her own. She had resources and loving parents she could count on. Most people I work with have been marginalized by society—whether because of race, gender, illness or disability, or sexuality—and have to fight to get past barriers and discrimination. An unplanned pregnancy, even at age thirteen, doesn't mean a girl's life is over, but she will have to work hard and she will need help if she's going to achieve. This is a fight that the person in crisis can rarely undertake alone. And people rarely engage in that fight unless they believe in their own capacities and their own worth.

"WILL YOU COME WITH ME?" asked Carmen. "I'm scared." Breast cancer had progressed in her body to the point where her doctors had pronounced the case *desahusiado*—one they'd given up on—and so she had decided to seek help from Dr. José Gregorio Hernández. He was a Venezuelan physician who had studied for the priesthood and was renowned both for his extensive medical expertise and for his charitable works treating the poor. The only catch was Dr. Hernández had died in 1919.

Patients and physicians in Venezuela often pray for his intercession and for a good outcome. Miracles have been attributed to him—so many in fact, that Dr. José Gregorio is well on the way to canonization as a saint in the Roman Catholic Church. He is also celebrated in Venezuela as a minor deity in the María Lionza cult, which includes Che Guevara in its pantheon. In the slums of Medellín, belief in his powers was at least as strong and his adherents claimed that his spirit could travel back to this earthly plane and perform healing surgery.

Carmen—a Marxist, rationalist, avowed atheist—had begun to fear that her family was right and that her cancer was punishment for her sins. Instead of thanking her, society had condemned her, and now, in her desperate state, every accusation that had ever been thrown in her face hit its mark. Her thinking had become so irrational, I wanted to shake her and remind her how much good she had done. She had saved many women from taking desperate measures and I knew she still felt there was no point in giving birth to children who would not or could not be nurtured. But now, Carmen feared not only death, but the afterlife. She was looking for a miracle and was ready to try anything. However, as an upper middle class woman who lived in a rich neighborhood, she was afraid to venture into the barrio without me.

In a better world, Carmen would not have had to dedicate herself to performing abortions. That would have been only one service, one aspect of her work. She would have provided prenatal care and she would have attended deliveries, bringing forth life, and only occasionally terminating a pregnancy. But no one else was willing to do it, and so her days revolved around abortion. She never had the chance to deliver a loved and wanted child but instead ended the possibility of life again and again and again. The wound near her heart became a spiritual one.

We found the address and entered a room lit by dozens of candles. A strong smell of cheap perfume and of patchouli and church incense filled the place. Like the other patients, Carmen had been instructed to dress all in white, and white-clothed people lay everywhere, on beds and cots, on the floor, and on rickety tables that had been pushed together. There were the blind, lame, and terminal patients carried in by family members. There were indigent people who couldn't afford conventional medical care, and there were desperate people, like Carmen. She clutched my arm until an assistant in white took her to lie down and covered her with a sheet.

The room was quiet. Just coughs and moans from the very ill, the rustling of clothing as the white-robed assistants moved people around the room or draped them or led them away to where I wasn't allowed to follow, where patients prayed as the spirit of Dr. José Gregorio performed invisible surgery.

O, my all-powerful Lord!
You have brought your beloved servant
José Gregorio to Your heart,
to whom, with Your great mercy,

You gave the power
to heal the sick of this world.

Give him now, Lord,
as my Spiritual Physician,
the grace to heal me,
both in body and soul.

I didn't believe for a moment in invisible surgery and yet Carmen was so strong and so beautiful even as her body was ravaged, I was unprepared. It came as a terrible shock when she died.

YEARS BEFORE HER DEATH, I'd already stopped serving as her go-between.

One day in Medellín I staggered off a bus in such pain that I fell coughing and in spasms on the ground.

In the emergency room, the doctor said, "You ought to be dead."

Next to me a man screamed as the machete wounds on his neck were stitched. "Your right lung is entirely collapsed," the doctor said. "You have air trapped in the chest cavity." The nurse arranged the instruments. "We'll get rid of it."

The doctor punctured my chest wall and inserted a tube, a *sonda* like the probe I'd pushed past Julia's cervix. The chest tube emptied into a jar where water bubbled away with released air. "It's coming out. We'll get rid of it," the doctor said. My lung began to inflate; my chest rose and fell. Breathe. And I was back in that bathroom with Julia seeing the last breath of the fetus, the little chest inflating for the last time.

"Are you all right?" the doctor asked.

There was a wound in my body and a tube probing me through the wound. I pulled the probe from Julia's body, out it came, and then the fetus pumping out, and we got rid of it.

The procedure was done.

I lay in a hospital bed, recovering. But the pictures played over and over again until they overwhelmed me. I couldn't make them stop. The doctor's hands, my hands, the wound, the probe, the breath. I saw Julia. The *sonda*, the fetus. No, I thought, I'm not all right. Like Carmen, I'd participated too many times in cutting short the possibility of life. I still believed firmly in a woman's right to choose, but someone else would have to do the work. I couldn't do it any longer.

Chapter 3

Hidden in Plain Sight

Hernán Darío was a sissy. He was a Mama's boy. When we played soccer in the street, he cried, afraid the ball might hit him. *Was it my fault?* my mother sometimes wondered. *After three boys, I wanted a little girl so bad, is that why Hernán Darío came out like a girl?*

I was also capable of crying like a girl. One night, I heard terrible whimpers and found a kitten in the yard. It had been horribly injured, its body half-crushed, and I looked on its suffering and had no idea what to do. Then along came Hernán Darío, incapable of hitting a ball or hurting a fly. *Do something.* I was crying. *Someone has to do something.* My brother picked up a rock. *Do you want me to put it out of its misery?* All I could do was cry. *Do you want me to kill it?* he said. *Hector, please stop crying,* and he smashed the little creature's head. I should have realized then that when it came to killing pain, Hernán Darío wouldn't falter.

He was a drug addict, a prostitute, and thief.

My brother's homosexuality was an open secret that no one dared speak out loud. We thought we loved him. We didn't know how. My other brothers and I taunted him, rejected him. When he didn't want to go to school, afraid of a certain mean teacher, my father marched him to the classroom and announced, "Here is the Colombian Pinina," giving him the name of a lonely female character from an Argentine soap opera. School was a nightmare. Some kids attacked him. The few that befriended him were told by their parents they mustn't see him. The scary neighbor, Peligro, took him for walks and raped him. Another neighbor molested him regularly after inviting him in to watch TV. I don't believe either of these men was gay. What they saw was a pretty little boy with big eyes and long lashes, a faggot who therefore had no rights. A boy like that deserved no respect. They could do with such a child whatever they wanted.

We knew nothing about those men at the time. As we grew older, I did know that Hernán Darío slipped out of the house sometimes secretly at night. Sometimes he tried on women's clothes. I used him, too, in my own way. Julia was my official girlfriend, but when I cheated on her, I'd send Hernán Darío to visit her and keep her distracted while I pursued Adriana or Tota. I knew he would be charming and entertaining but would pose no competition or threat. I couldn't imagine my brother wanting a woman.

When Hernán Darío stayed home at night, he didn't sleep. I'd awake at 2:00 or 3:00 A.M. and smell the chemical odor that meant he was on the patio, smoking *basuco*, the marijuana laced with crack. The patio was lined with *macetas* full of plants, including the rare natural bonsai—the *bonsai criollo*—my brother found up in the mountains and brought home to tend. But I paid no attention to the plants he loved. Such an interest seemed to me effeminate, almost as bad as the romantic boleros he sang along with on the radio. In the family, we only paid attention to his drug use.

"Your eyes are red, you're losing weight. Look at you, brother, you're a drug addict. Let me help you. What can I do to help you?"

I went to work in a drug clinic; I studied alcoholism and addiction, looking for answers.

"Do you like this life, Hernán Darío?"

"Do I like my life?" he asked. "What a stupid question."

We borrowed money to take him to clinics. We sought out therapists and treatments. We tried throwing him out of the house after he stole and sold what few possessions we had that he could get his hands on: a radio, a tape-player, a wristwatch, loose change. We steeled ourselves against the sight of him in the street, hungry and dirty, begging my mother to let him come in. "You'll stay outside until you're ready to accept treatment," I told him.

We were ready to try anything except to tell him it was okay to be gay, anything but to acknowledge and honor this most basic fact in his life.

Our silence sent the message that what he *was* was unspeakable. And so he didn't speak of it either.

EVERY WOUND OF MY PAST has led me to my work. All the work I've done has helped weave the meaning of my life. My story makes no sense to me unless I bring these threads together: life and work.

In Los Angeles, as I lead a therapeutic group for kids, I hear the word "Faggot!"

When I work with middle school kids, "faggot" is the most common insult they fling at each other. It comes out casually when a boy shows vulnerability or emotion. It comes out automatically as the most demeaning word they know to say. Once it was a casual word to me, too. Now I recognize the damage that hate speech can do.

"Why did you call him 'faggot?'" I ask.

"Because he is one!"

"But what does it mean?" No answer. "It's a very insulting way to refer to someone who is attracted to people of the same sex. My brother was homosexual, or gay, and many of my friends are gay."

"Then you're a faggot, too."

"Well, I could be, but I'm not. And the fact is, that many of you could be homosexual or bisexual, or some of your close friends. If you are calling each other 'faggot' in a despicable way, you are hurting the friends who may be having these feelings. You are telling them how unacceptable they are." I give them the statistics, about the kids between the ages of fourteen and eighteen who commit suicide because they are gay, and are convinced there is no place for them in this world. I ask them to think about bigotry and the consequences of their words.

I wish I'd understood those consequences earlier.

Most of the time, though, rather than lecture at kids, I like to use the council circle, drawn from the Native American tradition, to open up difficult conversations. Sometimes the kids themselves ask for a circle when they're upset about something or want it aired. We start with four invitations: speak from the heart, listen from the heart, be succinct, don't prepare what you're going to say. With some groups, I also start with an agreement: no violence. We pass a feather or some other natural object around the circle, and the person who holds the feather speaks. It's not about convincing anyone of anything or arguing with anyone. It's about speaking the truth that's in you at that moment. And I present the questions: Why do you call someone a faggot? What do you feel inside when you say that? Where does it come from? How do you feel when someone pins that word on you? At the end of the circle, we each make a commitment or agreement about what we're going to do in the future based on what we've heard.

At the arts-based therapeutic program I helped create, some of the gay teenagers have come out to the group and it changes the dynamic. Once it's in the open, everyone becomes more comfortable. These are kids who've spent time together in our group every week for two or three years and so there's enough cohesiveness and loyalty to make it a relatively safe space. The gay child discovers he is not rejected. The straight kids discover that a homosexual isn't a faggot; he's one of their friends.

Of course, some kids in any group just won't like each other, but what has amazed me is that, even when the gay kid is in conflict with someone, once he's come out I've never seen his homosexuality used as ammunition against him. Now the question remains whether he can take the risk and come out to his family, or in school, or in his neighborhood. The answer may be that he can't, but at least there's one place in his life where he can be himself and is not just accepted but seen and valued as a whole person by his peers. I wish my brother could have found such a place.

HOMOSEXUALITY CAN OFTEN BE kept hidden, but there are kinds of Otherness that are in plain view. Martin has a short, stocky body, strangely shaped jaw and skull, and deformed ears. Since birth, he's undergone a series of surgeries on his skull to allow for optimal growth of his brain, and on his fingers to remove the webbing that stood in the way of functional use of his hands. Martin's feet remain webbed as separating his toes is considered a cosmetic procedure and therefore not covered by the state's Medi-Cal program. He most likely has some developmental challenges but at this point it's hard to tell how much of his apparent slowness is due to cultural and social deprivation.

When I met him, Martin was eight years old and his mother had tried to protect him from humiliation by keeping him away from the outside world. Though he'd been socially isolated, both of his parents were very loving. Their support and affection had given him a strong foundation and an innocent self-confidence that made it easy to gain his trust. When they allowed him to participate in our group, he was open and enthusiastic, eager to paint and sing and play, the first to try anything I suggested, and very happy to be among other children. It's true that when he first tried to make friends, some boys responded by rejecting him. Martin suffered and cried, but each time after I had the whole group process the incident together, he was so willing to forgive that the other kids were impressed by his big heart. He responded to any show of friendship with immediate warmth and, in our group, among boys many of whom were emotionally guarded, his cheerfulness and sheer enjoyment of life became contagious. Martin was soon an integral part of our small community. But when I organized a field trip to the beach, his mother said she couldn't give him permission to go.

"People will make fun of him," she said.

"Maybe some will," I said. "That's what will happen in his life. Some people will stare at him, some will tease him, but some will love him."

"They're going to look at him and say 'What's wrong with you?'"

Of course that was likely to happen, not because children are cruel, but because they haven't yet learned to censor themselves when it comes to subjects that adults consider taboo. I wanted Martin to learn how to answer that question: "I have Carpenter syndrome. It's very rare and even though I'm only eight, I've already had a lot of operations." If he could learn, as a child, to treat his difference in a matter-of-fact way, he could satisfy the natural curiosity of other kids. By opening up conversation, he could also open up the possibility of friendship. This would be a good start to develop the social skills and confidence that would serve him well as an adult.

His mother was still nervous, but she finally agreed to let him go.

The others boys were used to Martin's obvious difference by now, but they had never seen his feet. I talked to them individually. I didn't tell them to be discreet and polite. I didn't warn them, *Don't say this, don't say that*. I told them their curiosity was normal and that I was curious, too, but I was so glad that they all saw Martin as a friend, since we all knew what a great guy he was.

At the beach, Martin kept his feet covered with the sand. At first, all the kids were too excited and, some of them, scared by the ocean to notice him. These were kids who had lived all their lives in Los Angeles and had never had the chance to travel the fifteen miles from their homes to the beach. Eventually, all of them ran into the water with me, including Martin. By the end of the day, everyone had seen his webbed toes and no one seemed to care.

Martin's mother had also taught him to deflect hostility by always being nice. In our group, as in any group of kids, arguments broke out. There were challenges and insults and, even after he was well-liked and accepted, Martin got his share. He never disagreed or argued. He placated people. Whatever happened, whatever anyone said to him, he kept smiling except for when the hurt was so deep he had to withdraw and cry. The day he finally got angry, talked back, and stood up for himself like any other kid would do, I was so thrilled I gave him a kiss.

WHEN I WAS GROWING UP, I always stuck up for the underdog outside of home but at the same time, as the oldest son, I used to bully my brothers mercilessly—until they got big enough to fight back and stop me. I invite kids to look at ways in which we've all been the victim of bullies or have been bullies ourselves.

One recent summer, I took some of the low-income Catholic Latino kids I work with to an interfaith sleepaway camp at the invitation of Rabbi Lynn Gottlieb who brought them together with middle class Jewish kids, wealthy Iraqi-American Muslims, and Native American members of the Chumash tribe. We started and ended each day with a council circle. One day, we talked about bullying and teasing. A Muslim boy told how his sister wanted to quit school after 9/11 because classmates either shunned her or called her a terrorist. A Jewish boy said he'd been mocked and called a girl because he likes to wear his hair long. Another child was ostracized for being fat. To an adult, the Muslim girl's situation is clearly the most serious and most in need of adult intervention. But the kids seemed to understand that all kinds of cruelty hurt, and that pain is pain.

When I work with kids, it's not about condemning the bullies. It's about understanding that we all can be hurt and all have the capacity to use our power—whether it's that of numbers, size, beauty, intelligence, or wit—to take advantage of others. I find most bullies are vulnerable, too. They are kids who are not very comfortable with who they are or who come from places where they're not treated well. They've been bullied themselves by older brothers, cousins, their parents, or gang members in the neighborhood.

Most kids who are attacked, whether verbally or physically, don't know what to do. They are given the message, *Tell an adult*; but not only does that turn a kid into a snitch which can make matters much worse, but kids have learned that adults will rarely do anything to help. Teachers and guidance counselors will sometimes say, *It's a peer prob-*

lem, you have to solve it yourself, but don't offer any guidance on how that is to be done.

The traditional way of dealing with bullies is to fight them and gain their respect. I don't encourage violent responses, especially when bullies today may carry firearms. But the dilemma inherent in using a nonviolent response is that you don't want to be seen as cowardly or insultingly superior. If you turn the other cheek, will the other kids say, *Who do you think you are? Jesus Christ?* So, in my groups, we do a lot of role-playing, experimenting with ways to disarm a bully by using our wits. In improvisations, where kids know they won't risk real injury, they often start by putting up a fight, which I point out isn't very realistic in a situation if it's four against one. We use theater as training for life as kids experiment, trying out their own ideas in their own individual styles. I encourage them to practice trickster behavior. *Use your imagination,* I tell them. We practice using jokes, stories, and intelligence to shift the energy and defuse the situation. We've found one of the most effective responses is for a kid who's been cornered to "go crazy" and act so nutty that the oppressors don't know what to do.

"Shift the energy," I tell them. "Find a way to do that."

I've also seen kids come right out and say, *You're hurting me and I wonder why. I haven't done anything to you.* When a boy becomes very emotional instead of hiding how he feels, he's a person, not just a punching-bag, and it's not so easy for the bully to dehumanize him. Of course, there's no sure-fire formula that will always work, but what's important is we train so that a kid won't just freeze when confronted. When you're frozen, you become an object. So I train kids to keep themselves as subjects and to find allies, to make eye contact. Get the message across: *You are hurting me. I am here and I hurt.* Or *You're calling me names and I don't like it and I'm feeling very angry.* Responses like these won't reach the violent sociopaths who are staple fare on TV crime shows, but sadists of that sort aren't encountered very often in real life.

Most bullies aren't sadists, they're children who've also been wounded. When you say, *You are hurting me*, it carries the assumption that the bully is also human, and this may mean a lot to a boy whose own humanity has gone unacknowledged.

All kids are "at-risk," but services tend to be provided only to those who've been labeled so. At one LA middle school, this means I work with maybe fifty kids at a school of 4,000. I worry about the other 3,950, the ones who aren't acting out or smoking marijuana or joining gangs. They're in trouble, too, because no one sees them as trouble and therefore no one sees them at all. I'm as guilty in this regard as anyone. While I tell others to pay attention to the "ordinary" kids, the ones who hide their confusion behind façades of cheerful conformity, I myself have always been drawn to the outcasts.

While my brother Hernán Darío was sinking further into addiction, I was at the university, combining my study of psychology with my acting experience. I created the character of Xicotico, a street psychotic. It had always troubled me the way people like him were rendered invisible. Society doesn't have to address a problem if no one sees it, and so Xicotico wandered around the city causing so much disruption he was impossible to ignore. In filthy clothing and with wild hair and crazy behavior, I spent days and nights in the street among the homeless.

I grew up poor, but I lived in a house with parents who loved me. Now I met *los gamines*, the street kids who had been born in the mountains on the outskirts of the city. Their parents were peasants forced out of the small towns and farms, who'd come to Medellín looking for work. They would find a little space of ground somewhere and would build their little shacks with pieces of whatever they could find. That's how shantytowns began to appear on all the hills. There was no food, no jobs, and lots of alcohol and domestic violence and despair. To survive, children would end up downtown, looking for something to steal. Drugs were everywhere, especially *sacol*, the glue the kids sniffed to relieve hunger pains and help them endure the rain and cold and pain of their abandonment. They shoplifted the stuff, and every boy kept a bottle of it hidden beneath his shirt.

Sacol, resistol: by any name and any brand, glue is abused by street kids all over the world. Some U.S. kids also huff glue fumes and risk permanent harm, but their occasional high is nowhere near as dangerous as the constant use you find among street kids, like the *gamines* I knew in Medellín. *Sacol* damaged their brains and central nervous system, their kidneys and other organs. It stunted growth so that the little boy I thought was seven years old turned out to be thirteen. These kids died young of organ failure or sometimes from being so high they walked in front of cars. *Sacol's* effect on the cardiovascular system was so intense that if you startled a kid during the drug rush, you could see a ten-year-old die of heart attack. Death squads had just begun the practice of social cleansing—gunning down street kids, transvestites, whores—but during this era, the *limpiezas* were still rare enough that the odds of my surviving the street were good. It wasn't so good for the kids. One way or another, they would die with no one knowing who they were or even their names.

We'd make our camp on the steps of the Metropolitan Cathedral. In the real cold weather, we ventured inside the vast and echoing church, hoping the priest wouldn't kick us out. The luckiest or strongest kids would claim a space on the sidewalk outside an air-conditioned bank where the vents spewed out warm air. We slept in piles of newspaper or on pieces of scavenged cardboard.

The *gamines* got their clothes and shoes from the open air flea market that has since been closed down. They survived by begging, scavenging, and through prostitution, but mostly by stealing. Of course, to get money from this booty, kids had to rely on fences—adults who derived the greatest profit from the kids' criminal work. The kids gave Medellín drivers a good reason to keep their windows rolled up and to ignore red lights. If a bus was stopped, the kids would jump up and reach in through any open window to grab wristwatches, bracelets, and necklaces torn right off a passenger's neck. People in cars were even more vulnerable. A stopped car could be surrounded and the driver and passengers violently robbed. If I'd tried hanging out around them in my identity as a student, I could have been robbed or killed; but as Xicotico, I was one of them. Still, I must have given away some clues to my background: I once heard a boy explain to another that I was a university student who'd gone crazy for being too intelligent. *A good guy*, he said. *Crazy but harmless.*

During my student years, I had plenty of time to carry out my unconventional investigations, because the university was often shut down. During the 70s and 80s, students and workers often took to the streets to protest government policies or U.S. imperialism. One night, I had to hide in the bushes from the police after painting *Kissinger Go Home* on a cemetery wall. Demonstrations often turned violent. Soldiers would fire rubber bullets or lob tear gas to disperse us. They had all the gear; we had rocks. (These days, when I see news footage of Palestinian teens throwing stones, I see myself.) When soldiers used live ammunition, someone was bound to die. If a student was killed, protesters responded by overturning cars and buses and setting them on fire. Usually, what happened next was you'd show up at the university and find it closed for our own "protection."

One day, a huge commotion broke out on campus. My classmate Martha Nieves Ochoa—we called her "Blanca Nieves" after the fairy tale Snow White—was abducted by members of the guerrilla organization M-19. She was eventually released unharmed, but the militants had made a big mistake in targeting the sister of the three Ochoa brothers, bosses of the cocaine cartel. Her kidnapping unleashed still another wave of terror. The mafia joined with right wing paramilitaries and official government forces to create MAS—Muerte a Secuestradores, or Death to Kidnappers—and set out to assassinate guerrilla leaders. This movement, which was violent and illegal to begin with, soon turned into a free-for-all when the various factions discovered that by massacring peasants they could lay claim to huge estates of the best productive land. By assassinating students, teachers, judges, journalists, artists, union representatives, and human rights leaders they could continue to act with impunity.

Yes, we all needed protection, but the university closures didn't help. They sometimes lasted as long as three months, and so it took eight years to get my Masters degree. But I never stopped learning outside the classroom.

WHILE SOME KIDS ARE marginalized or bullied for being different, I made myself as different as possible and turned my alienation into adventure. As Xicotico, I especially liked to go to Parque Berrío and cause a disturbance, darting around La Gorda, the huge woman sculpted by our world-renowned artist, Fernando Botero. Then Xicotico, turned religious fanatic, would invade one of the nearby churches: la Iglesia de la Veracruz, with its white façade and pointy spires; or the domed Cathedral of Nuestra Señora de la Candelaria, dedicated to Medellín's patron saint. When I started speaking in tongues or rushed to the altar to beg God for a cure, the *gamines* would follow me inside and coax me to leave. "Come on. Let's get out of here. You're going to get in trouble."

They were right. I was arrested twice, and one day Xicotico was carried off to the mental hospital (where the head of the unit knew me and was expecting me), and where I was able to experience firsthand how the patients were treated. Many had been locked up twenty years or more, and while some were schizophrenics who certainly needed or benefited from drug therapy, everyone was medicated, mostly overmedicated. There were zombie-like patients who'd undergone lobotomies or multiple sessions of 1970s-style electroshock. Methods that would drive sane people mad such as prolonged isolation and restraint with straitjackets were used for control when many patients could have been reintegrated into society if support had been available.

When I spoke afterwards in staff meetings and at conferences, what stood out to me from my experience as Xicotico was that so many of these people who were considered violent, antisocial, and beyond redemption were in fact deeply imbued with and respectful of social norms. I told how the *gamines* looked out for me and tried to make me behave. They were filthy, but I followed them as they sought out public baths and fountains, any place where they might wash and get clean. Boys would bring me mangoes they'd been able to scavenge or steal. They didn't want me to go hungry. Similarly, when I acted out on the psych ward, the staff had been warned to leave me alone, but the patients tried to calm me down. They were considered trash, locked up in a place the director himself referred to as a landfill for humans, but these so-called pieces of garbage talked to me, took me to the isolation room, tried to get hold of medications to give me. They followed the exact same procedures they had endured from the nurses and staff.

I wanted the psychiatric establishment to accept that many "crazy" people had been broken by despair due to hopelessness and the social conditions they lived in. They displayed normal reactions to their abnormal situations. Many psychiatrists accepted this, but none was able to change those desperate conditions and so the primary beneficiary of my investigations turned out to be me. My experiments as Xicotico brought me to the attention of prominent professors, psychiatrists, and researchers, and that's how, even before I finished school, I was offered a position at CENIT, Centro de Investigación y Tratamiento, renowned not only for the quality and effectiveness of its drug rehab treatment, but also for its research into addiction.

The clinic was private, exclusive, and very expensive—so costly, in fact, that most of the patients were members of the cocaine mafia who'd become addicted to their own product. Who else could afford it? Though I was on the staff, there was no way my family could send Hernán Darío to CENIT as a patient. However, I told myself I could at least learn more about addiction and how to help him.

CENIT was located in a bucolic area, now very developed, in a historic old house on the outskirts of the city. (The hilltop nearby would briefly be home to drug cartel boss Pablo Escobar, who'd agreed to turn himself in to the police on the condition that he could build his own prison. From that luxurious retreat, he continued to run his drug operations, receive visitors, execute his enemies, and throw parties until the day he decided he'd had enough confinement and, without difficulty, arranged his own escape.)

At the clinic, patients stayed from one to three months. Their treatment was intensive and could be extremely individualized as we could accommodate only fifteen people at a time. Patients slept in dormitories, two rooms set aside for men, and one for women. Medical doctors helped them through withdrawal. Psychiatrists, social workers, and psychoanalysts, including me, worked on their psychological issues through individual and group therapy, as well as in an art therapy program. Alcoholics Anonymous and Narcotics Anonymous held daily meetings, often led by former addicts who had gone through the CENIT program and had stayed clean. Conchita, the cook, sat in on staff meetings. Sometimes she was the most valuable part of a treatment plan as she shared her warmth, showed her concern, tempted patients with their favorite meals, and fed them back to physical health. She even went to work on me: "Doctor, you don't look like a doctor. You're too skinny. I'm going to feed you and make you look right."

CENIT remains my model for a treatment program based on true teamwork. We looked at addiction from all our different therapeutic perspectives and we shared what we knew about each client. Everyone's point of view was valued because you never knew who—doctor, nurse, social worker, Conchita—might have the most insight or be best at creating rapport and a connection with a client. This may sound obvious, but in my experience in the U.S., staff meetings are rarely about taking a comprehensive look at a client and discussing the best way to help. We sit for hours talking about productivity, the new computer system, and billing procedures. When we do consider a client's case, it's usually to figure out how to refer the person elsewhere and get rid of him.

In the U.S., staff also lack the emotional support that would, at least in some cases, prevent burnout. At CENIT, meetings gave us the chance to process our own emotions. I, for example, needed to handle my own rage after listening to a twenty-two-year-old who had consumed 20 million pesos that year, when I still didn't earn enough to get an apartment of my own away from my parents. It felt sometimes as though I'd never be able to move out, marry, start a family of my own, and lead an independent adult life. Or else I'd end up like my father—different in that I had an education and a profession, but still destined to raise a family in poverty. Again and again, some patient I was trying to help would look at me and offer help of his own. "Doctor, you have nothing. You don't even have a car. Come work with us and you'll be rich."

Then, a year after I myself had been tortured, I found myself treating an addict who'd been an assassin and torturer for MAS. I had to deal with my feelings and listen calmly as he told me what he'd done to leftists and university students, how terrified they were, how they cried, and how he tortured and killed them. Getting high on cocaine was the only way he could do it, he said. He would go crazy from the killing and sometimes was so wasted on drugs and drink he didn't care who his victims were or what they said. He just tortured them without thinking. Hector the therapist understood that this man was suffering. Hector the human being knew this man could easily have tortured him. It tore me up, and talking about it at staff meetings helped me through it. In the end, I think it was also helpful for me to have a human connection to this man, to see how circumstances had led him to do what he did and become what he became.

As staff members, we were all living on the edge. The nurses were always confiscating cocaine from incoming patients. I don't know what became of all of it, but we did use some of it ourselves, as "research" at those staff meetings. When we learned lots of patients were coming in addicted to a new high, I offered myself as the guinea pig to test the effects. While doctors took notes, I injected myself with a mix of alcohol and cocaine. It was only after I worked in U.S. clinics that I realized how questionable our "research" methods were, to put it mildly. Now I see we weren't being researchers, we were just acting out; but our treatment methods were, as far as I'm concerned, first-rate.

ACTING IS NOT the same as acting out. At the mental hospital, an Argentine psychologist named Diego Cordón taught me about psychodrama, how enacting a scene engages your body, your energies, and your emotions in a dynamic way, cutting through the rationalizations that come so easily when we hide behind words. Dr. Cordón used the methods with staff rather than with patients as he had us explore our own attitudes about authority, power, and madness in order to make us more effective and compassionate healers. I was impressed, and so I brought psychodrama to CENIT.

There, I did with strangers what I couldn't with my brother: instead of addressing addiction directly, I focused on its underlying causes. In one psychodrama session, Beto, for example, chose one of the therapists to represent his father. The choice itself was revealing, as this was a therapist he had an intense love/hate relationship with. I hesitated a moment: Beto was volatile and we all knew he could get violent. It was a borderline call, but I thought I had a strong relationship with the kid and decided to let him proceed. Within minutes, he was hyperventilating and then suddenly grabbed a chair. "I hate you. I'm going to kill you!" My overconfidence had put my colleague at risk as Beto swung the chair at him, then smashed it down with enough force to break the seat. Once it was clear no one was hurt, I figured we might as well go on and have

Beto explore how these feelings about his father manifested themselves in his life. A simplified version goes like this: Beto was the son of a prostitute who'd become the mistress to the very wealthy owner of several successful bars. Although his father had a life with his wife and family, he did try to stay involved with Beto. He gave him a job; Beto robbed the place. His father sent him to drug treatment again and again. Beto would force his father to spend huge sums of money and make him face the fact that each attempt at rehab would fail. He was also struggling with his attraction to transvestites, with desires that both thrilled and terrified him. *Was he a real man?* he wanted to know. *Or was he gay?*

My brother didn't ask himself such questions. He knew. But by then, he was in the streets.

"LET ME IN, MA!"

Neighbors watched and gossiped, but I wouldn't let my mother open the door to Hernán Darío.

"I'm hungry, Ma. Please. Just let me come in and wash up and change my clothes."

I shouted to him out the window. "You can't come in until you're ready to go for help." Then I pulled my mother away from the window and shut it. Of all the ordeals we put her through, this may have been the worst, when I made her lock her youngest son out. "It's for his own good" I told her. "He won't go for help till he hits bottom." Of all the lessons I was learning about addiction, this was the only one we could afford to put into practice.

Here in the U.S. I've seen the dangers of this approach. Locking one child out of the house may be the only way to protect the rest of the family, but it rarely turns out to be for "his own good," when gang members and predators are waiting and ready to offer their own dangerous kind of family. When drastic measures must be taken, parents still need to get across the message: *you are loved*. The unconditional love a child needs doesn't mean a parent can't set limits. It simply means the child is loved, period, and not only if he conforms and not *in spite of*. He is simply loved. The child who knows this has at least some inoculation against self-destruction.

We thought we loved Hernán Darío unconditionally. But we weren't giving the simple message of *We love you*. What he heard was that we loved him, *even though* he was unacceptably gay.

I DON'T KNOW HOW she got the number, but shortly after her discharge from CENIT, La Negra phoned me at home. "Pack your bathing trunks and a change of clothes. I'm taking you to the country club."

La Negra had never been my patient, but the clinic was so small that everyone got to know everyone. We all took walks together in the countryside and played soccer in the yard near the gardens. I knew that she'd run base cocaine in Miami and been arrested but had somehow managed to avoid prison and was simply deported back to Colombia, where she continued working for the cocaine cartel, Rodríguez Gacha in particular. The other bosses thought the world of her, too. She was a favorite with the Ochoa brothers and even Pablo Escobar. Along the way, she'd become an addict and, hating what had become of her, she was determined to stay clean.

Though her nickname was La Negra, she wasn't black. Her sister was blond and she was the dark one of the family. Same with me. At home, I was called El Negro. I didn't really become "Hector" till I landed in the U.S. and people said, "but you're not black."

La Negra was smart and ambitious. She was also gorgeous. I packed my clothes.

She picked me up at home. Unlike other rich people, drug dealers didn't hesitate to go into any neighborhood. She drove us to the club outside the city where the rich spent their weekends. She changed into a bikini that almost made my heart stop. I knew immediately I was on dangerous ground and didn't mind it at all. Sitting by the pool while I drank *aguardiente* and she stuck to soft drinks, La Negra got to the point. Addiction was a horrible curse. CENIT was great but could treat very few sufferers. Her plan was to approach the Ochoa brothers and ask them to finance a big new treatment center that would bring CENIT's methods to many more people who needed help. "I want you to work there," she said.

That did it. I was seduced.

CARLOS LEHDER, ONE OF the first major drug traffickers from Colombia, called cocaine the revenge on the Empire, the means by which South America would poison the gringos. The other mafia bosses didn't take him and his ideas all that seriously. He was too crazy for the cartel, giving them such proof of insanity as his ties to the guerrilla movement and his deal with the U.S. to testify against Manuel Noriega, the Panamanian dictator. Noriega began working for the CIA in the early 1970s but was accused of drug trafficking and eventually imprisoned in Florida after the U.S. invaded his country in 1989 under the first George Bush. In my view, where Lehder was truly deluded was that he failed to see what drugs would do to our own society.

In the 1980s, cocaine became the new export business boom, replacing high quality marijuana, Colombian gold. Cocaine was compact, easier to ship, and much more profitable. Drums full of the stuff entered the U.S. aboard ships and planes quite easily till the DEA finally caught on that it was happening. By then, so much money was involved that traffickers came up with new routes and new smuggling schemes. Pablo Escobar was the most ingenious of them all.

At first, Colombians merely processed the cocaine and handled the marketing. The coca leaves were brought across the border from Bolivia and Peru, but soon we began to grow the stuff as well. The result: in the 1980s, while most Latin American economies struggled— in part because so much of the gross national product went to pay off interest on World Bank and IMF debt—cocaine kept money in circulation in Colombia. Cocaine turned some Colombians into the richest people in the world, virtually overnight. Cocaine served the U.S. economy, too, as traffickers spent their money here on luxury items. U.S. businesses and banks profited from money-laundering and huge cash deposits.

The strong economy on paper didn't help the vast majority of Colombians. In small towns, millions lived without running water while the rivers they used to rely on now ran toxic with industrial waste. Peasants were massacred. Teachers sometimes worked for months without a paycheck. Prices for food and essentials kept rising while wages declined for those lucky enough to have a job. High rates of unemployment might have destroyed the country altogether but for the many people earning a living directly or indirectly thanks to the cartels.

Cocaine implicated us in U.S. politics. Long before the world heard of Oliver North and the Iran-contra scandal, a client at CENIT told me how he flew cocaine to an airstrip in Arkansas, unloaded the cargo, and took on a shipment of weapons that he delivered to the right wing Nicaraguan contras waiting for him in Honduras. At the time, I didn't know whether to believe him. His story sounded so unlikely, but dangerous for me to know about if it were true.

Cocaine didn't just change our economy and our politics. It changed our psyches. By reaching into every aspect of our lives and by consolidating so much power, the cartels affected how we saw the world. It affected our imaginations: what we could do and what we could see ourselves doing. It set limits to what we could imagine and left us often unaware we were living inside those limits.

In Colombia, the mafia routinely buys up our best land, as well as policemen, soldiers, judges, and politicians—sometimes by financing their campaigns and sometimes by making them rich. While Pablo Escobar showed no scruples as he enriched himself, he liked to call himself a man of the left. He used drug money to finance public housing and other social projects in Medellín, and figured he could buy votes as well to launch a political career. The Kennedy family made their fortune in bootlegging and then rose to the presidency, he said, so why couldn't he do the same after trafficking in cocaine?

There are reports that on two occasions he and the cartel offered to pay off Colombia's international bank debt, which would have been an extraordinary boon to the poor, but the government, fearing a public relations disaster, turned him down. This left Escobar bitter over politicians who pretended not to know him, but who never hesitated to solicit cash from him to run their campaigns. When Escobar was elected to office in 1982, he was denounced as a criminal and removed. Resentment, in addition to the threat of extradition, fueled the carnage he unleashed.

Alvaro Uribe, now Colombia's president, was also removed from office in 1982 when he was mayor of Medellín due to his close ties to Pablo. In later years, I saw Uribe riding horses with the Ochoa brothers on one of their estates. But how did I get to see that? I was there, too, so how can I pass judgment on someone else? Cocaine and the people who profited from it were everywhere. One way or another, we were all connected.

A shiver ran up my spine when my co-author Diane wrote that, as director of Civil Aviation, Uribe came under fire for granting a record number of pilots' licenses and construction permits for landing strips, not to mention appointing as his assistant a man who was later sentenced to prison for his work for the Cali cartel. When he was Governor of Antioquia, his close associate and right-hand man illegally imported tons of potassium permanganate for which there was no other use in existing Colombian industry aside from the processing of cocaine.

"You can't say that," I warned.

"Hey," she said, "it was in *Newsweek*. And he was named back in 1991 in a Defense Department intelligence report."

Does my reluctance to repeat these charges come from fear or from fairness? I know too well how these things go. It could all be rumor. Or, to put it in North American terms, maybe they just made Uribe an offer he couldn't refuse.

In Medellín, that offer most often took the form of a choice: *plata o plomo*, silver or lead. Take my bribe, or take a bullet. In the countryside, when a mafioso wanted to get some small farmer's land for a pittance, the choice was *Sell to me today or I'll buy from your widow tomorrow*.

Through my affair with La Negra, I was drawn closer and closer into the cocaine-trafficking world. She told me about Griselda Blanco (also called La Negra, which in her case was short for La Viuda Negra— the Black Widow—as she was reputed to have killed all three of her husbands). Griselda established Medellín's drug business in Miami at a time when Cubans controlled that city's organized crime. La Negra sent one of her people to Miami to run base, with orders to refuse any payoff to the Cubans. The Cubans cut off the guy's hands and mailed them to her in Medellín with a message, "Pay up or we'll send you something else."

La Negra's response was to travel to Miami and slaughter not just a few of her rivals but members of their families. Heads and other body parts were soon being delivered all over town in the mail while the leftover pieces were cut into little bits and fed into the garbage disposal units of apartments in Miami's luxury high-rises. La Negra was ruthless, but her willingness to kill friend as well as foe left her surrounded by enemies. Finally convicted of ordering three murders, she spent twenty years in prison in the U.S. and was then deported home to Colombia in 2004. She wasn't expected to survive.

"CAN YOU GET SOME TIME OFF?" La Negra (my girlfriend, not the killer) asked one day. "We're taking a little trip."

We boarded a regular commercial flight in Medellín like tourists headed for a romantic weekend in the rainforests of Chocó. The only thing unusual was that La Negra checked so many cartons as luggage I didn't think the small plane could carry them all. I didn't want to know what the boxes contained, but she assured me it wasn't drugs or weapons, just food and staple provisions she was delivering to the Ochoas who were then in hiding. We landed in a small town where a car was waiting to drive us to the Pacific coast. Next came the scariest experience I've been through, several hours clinging for dear life in a small motorboat as we and all our cargo were thrown about by waves high as mountains. Only a skilled local pilot who really knew the tides and the dangers of the coastline could navigate safely to the Ochoas' hideout.

The brothers themselves traveled by helicopter. During the time the law was after them, they flew regularly to their mother's house in Medellín for lunch. Like any good *paisa*—as we people from Antioquia call ourselves, they were notorious for being unwilling to cut the umbilical cord. These visits were an open secret but never interrupted by a raid or any attempt to arrest them. I don't know if this was due to fear or bribery or the average *paisa*'s deep respect for motherhood.

When we arrived at the estate, the Ochoas weren't there. It was a disappointment, as I was curious about them, but also a relief. We were free to play and enjoy ourselves in this secluded paradise. We tried out their jet skis. I saw a VCR for the first time and we looked through their collection of hundreds of films and their stockpile of video porn. I'd never driven a car in my life but the three-wheel electric scooters they used to get around the estate looked simple. I jumped aboard one, turned it on, took off, and crashed. With reckless self-confidence, I decided okay, now I know how it works, got another, and crashed that one, too. It's a good thing the Ochoas weren't home.

I was also reckless about my reputation. Even some of my close friends began to assume I was trafficking. Certainly, I was happy to take advantage of some of the luxuries of life that my connection to La Negra afforded me, but I never considered getting involved in the business. I was too committed to my own path in life. Even doing one quick job to make a score made no sense to me. For one thing, my brother's mess of an addict's life was always in front of me. Then, the stories of my patients were cautionary tales. Rubén was the most like me. He'd managed to attend the university and had a graduate degree. But even with a profession, he couldn't earn enough to support the extended family that relied on him. He finally went to work as a cocaine cook. While you've probably heard of the cartel's amazing processing sites—complete with housing, recreational facilities, and clinics for employee medical care—operations that big are hard to hide. So many cooks were simply left in deep rainforest, where they'd spend up to seven months living alone except for an armed guard in a *cambuche*, a makeshift shack where they would process coca leaves into paste ready for transport and sale. It was lonely work and dangerous. Cooks weren't allowed to communicate with family or friends for fear their messages might be intercepted. The army was looking for them and so were the paramilitaries and guerrillas who might rob them of the product. Former cooks who knew where to find a *cambuche* were also known to put together a gang and rob and kill their replacements. So, while Rubén's family was calling him their savior, he, like many other cooks, was going crazy in the jungle. Bored and growing every day and every night more paranoid, he started using his product. He was a good man and strong, and yet his involvement in the drug trade had broken him.

Most of all, the closer I got to the trafficking world, the more I learned of its horrific violence. Drug traffickers were behind the assassinations of some of my closest friends. How could I ever be part of that? One day at a funeral, the friend standing to the left of me and the friend standing to the right of me were both struck down by gunfire. Somehow, the bullets never hit me.

I put all the killing out of my mind when La Negra and I danced all night in the glamorous discotheques built by Pablo Escobar. The Ochoas laundered some of their money through a Brazilian-style steakhouse owned by their father. Another girlfriend of mine used to sing there. I'd go to hear Tota, and waitresses would pile my plate for free with the best beef from Don Fabio Ochoa's ranch. I still didn't have an apartment or a car, but between Conchita and the Ochoas, I was putting on weight and growing into the body of a "real doctor."

•   •   •

HERNÁN DARÍO WAS SKINNY. Instead of eating, he smoked more crack. As a last resort, we borrowed bus-fare and got him into a clinic in Bogotá. CENIT would never have approved of the treatment. The plan was to shatter and destroy his identity: *You're an addict, you're nothing, you're a piece of shit. You don't love yourself, you don't love your family.* It didn't bother him to have his addict-self attacked; there was nothing about that identity he cared about or wanted to hold onto. But what was left after all his armor was destroyed was a boy whose real identity was one that no one could accept, a boy who was gay.

Through my brother's suffering, I began to see the limits of what therapy can do. It wasn't till he was dying that I came to understand his pain and the beauty of his soul, a beauty that had been there all along though none of us had managed to see it. He hadn't seen it either until, ironically, he found healing and a path to something better than drugs while working for a boss of the cocaine cartel.

Chapter 4

Life from Barren Rock

Throw yourself like seed. . .
from your work you will be able one day to gather
yourself.

—Miguel de Unamuno, translated by Robert Bly

"Once, I thought a lot about God in heaven," my brother said. "The staff in his hand shot lightning. He used it to strike people down and I dreamed of God and all his avenging angels taking revenge on everyone who ever hurt me. But now I dream of a God who comes down to earth and harvests everything that's good. He gathers all the flowers up to heaven and that's why you see flowering vines climb the wall. They want to leave the earth."

Hernán Darío, thirty-one years old, was dying.

In 1995, I'd been in the U.S. for six years. I'd fled Colombia for my life, but I booked a flight as soon as I heard he'd been diagnosed with AIDS. The treatment available in Medellín was ten years behind the advances that were saving lives in the U.S. and so my brother's deterioration was rapid. In health, he had been so handsome he'd turned heads, of both men and women, whenever he walked down the street. Now he looked like a cadaver.

I was a new father then and had recently acquired a video camera to record Gabo's early years. This wasn't premeditated, I hadn't thought it out. But now I brought the camera to Hernán Darío. "When my son grows up, I want him to know his uncle. Will you tell us about yourself, on tape?"

He was so weak he could hardly sit up. He said he was always cold, that his body felt to him like ice. It was difficult for him to speak, but he immediately agreed. He hadn't wanted anyone to see him with his beauty all gone, but now he roused himself and looked directly into the camera. I think the camera provided a buffer. He was speaking to himself and to Gabo and to the whole world, but he wasn't self-conscious because only the lens was looking at him. His words sounded like poetry. As he spoke honestly and openly, I thought this chance to create a documentary about his life with the help of my friend Juan Devis was evidence to him that his life mattered.

I began by wanting my son to know his uncle, but during the taping, I finally got to know my brother.

THE INFAMOUS CIA INTERROGATION manual known as KUBARK notes that prisoners held in solitary confinement develop an intense love for all living things. According to his guards, Saddam Hussein while awaiting execution saved bread from his meals to feed the birds. A released prisoner tells Diane how the sight of a spider on the wall of his cell filled him with amazement and joy. In Chicago, my friend and fellow torture survivor Neris González awakens a love of life in children exposed to gang violence by giving them, of all things, earthworms to hold. And yet it seems to work. These simple pink worms inspire a sense of wonder at the mere fact of their existence. As for my brother, society tortured him and kept him in isolation and he too looked for love in the world of nature. Hernán Darío loved trees.

"They are so beautiful, and strong. People cut them down and burn them. People damage them, but look at them: they stay serene." He had erotic dreams about trees, making love with them, being wrapped in their arms, penetrated in every orifice by their branches. According to our father, *Aristiźábal* is a Basque word that means forest, or a grove of many trees. Hernán Darío said, "If I'd been born a tree, I would have been a good one." And he asked me, "Do you think trees feel pain?"

He rarely mentioned his own pain. My brother was stoic and proud. In our videotaping sessions, he talked only of the destruction mankind has wrought on the earth, on its forests and rivers, the plants and flowers and trees. When he told me about the men who molested him, he was matter-of-fact and cast no blame: "I became friends with Rafael. He seemed intelligent. He used to touch me lightly all over my body and it felt good. And then he'd give me 100 pesos to buy things for school." I thought about how vulnerable a gay child must be to predators when an invisible wall separates him from everybody else.

Like any lover worthy of the name, my brother was willing to brave danger for his beloved. I thought of the little boy who was a scaredy-cat, the one who cried in the street till the other kids taunted, *Are you a boy or a girl?* (Once Hernán Darío answered *Soy las dos! I am both!*—too young to even know what that might mean.) Now I learned that this same timid child would climb up to Monte Quitasol, traveling through territory controlled by vicious criminals and violent gangs. He could have been assaulted, raped, or killed, but he took the chance again and again because up there on the mountaintop is where he found the natural bonsai trees. They survived in places where no one would ever expect them to grow, he told me. High up, on barren rock, a seed would find just a little bit of earth to cling to. Growing small and stunted, the bonsai would cling to life. But as new shanty-towns spread higher and higher up the mountainside, the trees were threatened, all the vegetation torn up to make way for the homes of the poor. My brother would explain to the trees that he only wanted to protect them. He would ask their permission before he dug them up to carry them home where he could take care of them and love them. These were the tenacious little bonsai trees that graced our patio and that we all ignored, and in ignoring them, ignored my brother's loneliness and disrespected his great gift.

THE PUERTO RICAN SOCIOLOGIST Manolo Guzmán coined the word *sexilio* for the plight of gay Latin Americans who've felt compelled to leave their nations of origin in search of a place where they could live freely (or comparatively so) as homosexuals. I met many sexual exiles when I returned to California. In my brother's honor and driven by my own regret and guilt, I went to work for a grassroots nonprofit that offers medical and social services to lesbian, gay, bisexual, and transgendered Latina/os infected with or affected by HIV/AIDS.

For me, living in exile from my country has meant tearing up all roots and living with a pain that doesn't quit. I began to understand Hernán Darío had always felt like an alien, a stranger in his own land. He set the *macetas* of bonsai trees close together on the patio. Up on Monte Quitasol, he said, they looked so lonely. When he talked of loneliness, he was, of course talking about himself. He had no native earth, just a place as inhospitable as barren rock. The way he saw it, humans created a toxic atmosphere for him. Plants were different: "So generous. They give us oxygen even while we sleep."

Being born gay doesn't mean being condemned to a tragic life. Gay men can be as happy and well-adjusted as anyone else. I'm heterosexual and hardly the model of an untroubled psyche. But during the eight years I worked as a bilingual psychotherapist for gay Latinos, men came to my group when they were in crisis or in pain and much of that pain was rooted in society's rejection and condemnation.

My group sessions didn't focus on AIDS and HIV. There were plenty of other support groups where people could talk about their T-cell counts, the latest cocktail, and problems with side effects. Instead, we talked about life and wounds and turning points and change: "It's not a death sentence. Everybody dies of something. You didn't ask for this horrible thing to happen to you. You don't deserve it. But now that it's happened, what strengths do you find in this moment? What opportunities?" For some of my clients, the diagnosis made them take stock of their lives and opened the question of whether to reconnect with the loved ones they'd left behind.

Toño was the oldest child of a traditional Mexican family. When he was sent to military school, his inability to be the young man everyone expected him to be proved so painful that he fled to the U.S. For seven years he'd had no contact whatsoever with his family. They had no idea where he was, even whether he was dead or alive. Far from home, he felt free to explore his sexuality. Because of the values that had been instilled in him, however, he hated himself for being gay. He turned to alcohol the way my brother had turned to crack. Toño ended up on the streets, had promiscuous sex with whomever he found there, and was near death several times because of alcohol poisoning.

One day in detox, he was told he was HIV+. He'd never heard of HIV and had no idea what it meant. His diagnosis led him to my therapy group. For the first time, he found acceptance in a community. We talked a lot about the ways in which his rejection of himself had affected every aspect of his life. While medication kept the virus in check, he stayed sober and started a small business selling belts and other leather goods at the Grand Central Market downtown. It's not like he was a news-making success story in achieving the American Dream, but Toño—up on his feet now and building his life—finally contacted his family. "I'm alive and I'm in Los Angeles. I'm HIV+, but I'm earning a living and I'm okay."

En familia—In the Family—was the title of a group of short plays I directed in collaboration with Fernando Castro's performance group, Ta'yer. We invited gay Latinos to write pieces drawn from their own experience. We produced the show at a local church to give the men a chance to perform in public and at the same time sensitize the community to the realities of their lives. One of my favorite short plays in the evening, *La mamá de todos*, honored the woman who, after her own son died, dedicated herself to visiting AIDS patients in the hospital. All the men called her "Mom." She made note of everyone's birthday. For many of these men, no one had celebrated the date since they left their countries of birth behind, but she did. She brought love and comfort to people who'd been abandoned by everyone else.

Some AIDS patients were mothers themselves. Otilia found out she was HIV+ during routine tests during her pregnancy. "How did this happen to me and to my baby?" she asked. "I never used drugs or had sex with any man but my husband." She was infected by him and didn't know—may never know—exactly how. Was he bisexual? Did he shoot drugs? Did he get it from a prostitute? He told her to shut up and refused to discuss it.

For women like Otilia (and, unfortunately, I've met many) the diagnosis was the wound—unsought, undeserved, unexpected—that led them for the first time to question years of silent obedience. Women shared their stories with me and with each other. *Why did I trust him completely even though I suspected? Why did I stay with him even though in many ways he lied to me and abused me? What example am I setting for my children?* For some, it became a time of great personal empowerment. Instead of taking the diagnosis as a death sentence or pathologizing this critical time, I encouraged them to take steps towards a new way—their own chosen way—of living their lives.

BIOLOGICAL WOMEN START OUT with flat chests. They have to wait for their breasts to grow and they wait impatiently for it to happen, with the same impatience I found among the transgenders in my groups. My clients relied on hormones and, just like some biological women, on implants. Over the years, I watched them create the bodies they dreamed of.

Our group became a place to build the family most of these people had found nowhere else. I was honest with them: I couldn't pretend to know their experience. With my brother, by the end I'd come to see how very much we were alike. We both craved excitement and attention. We lived intensely and refused to let any experience pass us by. But while people smiled indulgently and called me a playboy, they turned away from Hernán Darío in disgust and had nothing for him but insults and dirty words. When I asked myself what I had in common with my transgendered clients, I realized that being an actor is an essential part of who I am, and they were much better at it than I was. No method actor ever studied a character or prepared for a role with such total commitment as these men in transition to womanhood. They learned every aspect of femininity and integrated it into their daily lives until the performance became natural. They knew I admired their remarkable skill at self-transformation. As we shared tricks of the actor's trade, most came to trust me. They understood I saw them as fellow artists and that they had my respect.

It's amazing what a person can accomplish in two short years. I saw

young boys turn into women, completely unrecognizable from their former selves. I saw the success stories, the women who disappeared seam-
lessly into society as they married, achieved the ordinary female lives
they'd always longed for. For most of my clients the road was much harder.

It's unlikely Antoinette and Marianne will ever pass for women no
matter how many hormones they take to make their angular bodies
rounder, how many sessions of electrolysis they pay for to remove
facial and body hair, and how many surgeries they undergo not only
on their genitals and breasts but their square chins, their heavy brows.
Their souls were born in the wrong bodies, exiled into masculinity, and
now as they try to reach home, it's as though no matter how well they
learn the female language, its vocabulary, its grammar, its slang, there
will always be an accent to give them away.

But sometimes all the new women are beautiful. Sometimes everyone glows with excitement. I've gone with them to clubs in West Hollywood, to a Mexican nightclub near Grand Central Market, to the
hotel ballrooms downtown where they stage beauty pageants to celebrate what they've become. These are not drag shows. I am looking
not at men dressed in women's clothing. I am admiring women.

Some dazzle with their smiles or the flash of a flirtatious glance. The
clothes are incredible. The women are often uncomfortable shopping in
stores or letting ordinary seamstresses measure their changing bodies.
Madga has developed her own talent and become fashion designer to the
group. As an actor, I'm used to costumes that may look expensive but are
made from cheap materials, quickly sewn. Here, Magda works from the
finest fabrics, rare silks, sequins hand-sewn, spangles, and seed pearls.
Other contestants have sewn their own cocktail dresses and ballgowns.

Some walk with a sway, some with a serene and regal step, but I
know the price they have paid to be here. If Hernán Darío's life was
hard, how much harder it had to be to tell the family, "I'm no longer

Carlos, I'm Carla." Besides having lived as both a man and as a woman, like many of my clients, Carla leads a double life: working as a secretary during the day and prostituting herself at night to come up with enough money to cover hormones and surgeries. Even though she's got health insurance through her job, sex reassignment services aren't covered, and Carla is determined to transition safely with legitimate medical providers.

Most of my clients know they'll never be able to afford real doctors. During a single year, four members of our group died after injecting contaminated hormones purchased on the black market. Many of them sleep in cars or on the streets and prostitute themselves there. They live clandestine lives, trusting their bodies to the self-taught unlicensed surgeons they themselves refer to as butchers. I think of Claudia bleeding to death, of what I did to Julia, of Carmen trusting in the spirit of Dr. José Gregorio, and I know the risks people will take when they are desperate.

In group, we talk a lot about danger. Women who have had to transgress every idea we have of identity are too often incarcerated, beaten, tortured, and killed. So much abuse leaves them mistrustful and hyper-vigilant. Alone, they try to cope with medical complications: breast implants that shift, allergic reactions, scars all over their bodies where skin was removed from one place to be transplanted elsewhere. For many, there are legal complications. Newly female immigrants with permanent resident status find themselves carrying green cards that identify them as men.

I have to admire people willing to pay so high a price in order to live authentic lives. But it also concerns me how single-minded these men in transition to womanhood often have to be. Some are so occupied with transforming themselves, they don't have time to educate themselves. Yes, they can tell you the going rate for a new nose, for a remodeled chin, for female breasts. They can share makeup tips. But aside from the process of feminization, many are entirely unsophisticated. Unless they can develop a broader sense of themselves and the world, once the transition is accomplished, who and what will they be? One gift they have discovered in group is the chance to meet leaders and elders of their own community: a very powerful woman who herself became a therapist; an intellectual who shared her wisdom and experience while seated in her wheelchair.

In the ballroom, everyone wants to be seen as a woman, a beautiful woman, the most beautiful woman in the world. I don't want to stay to see the winner crowned because, to me, everyone here tonight is beautiful. But for the women, the competition is intense. Jealousy leads too often to the violence that surprised and shocked me. I sometimes have to ask someone to leave the group. "You're dangerous now. Maybe you can come back at some time, but not now." When the women fight, they try to mar each other's beauty, raking a rival's face with the pointed end of a teasing comb, stabbing at the breasts. Most of the people in the group though are loyal to one another and to the organization. Many come back as volunteers after no longer needing support from a group. It's where they can be themselves and form friendships and begin love affairs and find the genuine human contact that had always eluded them.

Alexa shows off her curves in a tight, sequined dress she's told me cost more than $3,000. I want to offer her the admiration she seeks so desperately, and yet it breaks my heart. She sleeps in a car. She's gone hungry unable to buy food. Her fabulous appearance tonight—paid for through prostitution—matters more to her than anything else in her life.

"I USED TO GO to an apartment downtown," my brother told the camera. "I'd leave the door open. Men knew they could find me there and sometimes I'd have relations with ten men or more in a single night." Some men paid him. "But I didn't do it for the money. There were guys who did it to be paid or so someone would buy him good clothes. I never cared about clothes. I like myself best wearing nothing. I did it for the caresses that were so delicious. I did it because I wanted to be touched."

He also wanted to be loved. He had loved, he said, and deeply, but his love was not returned. "I just wanted to have someone near me," he said. "But one night, I was with so many men, and not one of them asked my name. Finally, I began to choose solitude." Still, there were men, and the men didn't always touch him gently. Some hit him. Some hurt him. Some burned him with cigarettes as five years later Juan Fernando would be burned by torturers; but Hernán Darío didn't call these experiences by the name of torture. He called it being made to feel.

He told his story without blaming anyone: not the family, not the men, not himself. He opened himself, simply, honestly. He and I had lived beneath the same roof for more than twenty years. I had finally asked him, "Who are you?" and he was relieved to be asked and to have the chance to answer.

I HAD LEFT COLOMBIA soon after my brother returned from rehab in Bogotá and, until I showed up with the camera, I'd never heard the whole story of what happened after he came home. Though my parents welcomed him back, eight months of attack therapy had left him, if anything, less trusting of people and so he turned to his one true love, the love that had sustained him ever since he was a child. He was just a boy, he told me, when he saw some bushes being devoured by insects and made up his mind to save them. He tried to teach himself as much botany as he could. He hated school, but spent hours—though we didn't know it—at the city's Botanical Gardens. Now, aged twenty-four and determined to stay clean, he got a low-wage job as a gardener and sales clerk in the nursery. He spent the days with the plants he loved but life had become narrow and he saw no escape. Every day, he went to work, then returned home to our parents. Work and home, work and home, as regular and unvarying as Ignacio's routine, except that Ignacio could expect to find love someday and marriage and his own home and Hernán Darío could see no such future for himself. So he focused on his job and charming the rich who came to buy orchids and other rare plants.

In Medellín, "rich" usually implied drug money and Hernán Darío's charm wasn't lost on a certain trafficker's wife. Next thing he knew, he'd been offered what seemed like an astronomical salary not to sell cocaine but to landscape the kingpin's estate. No limit to what he could spend. No limit to his imagination, except that hundreds of valuable Canary Island palm trees were already on order.

At the hacienda, cocaine was easily available but Hernán Darío was too happily engaged in his vocation to want drugs. He supervised the planting of the palms. He dredged out the earth to create a lily pond and surround it with exotic flowers. He always had a magic touch with plants, and in this climate everything grew and blossomed. The estate was surrounded by acres of untouched rainforest where my brother found new varieties of orchids that had never been identified or classified. In doing so, he discovered himself and was for the first time discovered and seen by others, respected by the boss for his landscaping work and by the university professors with whom he shared his botanical finds.

"It was paradise," he said, as long as he stayed out of the boss's way. "Not that he ever threatened me or hurt me. He liked me. But he was a crude, ignorant man who wanted to be treated like some kind of Roman emperor and sometimes it just made me sick."

Hernán Darío's paradise would be lost within a few short years. The boss's wife objected to the ornamental pond—"too many mosquitoes"—and complained about the frogs. "Their singing was just noise." The pond was drained and replaced with an Olympic-size swimming pool. One day, my brother awoke to the roaring of engines, to squealing, buzzing, crashing. Outside, tractors, bulldozers, and backhoes were at work toppling the palms and clearing acres of pristine forest. Chain saws tore through tree trunks and Hernán Darío felt as though his own body were being torn apart. Over the next few days, all his work, everything he'd loved, was destroyed. Soon the area was paved over with new roads and parking areas for luxury cars. Acres were cleared and developed for luxury housing. Stunned, my brother was too demoralized at first to do anything, even leave.

Eventually he did leave, in the middle of the night. Now, I don't know if what he told me is true. The man he worked for has never been charged with a crime and, once again, is it fear or is it fairness that has made me decide not to name him? My brother said he witnessed the sexual abuse of children. He told me that one afternoon, the drug boss invited a group of business associates over to lounge around, relax, and swim. But the boss had no intention of relaxing. He came out with a machine gun. My brother witnessed the massacre as the water in the swimming pool turned red.

In spite of how it ended, the experience at the hacienda gave my brother confidence and showed him his gift. He came home to start his own plant and garden business and finally knew that he was valued. Then came the diagnosis and the swift decline.

"Brother, let's throw a party," I said. What I meant was he should take the opportunity to say goodbye, but I couldn't bring myself to say it. "Invite everybody that you love," I said. "Everyone who loves you."

"Then I'm not inviting Ignacio or Estela or my father," he said. "Estela is disgusted by me. Ignacio rejects me. Dad won't even talk to me."

"They just don't know how."

"No," he said.

I went to my father, the man who spent hours tending Hernán Darío's plants so tenderly, making sure they were cared for now that my brother was too weak to do so.

"Talk to him," I said.

"What do you want me to say?"

Pedro always showed his love through his actions, not his words. I remembered lying in the hospital with the collapsed right lung and desperately needing to empty my bowels. I was ridiculous then. Tormented by discomfort and self-loathing and ashamed to ask for a bedpan. *You can kill babies*, I thought, *but you can't defecate in front of a nurse*. My father, inches shorter than I am, lifted me and carried me in his arms to a toilet.

"Tell him you love him," I said.

"Telling people you love them," said my father, "that's a load of shit."

"Did your father ever say he loved you?" I asked.

He looked away from me. "I don't think so."

My brother chose twenty guests. I asked each of them to bring an object that symbolized their relationship with Hernán Darío. We would let him know he was loved while thanking him for the gifts he'd brought into our lives. I knew he was suffering and I hoped our presence would conjure a force that would allow him to leave us if he was indeed ready to go.

We invited his doctor and his therapist even though they thought the party would be too much for him.

"We're not going to dance," I assured them. "It's not exactly a party. It's a ritual."

I'd begun to suspect that as human beings we needed to place ourselves inside the cosmos with the support of mythic structures. This was a departure from my deeply engrained skepticism. I was the one, after all, who had discarded the religion of my childhood. I'd put no stock in ceremonies and had made a point of not attending either my high school or college graduation. When I became a U.S. citizen, I was taken aback to see the other new Americans surrounded by celebrating family and friends when it hadn't even occurred to me to invite anyone.

But over the years, as I'd observed teenagers wounding their bodies in gang initiations, hazings, with tattoos and piercings, or seeing their first prison term as the rite of passage into manhood, surely some primal need was erupting that modern society failed to satisfy. My brother's coming of age, his initiation into sexuality, had surely marked him with terrible wounds; but unlike what would have happened in a traditional initiation, it had left him stigmatized and outside of society instead of being welcomed into the company of respected adult men.

Just as our society has forgotten the need to initiate the young, we falter when it comes to the last initiation, accompanying a loved one to the threshold that marks the transition from life to death. My brother, like me, was raised Catholic, but what comfort could Hernán Darío find in the Last Rites. Ideally, this ancient ritual brings reassurance and peace as the priest, an elder, helps the dying person cross the threshold. But how could a priest give ease to my brother if he'd be expected to confess his sexuality as mortal sin? We gathered, instead, to affirm the beauty and value of his life.

It's funny how I only remember the words the women spoke. Tía Gabriela who laughed at me when I asked the guests to ring a small bell before speaking: "Oh, Hector. You say you're not Catholic anymore, but this is just like church!" She brought a bonsai tree and told how much she loved the plants Hernán Darío brought her from the mountains: "You have so many aunts, but of them all, you only chose me. I love you so much and I am so grateful, Hernán Darío." Our cousin Raquel said, "You were my confidante and I was yours. We could tell each other anything. When I lent you money, I knew I could trust you to pay me back." She brought a portrait photo of my brother. "The day of your diagnosis, you came to me and asked for money and you didn't say why. You used it to have this picture taken and then you came back and gave me this picture. You said *I want you to always remember me the way I look here.*" A friend who had a handcrafts stall on Avenida La Playa sewed a robe for him and brought a conch shell to recall a trip they had taken to the sea. "Hernán Darío, do you remember all the times we went dancing? And how sometimes you used to mind the merchandise for me?" she asked. "As soon as I stepped away, he sold everything. Customers couldn't resist him." She gave him a friendly slap. "Neither could my boyfriends!" Seven-year-old Laura, Juan Fernando's daughter, drew a picture of a flower and told him she didn't want him to go. What did my mother say? She was present, but neither of us can remember.

"Now I have something for each of you," my brother said. He'd found the strength to set up a selection of terra cotta pots, one for each of us, and paints with which he wanted us to decorate them. One by one, as we finished painting our designs, we approached his bed so he could fill each pot with soil and place a seed inside. "Grow this plant. Take care of it for me." Before the party, he'd complained bitterly, "They won't, you know. They'll let the plants die," but now, warmed by the presence of people who loved him, he seemed shy with hope.

He handed over a pot and closed his eyes.

It was Tía Gabriela who panicked first. "My God, he's not moving!" She crossed herself. "No!"

I froze in my seat, unable to look at my brother or the people around me. Tía Gabriela was babbling away. "Hernán Darío, please! I want you to grasp to life like that little tree on its rock." I'd pushed him so hard; I'd exhausted him. I couldn't believe he had just died in front of our eyes. Everyone would blame me. Everyone would hate me. "Héctor," cried my aunt, "why did we do this? This is pagan!" I should have smuggled him into the U.S. and arranged for the latest up-to-date medical care. I should never have left, or never come back. But at the same time I was thinking *Hernán Darío, you drama queen. You're faking, aren't you?*

My brother had a perfect sense of timing. He held out for maximum suspense before opening his eyes. "I think I fell asleep," he said. "I dreamed that I died." We all breathed again as he told his dream. "I was floating up, but all these little things were floating down. Little stars maybe? Angels, cosmic dust, human souls? Then I realized they were seeds falling out of the universe, all kinds falling into the earth to take root again. Species that no longer exist were coming back, the plants that disappeared from the face of the earth were all coming back, penetrating the earth to take root. I can leave," he said, "because I know that after all the destruction here on earth, it's going to be okay. The earth is going to survive and it will once again be a place of beauty."

HERNÁN DARÍO DIDN'T RELENT. My father wasn't invited, but again and again I watch a segment on the videotape in which my brother and my father stand together on the train platform in downtown Medellín. Hernán Darío has his arms around my father, and both of them are smiling. Then I notice my brother is smiling in a rather sly and provocative way. If I didn't know the two people in the picture, I might not be sure whether I was looking at a young man and his Sugar Daddy or a father and son. My father's smile looks forced.

Well, of course, he knows his son is dying. But beyond that, his whole posture suggests he is uncomfortable as he stoically accepts this very public embrace. Every time I watch this tape, I understand it differently. Sometimes my brother is deliberately provoking my father, trying to embarrass him. But that's okay: the Hernán Darío I most like to remember was no victim; he knew how to prod people, put them in their place. I also take the picture at face value: in spite of everything, my father and my brother loved each other.

After the ritual, I flew back to California. Hernán Darío died two weeks later. The body that had been the source of so much pleasure and so much pain was little more than a skeleton. He was thirty-two years old and weighed no more than sixty pounds. It was Palm Sunday, 1996, and all over Medellín people were carrying palm fronds to church as though all the fallen trees had come to mourn the man who was their brother, too. So many miles away, I mourned him, feeling the wounds of guilt and loss.

Some people, my brother among them, are like sacrificial lambs. They don't take on our sins or redeem our sins, but they reveal them: our cruelty, our narrow-mindedness, our discomfort with difference, and our baffled incomprehension. They awaken compassion and open the heart. Without their stories and their sacrifice, the conscience goes on sleeping. I'd loved my brother, but now I was grateful to him. Hernán Darío woke me up.

Chapter 5

Resurrection

*[H]ealing doesn't mean that our pain and suffering go
away. Healing is learning to live in a different relationship with our pain and suffering so it does not control us.*
—from *At Hell's Gate: A Soldier's Journey
from War to Peace* by Claude Anshin Thomas,
a Vietnam War veteran who became a Zen monk

I could never forget what he looked like. If I ever found him
again, I would have my revenge. Short curly hair, stocky body. The
thick eyebrows and a small mustache, broad shoulders, a small but
noticeable belly, and penetrating greenish eyes. But when I try to picture him now, I'm confused: the image of my torturer merges with a
picture of Peligro, the man who raped my brother.

My torturer. That's a pronoun I need to lose, and one I hear from so
many other survivors—*my* perpetrator, *my* rapist; because while the
state-sponsored violation of a person's body is a very specific assault, it
has much in common with other atrocities. When you're in that room,
that isolated place where no help can reach you, where you can no longer count on family or friends or human decency, one person is with
you. He was entirely focused on me, controlling me, watching me, listening to my breath, keeping me alive while holding over me the power
of life and death. And I had never in my life paid such close attention

to anyone. I was alert to him and to his every response, trying to predict his every move with all my senses, until pain overwhelmed everything and I lost my very identity. In that moment of utter surrender, when everyone else had abandoned me, when my own body and mind betrayed me, only he was there.

For a long time the man who tortured me was a primary figure in my mental life.

I now understand that one of the long-lasting effects of the trauma is to confuse that enforced and claustrophobic connection with intimacy. I need to break that connection and recreate the loving connections in my life. I need to think of that man as *the* torturer, and not *my* torturer, and to understand that he belonged to the army, to the system of repression, and not to me.

STILL, HE MARKED ME. He led me away from the wall. "They already know you are an urban commando leader and they know you are training those kids." *They.* He dressed in civilian clothing, as though he was different. "I recommend that you cooperate. If you don't tell them everything they want to know, you will be killed, and your brother, too."

The handcuffs came off before they took my mug shot. Then the handcuffs went back on and a blindfold. Someone pushed me and I heard a door slam and lock. I listened to footfalls leaving. After a while, footsteps returned. Someone entered the room. He barked out questions: *Name? Nickname? What organization do you belong to?*

"Sir, I don't belong to any organization."

The blow knocked the wind out of me. The fists slammed into my stomach again. I doubled over and he kicked me.

"What actions have you planned? Where do you cache your weapons?"

I had no answers for him, and so he beat me. Except for when he knocked me to the ground, I was not permitted to lie down or sit but had to remain standing day and night. When he left, the torture became psychological as I waited with no hope of rescue for his return. The door creaked open. No food. No water. No sleep. More questions for which I had no answers and gave him evasive lies.

A second interrogator came to see me. From his way of speaking, this one seemed to be an educated, well-mannered man. He pretended to be my friend; I pretended to believe him. "If you don't give me names," he said in a kind voice, "that man is going to come back. Your brother is already in very bad shape, and if that man comes back, I can't guarantee you will survive." But I had no names to give them.

The torturer called soldiers to help him. They hold my head under water. They strip me and attach the electrodes. Only they can hear my screams. Then, *el potro*—an ingenious technique that can leave permanent damage but no scars. Soldiers I cannot see cover my hands and lower arms with what feels like a wet sweater. Something is pulled tight, then my arms are jerked behind me and somehow I'm hanging in space over an abyss of pain, arms wrenched from sockets, my body extended so that the pain is everywhere.

I'm utterly abandoned. The pain disseminates itself to every cell. It extends to the brain and blows out all conscious thought, all sense of self. Was there always a void in the center of me? It's there now. I disintegrate and fall into it.

ALL OF THAT is true, but it's not the whole truth.

The narrative I tell myself is a form of recycling. I look again at a dirty experience I instinctively wish to get rid of, and instead try to find in it what's of value and of use; because any time you go through a difficult ordeal, it can awaken inner resources and reveal strengths. The torturer treated me as an object. But I resisted.

WHAT DOES IT MEAN to resist? If you have lived through physical or emotional violence and survived, you have resisted the attempt to extinguish your being. Legal definitions about what is or is not "resistance" confuse the issue and may leave survivors wrestling with guilt: *I should have fought back. I should have screamed. I should have gotten out before it was too late.* Maybe dissociating, dividing yourself and separating from your body is what helped you live through trauma. It's not that at the time you were thinking *if I use this, if I do it, I'm going to be able to survive,* but your mind and body knew instinctively how to protect you. Of course, you'll always have doubts—*Could I have? Should I have?*— but if you don't honor your own survival you keep perpetuating what was done to you.

Then there are people who survive the experience of having willingly, or under orders, violated deeply engrained moral law. Our binary way of thinking—victims on one side; perpetrators on the other—often oversimplifies. You would think I would hate anyone implicated in the practice of torture, but then I hear about former interrogators who've returned to the U.S. tortured in conscience. Just as my identity disintegrated in the torture chamber, I've heard one anguished man cry, "I am not who I thought I was."

In my own life, I prefer to see posttraumatic stress as an essential part of the healing process rather than pathological symptoms that need eradication. The nightmares and recurring, intrusive thoughts are the psyche calling attention to the wound as it seeks to rebuild itself. To remember, to put the pieces back together. I ask myself what my psyche is trying to say. What needs to be forgiven and absolved? What do I need to understand and to learn? I don't resist revisiting the wound, but I fight against obsessive thoughts of my weakness. Instead, I go back to find out what made me strong enough to survive.

So here's the other equally true version of my story, the narrative not of my helplessness, but of my resistance.

He blindfolded me and someone pushed me into a room. About twenty minutes later, I heard the lock turn, the door creak open and I recognized the same smell of tobacco and sweat. Though the man who came to torture me tried to disguise his voice, I realized I was dealing with the same fat individual in civilian clothes who led me up the hill. At that moment, I lost all respect for him. He thought he could hide his identity; he thought I was completely vulnerable and at his mercy. But at that moment, I felt superior. I could identify him. That meant I was holding a card he didn't know I had and that gave me a feeling of power.

It's true the pain was often unbearable; it's also true that I often exaggerated it. I'd done so much physical training as an actor, I could make myself fly back through the room when he hit me. I'd land back against the wall, and get some idea of the dimensions of this terrible space. When they submerged my head, I put on such a great act of drowning, I scared them. I pretended to be more exhausted than I was, falling against the torturer. When he instinctively reached out to catch me, I sighed and pretended to fall asleep in his arms. He didn't like that one bit! Though I could not resist the things they did to me, I refused to be passive. Would my ploys be of any use? I had no idea, but each time I believed I'd outwitted my tormentors, I felt stronger.

I was not an urban guerrilla. In reality, I had nothing to hide, but still I played a role. I would not let that man see me as I really was. I tell myself my performance helped save me.

I tried to learn as much about my situation as I could even when I had no idea how the information might serve me. A loose paving stone in the passageway echoed with a clunk every time the torturer or a guard came within nine or ten steps of the cell. At first, the sound made me panic; it meant I was going to be hurt. But then I realized it gave me warning; I knew when the torturer was coming back. More important, the sound let me know when I was alone and when I was being watched. I counted out the time it took for the guard to make his transit up and down the passage. Then I knew how many minutes I had when I wouldn't be seen. There was something else I could use to my advantage. My hands had been bound behind my back when I was arrested, but after the mug shot, the soldier had handcuffed me in front. This meant I could raise my wrists and push back the blindfold, if I dared.

Clunk. Heart pounding, I waited. I slowly raised my wrists but I didn't have the guts to go further. I counted the minutes. I waited. Clunk. I tried again. Were they watching? I let myself touch the blindfold. I scratched my forehead, waiting to see if anything would happen. I waited. No one hit me. I counted out the time. Clunk. I had to remove the blindfold but. . . . *Next time*, I kept telling myself. *I'll do it next time. . . . But they'll catch me*, I thought, and then again promised myself *next time*. It took me what felt like forever, but then I did it. I pushed the blindfold back.

Through the bars I could see down the hill. I saw the wall, and Mono, alive, looking scared. Even at a distance I could sense his tension, but he was alive. He was okay. They had lied to me.

In the story I tell myself now, I saved my brother and he saved me. Every time the torturer entered, all I could talk about was Juan Fernando. *Where is my brother? What are you doing to him? Please don't touch him. He has mental problems.* I'm convinced this saved him from torture. *He's fragile. If anything happens to him, our mother will die.* I named people I knew at the mental hospital and claimed they had treated him. By holding onto my love and concern for Mono, I never entirely lost my connection to humanity outside that room. My emotional ties were not completely broken.

Once I finally pushed the blindfold back and got away with it, I did it again and again. But each time the torturer returned, I was standing obediently in the exact same place in the room. Each time I *looked*, my first act was to reassure myself that my brother was still all right. Then I went further. To my surprise, I saw my cell had a toilet. Though I kept complaining of hunger and exhaustion and thirst, when I was unobserved, I was able to drink from the tank. The interrogators had left a pile of evidence in the middle of the room: the ELN pamphlet, a photo of one of the mental patients from the hospital in a barred cell, the so-called guerrilla hostage. At the bottom of the pile was the only evidence with my name and with my handwriting: the copy of the letter to Radio Havana Cuba. I tore it up and flushed it down the toilet. The noise was a risk, but not taking that risk seemed the greater danger.

At the end of ten days, we were brought before a military judge. Juan Fernando and his friends were sent to prison as the machete they carried for their camping trip was labeled a subversive weapon. I was released for lack of evidence. I'd gone through an ordeal, not at the hands of the elders, but at the hands of a perpetrator. In this perverted form of an initiation rite, I was told lies instead of myth. I'd survived but I wasn't brought back to the community and celebrated. The perpetrators left me in the wilderness and it was up to me, through my own resources, to find the way home. The people who loved me weren't prepared for this situation either. I would have to figure out for myself how to reconnect with my society.

I WOULDN'T PRESUME TO claim the title of a shaman, but I have tried to resignify what happened to me at Batallón Bomboná in 1982 with the shamanic experience in mind. The shaman is someone who's undergone a break with the reality most of us rely on. His or her identity has disintegrated. He has descended to hell, but has also returned, and that means he knows the path. He can go and come back, descend and return, and from those terrible depths the shaman brings back medicine and knowledge. Since my arrest and torture, I have carried the knowledge of how fragile we are, how tenuous our safety. I know I can fall apart again, and I have done so. But I've also had the experience of rebuilding myself, and that, too, I know I can do.

The shaman doesn't merely return from hell for his own sake. So I feel I must bring a story back to the world: I must speak out against torture, I must bring healing to those who've been to hell and are finding it hard to rediscover the path back to life on their own. Initiation remains at the stage of ordeal unless I find a way to share the gift of medicine I found with my wound.

A woman approached me one evening after one of my performances. She said she could not imagine how I'd been through such terrible events and come out of it seemingly whole. I explained that we human beings seek meaning by creating narratives about our lives and I refuse the narrative that casts me as "poor victim." Those of us who've survived torture or any other trauma need to see it as simply one event in our lives, not the definition of our identity. I don't want to hold onto the trauma but rather to reimagine it, see it with new eyes. The wound can be both tomb and womb, I explained. Something was killed within me, but something else was born. What dies needs to be mourned, while what is newly born demands recognition.

As our conversation continued, she told me she had never known her father. That is a pain I cannot even imagine.

WHAT COMES AFTER SURVIVAL?

At that moment I felt relief and joy and a full appreciation of life and of freedom. Julia feared I was dead. She thought she'd never see me again. What sweeter memory than the look on her face when I appeared at her school as she was leaving class? I learned that all the time I believed myself abandoned, my parents were searching for me. My mother pulled strings and got into the army headquarters but was not allowed to see Juan Fernando or me. My father contacted anyone he could think of who might help. So there was love.

There was also fear. I worried about my brother and I couldn't forget the high-ranking officer who'd made a threat before my release, pressing his index finger against my head. "If I ever see you again, you're dead." Soldiers often took matters into their own hands when they considered the judicial system too soft, and so I went into hiding. I wasn't free to go wherever I wished, but I felt very free because I was contained by love. My friend Alvaro Díaz took me to stay at his beautiful home where I felt cared for and safe. He protected me not only from the soldiers but from myself because my desire for revenge had me burning with rage. I had wild fantasies of returning to Batallón

Bomboná and killing the man who had tortured me. The rage was real, but the fantasy had little basis in reality. I had no weapon and no plans to get one. I saw myself grabbing him and breaking his neck with my bare hands, none of which was likely to happen. However, if I did go back to the barracks, I would almost certainly be shot.

Aside from the rage that came roaring up uncontrollably, I had changed in other ways. One friend said I'd lost my innocence and my sense of humor. I could still clown around and make people laugh. I could still make the sounds of laughter. But my capacity to be light-hearted and carefree was gone. Strange to say, I could have fun but I couldn't feel the deep happiness we call joy.

I took chances. I slipped away for brief visits to my family so that my mother could see I was all right and to find out what they had heard about Mono. And one day, I got a message that Chucho Peña, the poet of the barrio, had disappeared. Chucho's brother was looking for me. When he reached me, he explained that someone had called the family. "They say there's a body and it might be Chucho." He asked me to meet him and go with him to see. Somehow, in spite of the danger, I agreed.

Chucho's body had been thrown in a ditch and it was already starting to decompose. One of his eyes had been plucked out and so were his fingernails. His face and body were burned with acid and he'd been shot in the head. I looked and knew this was exactly what could have happened to me and to my brother. I was enraged and also terrified. This is what Chucho got for writing poetry; this is what I knew could happen to me if they captured me again. This is what did happen years later to my brother Mono.

I don't remember how long I stayed in hiding. While I was in the hands of the army, I'd been focused on keeping track of day and night and counting the days they held me. But for a long time after my release, I remained disoriented, unable to comprehend calendar dates or the passage of time. Whole periods leading up to my arrest also remain a blur.

"When were you arrested?" Diane asks me.

"1982."

"I mean, what month?" I don't answer. "What season of the year?" but I don't know.

She asks my parents and they both promptly answer, "*Agosto*."

WHEN I TELL PEOPLE the story of my arrest and torture—in an interview, for example—they always want to know what was done to me, and how many times, and how much it hurt. Though I talk about many other subjects, everyone focuses on what happened to me more than twenty-five years ago. It no longer troubles me to tell my story, but I no longer want to give the sensational details of what occurred unless at the same time I can talk about putting an end to torture and can talk about healing.

I travel the country performing and speaking out: the only thing that torture guarantees is pain; it never guarantees the truth. My friend Carlos Mauricio, for example, was a university professor in El Salvador when men dragged him out of his classroom one day in 1983 and demanded information about the guerrilla movement. According to the torturers, his failure to confess proved he had been to Cuba to learn techniques of resisting interrogation. "Admit you've been to Cuba! Confess!" At last, beaten bloody, Carlos made a false confession to stop the pain. When the interrogators next wanted to know everything he had done in Cuba and everyone he'd met, the torture started up again because he was unable to provide details about the place he had never been.

Now and then, someone will tell you that torture works. Former U.S. Vice President Dick Cheney's claims that torture led to actionable intelligence have been shown to be false. Many people will tell you that torture worked for the French during the Battle of Algiers. However, this assertion has been debunked by Darius Rejali in his exhaustive study *Torture and Democracy*. Rejali reports that the tortured Algerian insurgent did give up the location of a bomb factory but he held out long enough so that by the time the French arrived the place was cleared out and the bomb-making materials all removed. Not only did torture discredit the French mission, but it turned out that the French soldiers had been so busy torturing, they failed to notice their prisoner had a map in his pocket with all the information they needed.

Torture doesn't stop or prevent terror. The purpose of torture is to *sow* terror, and so many survivors speak reluctantly, if they are able to speak at all. We Latin Americans who survived the horrific repression of the 1970s and 80s have had decades to process our emotions and to learn that breaking silence is part of healing. We have learned we need to reconnect to the world outside. The trauma robs you of your community, your language, and your relations. All these connections are broken and must be forged anew. For me, the most effective way to do this was to join with others to work for justice.

TASSC, the Torture Abolition and Survivors Support Coalition International, was founded by Sister Dianna Ortiz, a North American nun who went to Guatemala as a missionary, living among the indigenous poor. In 1989, she was snatched by soldiers (with a CIA operative apparently among them), and they inflicted horrific physical abuse upon her, including rape. For me, in a way, torture confirmed my identity. You can never really be prepared for it—being detained, held in secret, physically abused—but all of this was what a Latin American dissident of my era had come to expect. Sister Dianna, though, had trusted in God and humanity. She had trusted in the U.S. government, and suddenly everything was thrown into question. She lived through all this trauma, as well as the disinformation campaign of accusations and personal attacks launched by U.S. officials once she grew strong enough to seek justice. Founding TASSC was an act of great courage and a huge step in her healing.

In June 2006, we gathered in a beautiful meeting place provided by Catholic University in Washington, DC. Survivors, therapists, and other supporters sat in a circle around the altar we created with flowers, stones, and fruits of the earth. We lit candles—more than 150 of them—to represent every country on earth where torture is used. There were survivors from Latin America, the Philippines, and Vietnam. We met Iraqis who'd been tortured under Saddam. Some survivors had been tortured for being Communists, others were tortured by Communist governments, making it clear that torture isn't a matter of ideology, but of power. Maybe, I think, it comes from powerlessness: a regime that lacks the loyalty and support of the people can only maintain itself through violence.

We told our stories with psychotherapists standing by to provide support if needed. A Rwandan survivor proved to me again that when oppressors try to break our most important connections, some of us resist instead by strengthening our commitments and our love. He told of the terrifying sacrifices he and his wife had made to protect one another and their children. They held onto love, but in the end, only he and one child survived. One woman told her story for the first time, in a voice so low that no one understood a word she said, but we honored her courageous first step.

I was fine—angry, of course, but fine—as Carlos Mauricio told how the soldiers broke his bones, and how they smashed his eyeglasses so that shards penetrated his eye. But when he told about being confined in a basement while the Red Cross was searching for him and other prisoners, when he described the cold and damp and the cockroaches running over the low ceiling, I was immediately back in that dungeon. My heart went wild with tachycardia and I broke out in a cold sweat. Posttraumatic stress does not control my life, but I recognize that it's beneath the surface, and that the terror will never be completely gone.

I met many remarkable human beings in Washington, but two encounters stand out. A tall man approached me at TASSC and introduced himself as Patrick. "So I finally meet you," he said. "You're the guy we were looking for!" He'd been part of the human rights delegation that stood directly above the dungeon where we were held, demanding to see us. Though the army denied holding us, this show of concern may have been what saved our lives. It had taken me twenty-four years to meet Patricio Rice and to thank him face to face.

Then, one rainy afternoon in the nation's capital, I went with other survivors to stand outside the White House and saw a man kneeling on the sidewalk dressed in an orange jumpsuit and black hood. He turned out to be an ordinary citizen who works in the area. He'd been kneeling like this every day during his lunch hour, rain or shine, no matter the cold. He wanted government workers and tourists to be reminded of the injustice, of hundreds held without charges in Guantánamo, and of the denial of basic legal and human rights. I wish I knew his name. This anonymous citizen—one person acting quietly on his own—said he would continue bearing witness until the prison camp at Guantánamo was closed and the prisoners received fair trials or were set free.

To help others to heal, I became a member of the board of the Program for Torture Victims (PTV), the first program in the U.S. dedicated to treating survivors suffering the physical and psychological consequences of state-sponsored violence.

PTV got its start in 1980 after two Latin American exiles met in Los Angeles. Dr. José Quiroga, a cardiologist, had been Chilean president Salvador Allende's personal physician before the military coup that cost Allende his life. Ana Deutsch, a psychologist, survived the dirty war in Argentina, escaping to the U.S. along with her family after the military government threatened to arrest them for their opposition activities. Ana and José knew survivors in Los Angeles who weren't getting the care they needed and they simply began offering their services, often in their own living rooms, free of charge. They recognized that survivors often find it hard to concentrate, to go to school, hold a job, or accomplish the tasks of everyday life. They can experience pervasive feelings of distrust, disconnection, rage, and desire for revenge. Asylum-seekers and refugees are often extremely withdrawn. They don't want their names known, or even their countries of origin. They fear agents of their governments who are here in the U.S. and most of all they fear endangering the family, friends, and colleagues they've had to leave behind. In addition to medical treatment for their physical injuries, they need a safe supportive environment in which to find emotional release. They need people they can trust, a new family. José and Ana tried to provide all this.

In 1994, PTV gained nonprofit status and the founders were finally able to seek outside funding, rent offices at Mercado La Paloma, and expand a staff of therapists, social workers, and administrators, as well as a roster of cooperating doctors and immigration asylum attorneys.

At first, most clients came from Latin America. Today, PTV serves people from more than sixty-five countries around the world from Afghanistan to Zimbabwe. As a board member, I often speak on behalf of PTV, while as a therapist I reach out to my fellow survivors through the Healing Club. We get together and play theater games. We play soccer. We dance. We go to the beach and to parks. We have fun, but in service, too, of a serious purpose. When you have a severely traumatized person who can't meet your eye and can't get articulate words out, how will this person be able to go to an asylum hearing and face the immigration judge and answer questions about torture and rape? The games we play are a way to prepare them. I don't do anything threatening. I don't bring up the big issues, at least not at first. We play. Nothing is at stake. This allows people to come back into their bodies and reclaim their voices.

After months of working, or playing, a survivor from Cameroon who arrived in the U.S. rendered mute was able to make a statement to a group of college students. Admittedly, his presentation was brief and he spoke in general terms, offering no personal account. More privately, he told me he loves the U.S. because in this country, everyone gets a fair trial and only terrible criminals go to prison: "Why doesn't the U.S. care about Cameroon?" he added. "President Bush invades Iraq to get rid of a dictator. Why won't he invade my country?" This man had suffered horribly for speaking out in dissent in his homeland. Much as I quietly disagreed with his opinions, what mattered to me was that he could express them.

MUSICIANS HAVE LEFT THEIR handprints on Hollywood's Rock Walk, under the red awning of the Guitar Center. I'm with Meluleki. He's a tall, handsome young man, always clean-cut and, like many Africans I've met in LA, always rather formal. We look to see if an African musician has been honored. Instead, I spot a pick embedded in cement, and a gold-colored bottleneck for slide guitar, and then the hand-prints and scrawled signature of Joe Cocker, one of my adolescent heroes. At parties, I used to imitate him, playing "With a Little Help from my Friends," Woodstock-style, on what Americans call "air guitar" and what I referred to as playing my bellybutton.

My friend Meluleki has been in the U.S. for two years, sitting in an apartment, doing nothing, just depressed and waiting while the government decides whether to grant his application for asylum.

"Go out," I suggested once. "Get a job. Even if it's a crummy job. Just something to do."

"No," he said. "They told me since I ask for asylum I'm not allowed to work. If they catch me working, I don't get it."

Asylum-seekers who aren't independently wealthy have to rely on family, friends, and charities, or else they eat air. People who've been through hell spend years in limbo. So Meluleki waited, with no money and nothing to do. All he had were memories of the life he used to lead and the political violence and torture that made him leave that life behind.

I imagine he was like me in that chamber, tormented not just with the pain or the interrogator's questions, but the bigger questions that never leave you: *Where is everybody? Where is my family, my friends, the country, the values of this society? Why can this happen apparently with such absolute ease? How can these people treat other human beings like this? Why doesn't anyone care? Where are the people?*

I don't want Meluleki to be alone. I want him to know *your people are here.*

In Zimbabwe, Meluleki was an actor which is why his therapist, Ken Louria, wanted us to meet. Now he speaks so softly the words come out and are swallowed back almost before I can hear what he's said. Someone who doesn't know the long-term consequences of torture might find it hard to believe this man was once on the stage, that he projected his voice in street performances in the open air.

Inside the store, he takes a quick look at the shiny new electric guitars but we are here to buy a drum. And not just any drum: a *djembe* drum, a healing drum. We hear a beat that leads us up the stairs to where a man dressed as if for the office in suit and tie holds a snare drum head detached from its drum and raps it sharply with a stick. I take Meluleki to the alcove decorated with African masks. There are claves, cowbells, shakers, everything you might need for Latin percussion; cane and gourd rattles from Ghana; and, in the corner, *djembe* drums—drums painted in the colors of Africa, another in a multi-mask design, more adorned with brightly patterned swirls. The drum Meluleki chooses isn't painted. Instead, it's the grain of the wood and the simplicity of the braided cord around the drumhead that give it beauty. The sales clerk comes over to offer help, but for the first time since I've known Meluleki it's clear he needs no help from anyone. As soon as his fingers and palm touch the goatskin, my friend is fully alive.

Over lunch, I ask Meluleki about the initiation rites of his tribe.

"The older men of the village initiate you," he explains. "Your uncles, not your father. If something is bothering me or I am in some trouble, I tell my uncle. He may then talk to my father or instruct me to do it, but in our custom I never go directly to my father."

"Who would be the equivalent of your uncle in Los Angeles?" I ask.

He names his therapist. He names the whole PTV program. "And you," he says, "because you were with me to get this drum."

"To celebrate you getting your asylum, your uncles should offer you a welcoming ceremony," I say.

He smiles. "That will be good, and I will tell you how."

And so one afternoon we sit in a circle in the meeting room down-stairs at Mercado La Paloma. The conference table is gone and the walls are decorated with African fabrics. We are survivors and staff and children and friends. We come from the U.S. and Sri Lanka, Congo, Guatemala, Eritrea, France, Italy, Palestine, El Salvador, and more. We speak English, Spanish, Shona, Russian, Armenian, and Georgian, Tigrinya, Singhalese, Arabic, Italian, Amharic, and more African languages than I can name.

"I am Hector," I say, moving my arms in a flourish. Everyone repeats, "I am Hector," and the whole circle copies me, waving their arms. "I am Melu," says Meluleki. One by one, we introduce ourselves—a name and gesture, to be imitated and celebrated by all. At last, we're back to Meluleki. Now it's his chance to say more than his name, to tell us all exactly how he wants to be known.

He begins to drum. He speaks in remembrance of those who have died in Zimbabwe. Then: "My name is Meluleki. My umbilical cord was buried in the red soils of *kwaGodlwayo omnyama*...." Instantly, the Zimbabwean women in the room begin to ululate, galvanizing us all. They join in Meluleki's praise of his people: "... *umahlaba ayithwale owadeluku biya ngamahlahla wabiya ngamakhand' amadoda*." "This," he says, "is how I praise my chief and identify with the sons and daughters of the soil, the people of my origin, the Ndebele tribe. I remember growing up in the presence of the Fifth Brigade commonly known as the *gukurahundi*, one of the most ruthless armies that have ever existed on this planet. They massacred more than 30,000 of my beloved brothers and sisters upon the instructions of the so-called angel of death, Robert Gabriel Mugabe, who has successfully destroyed my motherland for the past twenty-seven years. I tried with my fellow comrades to voice our concerns through staging theater shows in the schools, crèches, youth centers, and the streets of Bulawayo, but the message was too clear to go unheard by the little dogs that he has planted all over. These people visited me without an invitation and, believe me, it was not a pleasant visit. This is what they did to me."

He doesn't speak now, but his hands fly as he drums, hard and fast, and faster.

"Today I have a scar on my forehead. When I look at the mirror I see a defeated warrior, but it's only for the moment."

Will Mugabe fall at last? Will Meluleki someday return home?

He taps his drum. His fellow countrymen join him as they sing the national anthem: *Mayihlom' ihlasele, nkosi sikelel' izwe lase Zimbabwe.*

We welcome him to the PTV family, first with words: a welcome from his therapist, Ken Louria. A man from Cameroon talks of the support people must give each other: "No matter where you are or how bold, you need someone in front carrying the torch." We welcome him then with our drums. I've got mine. Enzo Fina, the musician with whom I often collaborate, is playing too, and so is case manager Saba Kidane, who's brought a drum of her own and can't stop smiling as she joins in.

We teach each other songs in our different languages and, when we start to dance, I see the African woman—the one who has sat silent and stiff with tears on her expressionless face—suddenly rise. She's out in front now, leading the dance, swaying and clapping.

"Look, look," says her friend. "This is the first time I see her happy since she arrives in the United States."

Now we have welcomed Meluleki and this woman, too, into the PTV community. It remains to be seen whether they will be welcomed by Los Angeles and into the wider community of the U.S.A.

Where is everybody?

We are here.

Chapter 6

Torn up by the Roots

If they build a 25-meter high wall, we bring a 26-meter high ladder.

—anonymous, on the south side
of the U.S.-Mexico border.

Like many exiles, I became one almost without realizing it. I'd been critical of the United States all my adult life, I spoke no English, except for some rock music lyrics and *Kissinger, Go Home!* Yet one day in 1989, I boarded a flight for Miami, heading right into the mouth of the wolf. How long would I be gone? I didn't know. When I left Colombia, all I knew was that I had to get out.

I was twenty-nine years old and loved the life I was leading. But if I stayed, it was all too likely I would lose it. Aside from the constant threats and carnage, people who cared for me saw I was self-destructing. My life was a mess. For seven years following my release by the army I'd lived intensely, treating each day and night as if it were my last. I'd escaped death so many times, I felt invulnerable, and that made me reckless. I worked all day, caroused all night. I went to my parents' home only to sleep on those occasional nights when I went to bed at home. I only felt fully alive at the edge, flirting with death; and in Medellín at that time, death was always near.

Pablo Escobar called dynamite the poor man's atomic bomb and when he declared war on the government, he didn't hesitate to use it. Politicians who thought he should be extradited to the U.S. and the judges and journalists he'd been unable to buy were the main targets of his car bombs. But it didn't matter who else died along with them. He sent out his army of suicide bombers: *los desechables*, the disposable people. Some were rumored to be dying of AIDS. Some were homeless men who were taken in and fed and cared for and then tricked into carrying out missions from which they had no idea they wouldn't return. Still others agreed to die with the understanding that their mothers would receive generous compensation.

Explosions, bursts of machine-gun fire: when and where were unpredictable, but the horrendous daily body count was something we came to expect. Besides the war declared by Pablo Escobar, the army continued to kill as did the paramilitaries, who while in the pay of wealthy landowners, were often allied with the army itself. In the low-income *comunas*, street gangs claimed one political identification or another while battling violently for turf.

One of my mentors, Dr. Héctor Abad Gómez, created a new academic specialty, violentology. For years, he'd insisted on addressing disease and early death in Colombia by working to provide running water and sewer systems and vaccinations. He saw poverty and resulting malnutrition as the underlying cause of much illness. Now he began to conceptualize Medellín's violence as a public health problem and sought to discover its roots and how it spread.

For one of the first violentology research projects, I interviewed many of the *sicarios*, the teenage assassins who were so notorious at the time. These kids were trained to fire machine guns from motorcycles traveling thirty-five kilometers per hour. Then they commended their souls and their missions to their patron saint, María Auxiliadora, and carried out killings for the cocaine mafia and the extreme right-wing paramilitary militias. I would interview these boys in the *comunas* or in the hospital, because every weekend some of them got shot. Most of them were killed during the course of the study, often by whoever had hired them and didn't want them to talk. Their attitude was: *So what if I live only another two years, or another two months? Right now I've got a Kawasaki, and I can buy a house for my mom and support the family.* How could I hate them? They were a lot like the *gamines* Xicotico knew, who'd fled to the streets to escape domestic brutality. Now I saw how the sicarios used their new power to stand up to drunken fathers: *Stop beating my mother and get the hell out of here.* They were just like the kids I'd grown up with. In my neighborhood, juvenile assassins transformed their rundown houses into three-story buildings filled with the latest conveniences. Part of me could understand them, but kids just like these were killing my friends.

One afternoon I was with the mourners at the wake for a murdered union leader when we heard shots fired outside the door. We scattered in all directions, looking for cover. A boy with a gun ran in chasing my friend Dr. Leonardo Betancur. I took shelter with a mob of people crushed together in a claustrophobic room. We waited for the sicario to open the door and kill us. When it was quiet at last we dared to emerge. We found Dr. Betancur shot dead in the kitchen.

Outside the building, Héctor Abad Gómez lay dead in the street while his son, overcome by pain and rage, shouted: *Hijueputas! cobardes!* In any other country, I thought, Héctor Abad Gómez would have been honored. Instead, for addressing the needs of the poor, he'd been defamed, accused of being a Communist and guerrilla sympathizer, threatened, and now he was dead.

The thirteen-year-old kid who killed them both was shot dead a block away as he ran from the scene. No, that's wrong. Their assassin was never identified or caught. The thirteen-year-old who was killed to keep him from talking, that was another killing. The deaths all run together in my mind because it happened so many times. You'd be at a funeral or a meeting or walking down the street, going about your daily life, and the gunman would approach or the motorcycle would pass, one teenager driving while the shooter in the back took aim and fired. Over and over again.

We could always guess who was behind the killings. It was an open secret. Everyone knew when the mafia was involved. Everyone knew when the killings were politically motivated and who was implicated in giving the order, but no one said the names out loud, except for the kids I interviewed. That knowledge made me a target, along with them. One day, I'd just interviewed a kid named Flaco in his hospital room at San Vicente de Paul when I heard gunfire right there in the hospital. I threw myself on the floor. When it was over, Flaco had been perforated by a hail of bullets, but I'd survived once more.

Now, on board the jet, the flight attendant approached me. Feminism hadn't yet caught up with Avianca. You didn't get a flight attendant job unless you looked like a model, and this woman would have been a dream to look at, even if she hadn't given me a big smile along with a glass of champagne. "The captain sends this to you," she said.

The whole trip seemed unreal. People like me just did not get visas for the U.S. Especially if we came from Medellín during the Pablo Escobar era, we were looked at with great suspicion. Colombians applied for student visas or visitors visas again and again and were rejected by the U.S. Embassy. But I had met a man with the Lions Club who put together packages that took wealthy young Colombians to study at a Catholic college in Dubuque. I told him I wanted to go. At age twenty-nine, I was much older than the other students, and that didn't look good. But CENIT provided a letter saying they wished me to become proficient in English as we increasingly treated an international clientele. My application went right into the pile along with those of the rich kids.

My parents sold their house to raise the cash I needed. It wasn't as hard as we expected to give up the property they had owned for so long. That house had seen so much despair, moving out might give the family a new start. They kept half the money so they could rent a place to live until I could repay them. We were afraid I still wouldn't look prosperous enough to be granted a visa and so I turned to La Negra for a loan. But none of this really made sense. I didn't want to go to the U.S. If I were going to leave home at all, I wanted to go to France and continue my studies in the land of Lacan and Foucault. All I could hope was that once I got out of Colombia, I would find my way somehow to Paris.

The flight attendant returned. "The captain would like to invite you to the cabin."

As luck would have it, the pilot of the jet taking me to my new life was a friend of La Negra's.

"Miami, eh?" the pilot said in that knowing tone of voice I'd come to recognize. Even some of my closest friends believed I'd succumbed to the lure of drug money and was going to the U.S. as a trafficker.

"It's the cheapest flight," I said. "From there I need to get to Iowa."

"Where?"

Maybe he didn't know where it was either. It sure wasn't Paris. "To learn English," I said.

Whether he believed me or not, he welcomed me to the cockpit. "More champagne? Or would you prefer whiskey?"

• • •

VERY FEW OF THE immigrants I meet today reach the U.S. traveling, as I did, in style.

I'm called in to work with fourteen-year-old Genaro when he starts getting into trouble in middle school. It's nothing serious. He's simply talking too much, being labeled disruptive—being disruptive in Spanish, of course, because like me, he spoke no English when he arrived in this country. He's from El Salvador, a nation still reeling from the U.S.-sponsored civil war of the 1980s. So, here he is in Los Angeles where his mom works two jobs, neither of which pays a living wage. Day and night, she's always working and Genaro's out on the street with the homies. Who else is there? Who will fill his needs for love and respect and affection? And since his arrival, what kind of welcome has he received? The person who was renting the room to his mom said, "You can't have another person in here." They were evicted.

What do people see? A family of undocumented immigrants; a family in trouble; a boy who's disruptive in school, doesn't speak the language, and is far behind in his studies.

What do I see? A humble boy with milk chocolate skin and short black hair and almond eyes. Somehow, he manages to make eye contact even with his lowered head. He has a sweet and constant smile. His voice is breaking, what we call *el gallito*. He limps and walks a little bit hunched, but you can see the strength and power in him. And that sweet smile? It gets stronger and brighter as soon as he realizes you care. Other kids who can't speak English often shut down completely, but Genaro is gregarious and alert, aware, taking in everything that happens around him. I see a hero.

Genaro was twelve when his mother left him behind in El Salvador with an uncle who constantly beat the hell out of him. Every time his mom phoned to see how he was doing he begged her, "Please bring me where you are," and he'd get the same answer, "Yes, I'm trying my best. I'm saving the money but right now you're fine, you're with family." But he wasn't fine, and when she sent him a little money for his thirteenth birthday, Genaro joined up with some other people from his town who were going to attempt the trip north.

Somewhere in Guatemala, his money ran out. Then they ran into trouble trying to cross from Guatemala into Mexico and, in the confusion, Genaro got separated from the others. He just kept walking and walking and when he reached a town somewhere in Chiapas, he finally broke down and cried.

A man approached and asked why he was crying.

"I don't know where I am."

"Where are you going?"

"To Los Angeles."

"No way!"

"I'm going to my mother."

The man said, "Hell! I don't know how you are going to get there," but he gave him some *pesos* to get something to eat.

Next Genaro met a woman who turned out to be, like his mother, a born-again Christian. She offered to help him. Her family took him in and for months he stayed picking coffee beans with the family, a job he didn't like very much but a way to help the family and earn some cash.

From Chiapas, he phoned his mother again to say, "I'm coming."

"No, you're not!" she said. "Go right back home until I can send you money for the bus."

"I'm never going back there. The only place I'm going is where you are."

One day, he jumped from a truck and took a bad fall. The pain was incredible and he looked with disbelief at his left foot hanging from the ankle like a dirty rag. At the hospital, the doctor wanted to amputate. "That foot's never going to do you any good. It will just get worse. It's a danger. It will cause you trouble."

Can you imagine this kid, alone, no money, no education, standing up to the doctor and saying "No, you're not going to cut!"? A sympathetic nurse put a cast on the foot—"it won't heal, but at least you can get yourself out of here"—and then took him to El Buen Pastor. This charity shelter's mission is to care for migrants who've been severely injured while riding the rails, heading for the U.S. on what's been called "the train of death." Genaro didn't really belong there, but some of the residents befriended him. One was a twenty-one-year-old guy who'd slid off from the roof of a train. When he woke up in the hospital, he had no legs. Another man was missing most of the right side of his body, severed when he fell onto the track. Genaro was the able-bodied one, with merely a limp and lots of pain.

Once again he called his mom. Again she said, "Please go back to your uncle. Otherwise you are going to end up killed."

"No, Mom. I'm not going back."

Through the network of Christians, he got to Mexico City and from there to another house and then another, and then he was given the name of a family in Tijuana and the barrio where he would find them. He took the bus and it left him somewhere, and people there told him to take the *colectivo*. So he took that car and it left him at a *tienda* where he showed the name. "Oh yes, we know those people," and so the family came to get him.

Genaro phoned his mom. "I'm in Tijuana now."

"I'm trying, *mi'jo*, I'm trying, but a coyote charges $3,000 and all I have is $400. You'll have to wait till I can save the rest."

He waited three months, but all the time he was looking and asking on his own. Finally, he connected with a coyote who said, "I'm leaving in three days and I will take you there for $1,500."

Genaro phoned his mother. "Get the money," he said. "I'm on my way."

This boy traveled for more than nine months, without money, through all sorts of dangers, in order to be reunited with his mother. For nine months on the road, his warm and candid personality drew people to him. Again and again, he found angels and spirit guides to help him on his way. You meet him and love him, only now the other kids in school have been told he's a troublemaker. The school sees him as a burden. In my opinion, everybody in that school should recognize his courage, perseverance, and heroism.

Genaro walked the desert for seven days. This child, limping and in pain, lived through a journey that many healthy adults have not survived and he did it all for that moment he had imagined for so long, when the coyote knocked on a door in Los Angeles and said, "Hi, Mom. I have your son."

I VISITED THE U.S.–MEXICO border in 2007 and walked along the wall that at the time the Bush administration planned to strengthen and extend for 700 more miles (inspiring author and performance artist Guillermo Gómez-Peña to ask: "Who is going to build that *pinche* wall? Undocumented migrants hired by Halliburton?").

On the border, a man told me he didn't object to the wall. If fewer of his countrymen could get to the U.S., maybe the Mexican government would finally face up to its responsibilities to the poor. Others said, if you can't go around it, you go over it or under it. When your children are starving and you need to find work in order to feed them, you find a way.

In Mexico, I heard this joke:

"How much you think this wall is gonna cost Bush?"

"Oh, a few trillions."

"How much you pay for that shovel?"

"Five dollars."

As I stood by the border, I remembered another wall I'd walked along, the separation wall between Israel and Palestine. In 2004, when I traveled the West Bank with a Fellowship of Reconciliation group led by Rabbi Lynn Gottlieb, I asked almost everyone I met about that wall. Of course, I heard many different opinions. Ziad Allas, a Palestinian student said, "I'm happy with the wall. We have had invisible walls everywhere—fences, checkpoints, soldiers—so we have always had barriers between us and them, or obstacles to leading our own lives. We find a flying checkpoint on our way back from work, so then we have to detour for four hours or wait for as long as they want us to wait. This is a physical wall that the world can see. You can take pictures; you can take very nice pictures there. You can also see where the wall is not on the Green Line; how much more territory they have taken; how they have put the wall between us and our olive trees; how they put it between us and our sheep and our neighbors and our parents." Three years later, Ziad and I would very unexpectedly meet again.

I visited a house on the West Bank completely surrounded by the wall. A family of four lives inside the wall, which is high and cuts off the sun so they don't have natural light at home. They use a little gate to leave their house, but they have to wait for a soldier to open it.

Walls do not bring security. A Palestinian told me: "We will go under it, over it, or to the side of it to see the people we love and to kill the people we hate."

In Bethlehem, I led a workshop for a group made up of rabbinical students from the U.S. and Israel as well as Palestinian activists and intellectuals. Just as I do with torture survivors, I never addressed the big issue—the Israeli–Palestinian conflict—directly. I just said, "We're going to play some games." I asked them to walk around the space and choose partners, but not to be with people they already knew. I had them change partners again and again. I played the drum and they danced in groups of two, and then four, and then eight. I made no effort to match Israelis with Palestinians. What happened occurred naturally. When everyone is running around, it immediately democratizes the room. We were just playing. We were not Israelis and Palestinians, or men and women, or black and white. We touched each other, smelled each other. And people were comfortable with touching. I never said: *Now we're going to touch. If you have a problem with touching. . .* because that only invites people to say, *I have a problem.* I don't tell them, *We're going to act,* so no one says, *I don't know how to act.* I simply offer participants an invitation to perform some action.

Later on in the day, we played a game in which I invited people to turn around and hug the person behind them. The organizers looked at me like, *Hector! What are you doing? That's not possible!* So I said, "Wait, let's stop for a moment. My friends, I cannot pretend to know your culture. I have no idea what you can and cannot do. So remember: I'm just inviting. You do it your own way. When I work with seniors, maybe they can't move so easily. Maybe they can't bend down. But they do what they can. So you just figure out what you can do."

And you know what happened? Everybody hugged. I do things in a playful, respectful way. I don't force, although I do push, because life pushes us. Otherwise, as adults, we would be just the same as we were at the age of ten.

At one point that day, I asked two people to create an image of friendship or love. Then I asked them to transform that image into one of hate. Now they were strangling each other or showing their fists. Then I had them go back and forth: love, hate, love, hate! Now there was emotion in the room, but no one had to own it. Through the plasticity of theater, we could go in seconds from hate to love. You had an Israeli and a Palestinian, and they could show friendship or animosity. Either was possible.

After that, I asked the participants to use their bodies to describe the world they lived in. In the images they created, everyone was doing something different and the result was total chaos. Then, on the count of three, I had them transform that chaotic world into an ideal world. People ended up in a circle, making eye contact. Some were hugging. This is how we get people to work together without anyone saying, *Now you have to work together*. It just happens in front of our eyes. People are not forced to change who they are; they are invited to experience the Other, the unknown, through creating something together.

We need to be taking down walls of hate instead of building new ones. We need to discover that we all have an incredible capacity to transform ourselves, and the world.

GENARO IS NOT THE ONLY teenage boy who has managed to cross into the U.S. alone, but he was lucky enough not to get caught. As a volunteer legal assistant, Diane met with a group of kids from Honduras who came looking for work to help their families after their village was entirely destroyed in a hurricane in 1999. They were picked up in Arizona by immigration authorities and transferred to Los Angeles where they were housed in a Youth Authority facility with violent offenders.

"Let us go home. We won't come back here. Just let us go back home." The kids were begging to be sent back, but their own government, overwhelmed by a natural catastrophe comparable to Katrina, wasn't processing the necessary paperwork. One boy said, "Just let me be home by Mothers Day." The boys told of being disciplined with pepper spray when they didn't instantly follow orders given in English, which none of them could understand. The guard who sprayed them explained his interpretation of the Constitution: "If they don't obey, I don't care what language they speak. In America we treat everyone equally."

U.S. citizens have been mistakenly deported and dumped in Tijuana. Asylum-seekers with cases pending have been forcibly medicated with anti-psychotic drugs to stop their protests when officials tried to put them on planes, incorrectly and illegally, for deportation. Hundreds of thousands of families have been separated. So many people have been detained since 1996 that inadequate facilities intended for short-term questioning have been used to house thousands of people for months and even years, many immigrants dying in custody after being denied medical care.

Diane met women who for weeks spent their days in crowded and filthy holding cells downtown. Then they'd ride around on buses all night looking for a facility that could take them. Women slept under cafeteria tables at the detention center on Terminal Island in LA Harbor. They weren't allowed any personal effects. They were issued prison jumpsuits, but there was never enough underwear or toothbrushes to go around. People went months without knowing the charges against them or seeing a lawyer or a judge. The women weren't even allowed to have books or magazines as these were considered potential weapons. Families waited in line for hours to visit, and then got perhaps ten minutes sitting in a booth, separated by Plexiglas, talking to a loved one via phone. Or trying to. The one time Diane went into one of the booths, the phone didn't work.

Mothers weren't allowed to hold their babies or hug their kids, but since Diane was there as a legal assistant, she was allowed to be alone in a room with a client. The lawyers were overwhelmed by the number of cases and had to turn most of them down. So a lot of the time, Diane said, all she could do was hold someone's hand. That was the only friendly contact they were allowed, as their spouses and children were not permitted to touch them. "Sometimes I ended up holding a prisoner in my arms while she cried."

When I'm asked to introduce myself, the first thing that pops into my head isn't usually, "I'm an American," or "I'm a Colombian." Obviously, both these cultures play a huge part in who I am. In many ways I identify with each. I am a U.S. citizen, but when I think of myself, I think of an artist, a father, someone who most of all wants to help others access their own strengths and gifts. I hold many people and many places in my heart. I pay taxes, I vote, and I know how important my vote is. Given the role of the U.S. in the world, our own election results affect not just the daily lives of those of us who live here, but the fates of people all over the globe who have no say at all in the matter. I contribute in many ways to the community around me, whether it's coaching my kids' soccer teams and supporting their schools, or working with the most marginalized members of our society, or bringing joy to audiences through my clowning. And yes, I criticize my government when it fails to keep its solemn commitments to human rights, democracy, and the rule of law.

Undocumented immigrants also contribute and participate. It may be that in today's global world, *nationality* may not be the most useful concept. Maybe *citizenship* should mean taking responsibility for your community, something more profound than the passport you carry or the one you lack.

In Massachusetts, I meet with immigrants at a community center and listen to their stories: workplace raids, people dragged off commuter trains and buses, Immigration and Customs Enforcement agents banging on the door in the middle of the night to seize and detain their relatives. The immigrants here are unusually sophisticated; they are aware of their legal rights. But how easy is it to demand to see a warrant when it's two in the morning and the agents wake you with their hollering and the baby starts crying and the six-year-old is terrified and your undocumented husband is trying to pull on some clothes and escape out the back window? We spend hours role-playing situations so that words and actions will come more naturally and fearlessly if needed. And then, as it's late December, the group sings *villancicos*, Spanish Christmas carols. We reenact the *posada*, as the immigrants identify with Mary and Joseph turned away from door after door as they search for a place to stay.

I leave wondering how many of these fine and decent people will end up in shackles.

NO ONE SHACKLED ME. In 1989, I breezed through immigrations and customs, no hassles, no bribes, just Yanqui efficiency.

My first view of Miami from on high in the cockpit had been

mind-blowing. It was out of this world to see such a beautiful place. My first impression of the U.S.—and I still experience this every time I fly—was how orderly everything looked. When you fly over Colombia, it looks like everything is piled up on top of everything else. Streets go weaving everywhere like rivers. Instead, Miami seemed laid out in almost symmetrical quadrants. I couldn't believe how clean it all looked. It wasn't so much the number of cars that impressed me, but that even from the air I could see the streets were very clearly defined and were all paved. This was the country I'd considered the enemy and if it wasn't love at first sight, it was certainly admiration. Where were the potholes tearing up the roads? I didn't see any. How did Americans get the idea to put up walls and boards and fences around construction sites so the dust and dirt and noise don't invade everything? These people, I thought, had to be incredibly well organized.

I, alas, was not. I reached the terminal carrying a huge piece of luggage that weighed over seventy-five pounds. My only potential contact in this foreign city was an old friend of my mother's whose phone number and address I carried with me. I stood around in shock for at least half an hour, watching people from all over the world pass by me. Though Spanish is a second language in Miami, I couldn't quite bring myself to speak to anyone or ask for help. After an hour of trying to make a phone call and failing to reach my mother's friend, I went out to the curb and got into a cab. I gave the driver the address. Fifty dollars later, enough to feed my family for a week in Medellín, I was left outside a big house in the suburbs, sitting on my luggage like an orphan. No one was home. I waited. No one came home. And this was probably the best thing that could have happened to me.

The couple that lived next door found me sitting there. They didn't know my mother's friend, they didn't understand what I was trying to say, but miraculously they took me in. For years, I'd demonized Americans and now these strangers invited me into their home, fed me pizza, and gave me a bed. I didn't need much language to play the clown and make their children laugh. The husband took me to see where he worked at a U.S. military base. The next day, I went along with the kids to the Miami Zoo before the parents dropped me off at the Greyhound bus terminal where I bought my ticket to Iowa. Through their warmth and generosity, every stereotype I'd carried about North Americans was shattered. They gave me the best welcome I could possibly have received into this new society.

For two days, I traveled through this incredible land. I exchanged few words with people as I walked around the Greyhound stations in the big cities. I was completely numb. After many miles of unending landscapes and crossing through the cornfields of Iowa, I arrived in Dubuque. My friends in LA can't understand how beautiful and romantic this city in Iowa seemed to me. It looked like a movie set with its town square atmosphere, its leafy trees, and church steeples, everything so clean and orderly. It was such a contrast to the chaotic, noisy, complex life I was living in Medellín that I felt—and surely acted—like a kid in wonder. Clarke College was a paradise that I just seemed to be floating through.

Then I crashed. Yes, my life in Colombia had become a mess, but after years of work and luck all the doors of Medellín had opened to me. Coming from the barrio, I'd achieved a professional and social standing I could never take for granted and was accomplishing most of what I'd dreamed of. I'd painstakingly built an identity and now it was gone. In Iowa, I had no voice, no profession, no art. I was invisible; my money was already gone. One month's tuition at Clarke College had cost me as much as my entire higher education in Medellín. I missed my family and was conscious every minute that I had a very weighty commitment hanging over my head. I had to buy my parents a new house. The money they'd held onto for rent would not last long.

Gbanabom Hallowell, the poet from Sierra Leone, described his years of exile as living in a "claustrophobic room." For me, exile reawakened memories of the torture chamber. Not since my ordeal had I felt this way, as lonely and desperate as a person could be.

Medellín had been a battlefield, but as a psychologist and artist, I experienced it as a land of creative opportunity. Some of the greatest theater directors in the world visited Colombia and I learned from them. Jerzy Grotowski appeared before us dressed in a white robe and spoke of returning to the origins of theater in ritual. He told us the actor becomes holy by casting off the everyday masks we all wear, by revealing and sacrificing the most inner and painful parts of his being. Eugenio Barba, a larger-than-life figure, had us sit on the floor on cushions—something that to us, provincial artists, seemed eminently and thrillingly weird.

Theater people in Medellín tended to be informal in dress, attitude, and speech as we wanted to be seen as no different from the ordinary people of our communities. Art was to benefit the people, we believed. I was a member of El Pequeño Teatro, a theater dedicated to the classics and to contemporary works from around the world, an ensemble that has grown and thrived and still produces plays in Medellín. However, I was also a co-founder of the street theater troupe Mojiganga which performed free for the poor. We used broad physical humor and all our clowning skills. In a play about domestic violence, my friend Walter dressed as a woman. I was the fat, bald husband. The set was a rundown dwelling with spider webs and children, just dolls, hanging everywhere. I would go to a doll. "How beautiful you are!" and tear an ear off. We would talk about love and act with hate. We'd explore the economic despair that led to violence and would follow every performance with a discussion that let the audience speak up about their lives or come up onstage to portray their own domestic situations. Onstage, when I could feel hundreds of eyes watching me, I was as far as I could get from the room where I was alone with the torturer. Onstage, portraying a character, I felt safe, as I left myself behind to become somebody else.

After Xicotico retired, I continued my explorations of Medellín at night in the guise of Jairo Arrabal, a denizen of the underworld who combed his hair back with brilliantine, wore white patent leather shoes, and never took his dark glasses off. In this identity I would go to Guayaquil, the red-light district, and sit at a table drinking *aguardiente* and taking in everything around me. I didn't earn enough to drink as much as would befit a bad man like Jairo, so friends gave me money for booze in exchange for the wild stories I brought them in return. My braver friends came with me. We even staged a fake fight one night. Friends came in pretending not to know me. I got into an argument with one of these supposed strangers, "stabbed" him, and returned to my table to keep drinking, while my other friends carried the bloody body out to a waiting cab. That's how Jairo earned his reputation as a coldblooded killer. One night, leaving one of these low cantinas, a man staggered toward me, his eyes unfocused, and his belly cut wide open. His blood was real, and when he fell at my feet he was really and truly dead. That was also the end of Jairo Arrabal. After this encounter with reality I was too scared to continue his adventures.

Other realities I could not escape: mutilated bodies found thrown in ditches and ravines; people shot down in the center of town in cold blood; the photos that appeared in the newspaper every single day of faces of the disappeared printed along with pleas from their families who hoped to find their loved ones alive, or at least be able to find and bury their dead. The only escape was through exile.

At night in Iowa as I fell asleep I would find myself plunging at high speed into a vast emptiness. I would jerk awake without hitting bottom, without even a barren rock or a little bit of earth to hold to. I'd been uprooted, turned into nobody. I was in freefall, but I was alive.

Chapter 7

In the Mouth
of the Wolf

*Exile . . . is a state of spirituality in which body and soul
become disagreeable to each other because an identity has
been altered.*

—Gbanabom Hallowell

I have always found my salvation in women. In Dubuque,
Iowa, I found Cindy. As is my way, I fell in love with her at first sight.
We met at a dance. Later, she said I seduced her just by the way I
moved. I followed her through the hallways of the college, communicating with her in nonverbal language. My training as a mime and
juggler had never before been so useful. I started to learn English by
repeating all the sounds that came from her sweet lips. Then, and for
many years after, Cindy was my rescuer, my oasis, my source of hope
and energy, my only means of being human. But even her love didn't
ease my despair. As soon as I knew enough English to say it, I told her
I needed to leave Dubuque.

"This is a beautiful place, but there is nothing for me here. I have
to go."

To my joy and amazement, she said, "Then I'm going with you."

Cindy was a talented art student, nineteen-years-old—almost ten years younger than me. She'd been born and had lived most of her life in Springbrook, population 250 and dropping, where everyone was Catholic and of German descent, all of them farmers, and forty percent of them with the same last name. We went to meet her family. The men towered over me. What must they have thought of this dark little fellow who had come from so far away to steal their daughter? Without language, I had to sense who they were without words, and even in our brief meeting I could tell that Cindy's grandmother was the most important person for her, an extraordinary woman with a big and loving heart. For most of Cindy's family members and for most of the people of her town, I was the first brown person they'd ever seen outside of a TV screen. I still wonder what they made of me.

Much of the U.S. still doesn't know what to make of us—"us" being Latinos, which is in itself a misleading term. How useful is a label that includes people who crossed the border last week and people whose families have lived on what is now U.S. territory for hundreds of years? In California, the first stereotype is that if you speak Spanish, you're Mexican. Latin Americans share some culture in common, but we're also very different. Mexicans themselves are far from being a monoculture. There are urban and rural Mexicans. Huge differences exist in education and socioeconomic class and dozens of indigenous languages are broken down into hundreds of distinct dialects that are spoken in the country in addition to or instead of Spanish. As for Colombians, being a *paisa* from Medellín makes me very different from people who grew up in Bogotá, or come from the south, from Pasto, or from either of Colombia's coasts. People from the Pacific coast are very different from people living along the Caribbean. We have different music, different food, different idioms and idiosyncrasies, as different as a kid growing up in Brooklyn, New York, will be from a kid in Williston, North Dakota. Besides our cultural differences, we are individuals. I co-lead groups with Gisela Burquet, the skilled and sensitive parent educator from Argentina: where I am spontaneous, she relies on conscious thought; where I am outspoken, Gisela is reserved. "The way my family survived the dictatorship," she says, "was to keep quiet. The rule was *Never draw attention to yourself.*" Personality, background? Or both?

I still don't know what to make of the U.S. and its contradictions: the generosity and kindness of the Americans I met when I arrived as I tried to blame them, in broken English, for every Latin American tragedy. I harangued perfect strangers: *Your country conspired to overthrow the democratic government of Jacobo Arbenz in Guatemala! You're responsible for the death of Salvador Allende in Chile and the death of Chilean democracy! You plunder the resources of my country! You trained the soldiers who tortured me!* And I learned that in spite of freedom of the press, most people had never before heard the stories I felt compelled to tell.

Sometimes, I think perhaps the rootlessness that causes me so much pain is also part of my Colombian identity. I come from a country where people, including my grandparents, moved from place to place in search of a better life, just as North Americans have always done. But in my country, these travels have rarely been voluntary. In Colombia today, millions of people are refugees in their own land, in a crisis of internal displacement that rivals the horrors of Darfur in Sudan. Some leave home because they are caught in the crossfire of war, but these days, most leave because they are driven off their land by wealthy men with private armies, or multinational corporations backed by the government, their small farms replaced with biofuel palm-oil plantations, army posts, oil fields, and coal mines.

I'm convinced my dispossession is not complete as long as I hold onto and can tell my story.

SOMETIMES, WHEN I WORK with the children of immigrants, I ask where their parents were born and the kids don't know. They've lost their roots back in the highlands of Guatemala or in Oaxaca. Sometimes, I sit at the computer and type the parents' stories as they dictate them. Then I reflect their stories back to them in a mythical framework so they can see their strengths and can see themselves as heroes. I read back what they've written, and I ask them, "Would you watch this movie?" And they say *yes*.

I meet children who have incredible knowledge of botany and music, of how to fix and build things. Think of all the languages they know and the linguistic skills they bring. A lot of immigrant kids know firsthand about hunger and survival and they know about solidarity. They know about the angels and good Samaritans they've met along the way. A fourteen-year-old kid who has traveled thousands of miles without money, without even a map, is not an ignorant person. Yet educators too often look on their students as empty vessels, as people who don't know rather than as people with their own remarkable resources which the teacher can build on and also learn from. When native-born Americans think we are here only to take, society becomes unable to receive all our gifts.

I told one mother, "That's you! You crossed the Rio Grande when you were seven months pregnant. You didn't know how to swim, and you saw two people drown in front of you, but you kept going. And you got to the desert, and you didn't have water for three days, and you didn't know where you were going, but you kept walking. Isn't that a hero?"

Later, I read the story to her son. He couldn't believe it. "My mom did that when she was pregnant with me?"

"Yeah. You were the kid in that belly. You helped her float through the river and make it to the other side."

One year I worked with Kevin who, as an eight-year-old, tried to burn down his family's apartment. When I met him, he'd been diagnosed with a "conduct disorder," a very serious label that would indicate he was too dangerous and intractable for group therapy at the community clinic. But there was something bright and alive about him that made me unwilling to turn him away. I decided to visit him at home. I found Kevin living with five siblings in a one-bedroom apartment. His pregnant mother was sleeping with the newest boyfriend in the bedroom with the two youngest kids. The thirteen-year-old had cerebral palsy, and the rest were under eight years of age. So there were six kids in this place, literally crying all day long.

A child who tries to burn down his own home sounds like a monster; but if you go to that home, you understand this kid's spirit was crying for help. I would burn that apartment anytime. Who would want to live there? How could you take it? I wish I could change the world Kevin lives in. I did what I could: I expunged the damning diagnosis and made room for him in our program.

I think of one of the Apache creation stories: the Creator tells the people that everything in this world can be the cause of trouble and everything in this world can be the cure for that trouble. Sometimes an act of violence, frightening as it may be, is a sign that the life force is still alive inside a child, unextinguished. I have hope for Kevin because his spirit rages with energy. That energy is his strength and it needs to be honored and channeled, not crushed.

As for his mother, of course it's easy to condemn her. She has had six kids by six different men. These men come into her life, use her until she gets pregnant, and then leave. And yet that woman, who has been abandoned and betrayed so many times, still manages to feed her children. She doesn't leave them. She goes out to sell bedspreads in the street and puts a roof over their heads, I don't know how. This woman manages to raise her children—in conditions of great deprivation, yes, but I honor her strength and resiliency and her incredible capacity to survive. I can see her heroism, and if I can help her see herself this way instead of as a victim of circumstances, betrayals, and poor judgment, is it possible she would make different choices? If she can imagine and tell her story a different way, how might her life be changed?

One recent spring in Pasadena, following torrential rains, seeds of plants that had been dormant for centuries began sprouting. They had somehow kept themselves alive for all that time. I know this same potential remains always alive inside people. Creative seeds are buried in people, no matter how oppressed they've been, and you can find these seeds in their stories.

I believe our lives can be changed by the stories we tell ourselves, not just as individuals, but as communities. About ten years ago, when tensions grew in Pasadena between longtime residents and recent Latino immigrants, I learned the method of "appreciative enquiry" from Yolanda Treviño. We called a community meeting and about two hundred people showed up. Yolanda asked us all to close our eyes and imagine waking up five years in the future and finding everything exactly the way we would like it to be. People answered, *No gangs, no drugs, no crime.* But Yolanda insisted we shouldn't talk about what we wanted to get rid of, but rather what we wanted to see.

All of a sudden, people started imagining streets closed to traffic where people could walk and kids could play. They saw new parks, neighborhood schools that kids could walk to, and they even figured out where two new schools could go. Some of these dreams are actually coming into being, but perhaps what moved me most was what happened with a very aggressive white guy who came to several meetings. He kept saying things like *This used to be a nice neighborhood and I'm sorry but you people moved here and trashed it.* He was very upset with the changes in his hometown. But during the appreciative enquiry, he was constantly invited to think about what he valued and imagine what could be. He remembered a lake where he used to go swimming. He said he wished we could have a lake. Well, someone pointed out, there is a swimming pool at Villa Park. By the time the meeting ended, he had reconnected with a great pleasure of his own youth and had volunteered to teach some of the Latino kids how to swim.

Through this enquiry into community strengths, talents, and desires instead of complaints, we left the meeting with a plan.

CINDY AND I HAD no map and no real plan when we left Iowa in her Dodge Omni with our few belongings, most of them boxes of her paintings and art supplies. Our destination was no more specific than "California." Part of the time we drove; much of the time we had to be towed. Even when the compact car wouldn't run, it was still a place for us to eat—mostly ramen noodles—and sleep and this only made our trip more of an adventure. We visited Indian reservations and went to the Grand Canyon. We spent most of our money fixing the car and using our AAA card that was canceled shortly thereafter due to overuse. We finally ended up in San Diego, where Interstate 8 disappears into the Pacific Ocean. We sat there mute, scared, excited, not knowing what to do or where to go, like two *conquistadores* that had arrived at a place they'd thought existed only inside the maps of the imagination.

Cindy found a waitressing job almost right away, which earned us some money and also leftover food that she brought home for me. For her, the adventure was over. She was left with a crummy job, no way to continue her education, no studio space for her painting, and on top of that she was supporting a lover whose visa didn't allow him to work. Still I made the rounds of all the drug and alcohol rehab centers in San Diego. I didn't know if anyone would be able to get me papers, but I hoped my years of expertise would count for something. No one had work for me, but one man asked me to speak at the opening of a new clinic. "But I don't speak English," I said. "Then how have you managed to captivate me with your stories?" he asked. I realized my grammar might be bad and my accent strong, but I was already picking up enough language to make myself understood. I was making contacts but I still had no job. Cindy was depressed and I was desperate—dead though still breathing.

One day I met an African American body builder who sometimes performed at private parties as a sort of Chippendales-type dancer. He dressed me in a G-string and invited me along. "The ladies might like some Latin dance." They weren't crazy about this Latin dancer. "Too skinny," was the complaint. "Not enough meat." I wasn't invited again, but I was sexy or maybe pitiful enough so that sixty-five dollars in tips ended up tucked into my G-string.

Cindy and I had run off without thinking of marriage. To me, she was beautiful and perfect. I loved her, her painting, and her adventurous spirit. I knew she could be my life's partner. Now, with my visa about to expire, we decided to make our commitment to each other a legal one. My sixty-five dollars was enough to inspire a woman from the Dominican Republic to perform the ceremony in a storefront wedding chapel. She did for us what she had done for truck drivers and hippie desperados, as the photos under the glass of her desk testified. She was the secretary, the priest, and the decorator of this small space in which, after listening to a strange bouquet of words, I carried Cindy's precious body over a broom. We were married.

Six months after my arrival in the U.S., I was invited to give a talk in San Diego about the Colombian mafia. This led to my meeting a social worker who needed a Spanish-speaking counselor in his office in Pasadena. We packed the Omni once again, I got behind the wheel with Cindy beside me, and we headed for the biggest cement jungle in the world.

I ALWAYS KNEW I wanted children. And after Cindy and I got together, I knew I wanted to have children with her. She, however, wasn't sure, at least not right away, as she was almost ten years my junior and not quite so ready. One day, after we'd been married five years, Cindy came back from a friend's wedding very affected by the ritual which awakened her desires for permanence, community, and motherhood.

We were very much in love when we conceived Gabo. I still remember exactly when it happened. I think this was the happiest time of my life. I was fulfilled in every way: teaching kids, working as a vocational rehab specialist, performing in a play, going to Pacific Oaks College to get my U.S. Masters degree, and most important, Cindy was pregnant. We were also buying our first house, a fixer-upper. My father came from Colombia to help us and we all went to work painting and sanding. In true *paisa* fashion—and here's a cultural trait for you—when

I thought "family," I thought of my mother. I'd always relegated my father to the margins and when I did think of him, I was critical. He wasn't ambitious enough or aggressive enough. But now as we worked together and as I looked forward to becoming a father, too, I learned to appreciate him. I saw his competence, the way he knew how to do just about everything, how he was already looking at the small backyard and planning a garden, and the patience with which he instructed us. Most of all, what I saw was his goodness.

One evening he walked into the garage and saw me in a dress, stuffing extra filling in my bra. I hadn't meant to surprise him quite that way. He was supposed to get a kick out of the unexpected sight of my appearing in this costume onstage. But we laughed and he came along to the theater where Cindy, close to nine months along by then, worked the lights as I performed a satirical cross-dressed role.

Government support for the arts was something that thrilled and amazed me in the U.S. While Europeans have taken generous government subsidies for granted and think Americans are shockingly stingy when it comes to funding culture, in Colombia we learned to create art with next to no money at all. We learned a very physical style of acting so we could portray characters through our bodies alone because we lacked access to elaborate costumes and sophisticated stage sets.

Even today, I usually perform in sweat pants and a T-shirt. As for props, a length of black fabric serves many purposes—a rifle, a shawl, a blindfold, a helicopter—and I can use a single balloon to simulate pregnancy, play soccer, and by stomping on it, the sound of gunfire. In Medellín. we didn't worry about how to attract an audience to our theaters; most of the time, we *had* no theaters. And we didn't make audiences go to us, we went to them. That's one of the reasons we trained in circus skills. When you show up in public on stilts, juggling, and playing instruments, you quickly attract a crowd for your play.

In the U.S., I learned about grants. Wow! The first one I received, for $5,000, was exactly the amount needed to add to our savings in order to buy my parents a home in Medellín to replace the one they had sold to finance my escape.

GABO CAME into the world on September 25, 1995. Cindy had chosen natural childbirth and it turned out to be very painful. It was almost unbearable to me to see her go through so much, but we were very happy and the boy was beautiful, perfect. I'd attended other births and even videotaped the event at the request of other couples, but nothing had prepared me for the emotions of seeing my own child emerge. Somehow there was a connection, a feeling of humble awe that this creature had chosen me to be his father.

Cindy can go without eating for years, I think, while I cannot go without food for more than two hours. She, however, has always needed her sleep, so after Gabo was born, I always had the night shift. And it was wonderful. I didn't care how many times I had to wake up. I was happy to spend all night carrying Gabo, giving him water and milk and just being with him. When Camilla was born on February 25, 1997, it was the same. There's simply nothing more beautiful on earth than your child sleeping on your chest, nothing better than when they begin to talk to you and tell you things. Having kids has been the best part of my life.

Five days after Camilla's birth, Cindy's much-loved grandmother died. The loss was a hard one for Cindy, especially because she couldn't travel back to Iowa for the funeral. Camilla has always felt a strong connection to the great-grandmother she never knew. Sometimes, she cries even today thinking of this loving woman who meant so much to her mother.

Camilla's birth was also a test in physical pain for Cindy. "No more children," she said. I didn't want her to face another painful labor, but when she said if she got pregnant again she would consider abortion, I couldn't face that either. Her body had endured so much, I felt it was my turn to take responsibility. When I had a vasectomy, some people praised me as a male feminist, especially impressive considering the macho culture I come from. The truth was, as it usually is, more complex. I went to the doctor as a sincere act on behalf of Cindy. Eventually, though, I would find another reason to be happy with my choice. I could feel secure no pregnancies would occur outside of my marriage, that Cindy and I had brought into the world the only children who would ever be born from my seed.

While Cindy devoted herself to raising Gabo and Camilla, I conveniently ignored how trapped and blocked she might feel as I played around, enjoyed life to the fullest, and moved ahead as an artist and therapist with my dual careers. As far as I was concerned, everything was wonderful. I would come home and Gabo would run to me and Camilla, now that she had started walking, would follow. With everything in life I'd ever wanted, I believed I'd left all the pain and bad memories far behind.

Until the phone call.

Chapter 8.

The Latin American Dream

It was my Aunt Ligia, calling from Medellín. Her tone of voice didn't register at first as I babbled away about the latest signs of brilliance manifested by my two perfect children. Then, because my parents were visiting us I asked, "So, do you want to talk to Mom?"

"No," said my aunt. "I have to tell you something." And then I knew. This was it, the call I'd been dreading for years. "The paramilitaries took Juan Fernando. They've disappeared him."

"When?"

"Seven days ago."

My rage felt cold enough to freeze my blood, hot enough to melt the phone. Seven days, and no one had called me.

"We were afraid," Ligia said. "We've been trying every possible way to find him. We were afraid of what you might do."

I hung up and called the airlines to get us on the next available flight and thought I would explode when I learned we would have to wait three days.

"Why are we going home?" asked my mother.

All my life, I'd held nothing back from Nidia. I'd worried her, shocked her, burdened her with too much information about my life;

but now, I didn't have the heart to tell her anything. I told my father what had happened and also Cindy, but I let my mother think it was just Hector being impulsive as usual.

We headed for the airport at last. It was July 22, 1999, almost seventeen years to the day that Mono and I were both arrested. For years, I'd told the story that the soldiers had been so busy torturing me in 1982, they'd spared my brother. I liked to tell myself that the story about his mental condition and my very presence there had protected him. The flipside of such self-aggrandizement was guilt. Along with fear for him, as we flew all night over the ocean, I struggled with the understanding that while I went about absorbed in my new life in California, Mono had been left unprotected.

Landing, getting to the gate, going through customs, every minute of delay seared my nerves. Camilla slept in my arms; Cindy had Gabo by the hand and practically dragged him along. We were all exhausted. My mother, wrapped in silence, questioned me over and over with her eyes. She knew at once something was very wrong when the taxi left us at the house and she saw all our relatives, neighbors, and friends gathered. No music, no shouting, no drinking. It obviously was not a party.

"Why is everyone here?" she whispered. Some people hugged her; others couldn't meet her eye. We went inside. Outside the house, our neighbors knelt in prayer on the sidewalk, holding hands. My mother greeted all five of her sisters, but then she saw my brother's girlfriend, Margarita, sitting all alone.

"Where is Juan Fernando?" my mother asked. "Where is Mono? Where is my son?"

A truck driver had found his body thrown in a ditch.

My mother said, "I'd finally stopped worrying about him. How could this happen now?"

• • •

DURING ONE BIRTHDAY CELEBRATION for Mono, my father proposed a toast. "Here's to thirty-three years of silence."

My brother did not talk. By that, I don't mean he was an elective
mute, but he kept his thoughts to himself. He didn't much care for
words, but even as a child he was someone you could trust to keep
a secret. Like our brother Hernán Darío, Mono lived a hidden life in
the shadows. And just as I got to know my youngest brother as he was
dying, much of what I know about Juan Fernando Aristizábal I learned
only after his death.

When he and I were arrested, I assumed we were both innocent.
Later, after Mono became a *comandante* with the guerrilla army of the
ELN, I had to revise my thinking and suspect that more had been going
on than I'd realized. In fact, however, the Colombian army had virtually eliminated the military force of the ELN by 1973. Civilian members and sympathizers continued a propaganda campaign in the cities,
and that's probably all my brother knew of ELN militancy at the time
the army seized him.

Back in 1982, Mono spent only two months in prison, protected
from the violence and harsh conditions by the militants he met there.
The newly elected president, Belisario Betancur, repudiated the massive repression that had led to the indiscriminate arrests, torture, and
murder that had shocked to the core even the law-abiding apolitical
middle class. He negotiated a peace accord with another of Colombia's guerrilla armies, M-19, and as a condition of their agreement, all
political prisoners, including my brother, went free. Freedom, however, often meant death as right wing assassins stalked the prisoners as
they returned home.

While I myself was in hiding, my parents sent Mono away from Medellín for his own protection. A relative of ours who lived in the town of Montería was happy to shelter my brother.

After years of violent repression followed by the murders of many left wing activists by death squads, the peace accords were bound to fail. Militants of all guerrilla groups found that recruiting had become remarkably easy. Within the year, the ELN had reorganized its military and Mono had returned to Medellín with a pregnant girlfriend and a life-altering commitment to the armed struggle. The girlfriend gave birth and left. Mono remained in my parents' home with the baby, Laura, on whom he lavished all his gentleness and attention. But every now and then, for weeks or months at a time, he would disappear.

"That's when I started to suspect," says my father, Pedro. "Then one day, he came home in pain and running a high fever. When I saw his back and shoulders, that's when I knew for sure. The worms that hatched in his flesh, you only get those in the jungle, and I could only think of one reason for Mono being there." My father knew the rural way of treating worms: blow tobacco smoke into the air holes marked by tiny black spots in order to force the worms out. Instead he took Mono to a doctor who used a scalpel and tweezers to remove dozens of hairy gray larvae.

"You like the jungle so much," my father said, "you can come with me."

Pedro had retired from the textile mill and had found work as a traveling salesman for a pharmaceutical distributor and a cosmetics company. The cheap perfumes, colognes, and lotions all had English names, none of which my father understood. Years later, when he learned the meaning of *Cowboy*, one of the most popular products, he slapped his head. "So why didn't they call it *Gaucho?!*"

Every so often, the driver would show up in an old Chevrolet and my father would take my brother with him for twenty days of hard traveling across the mountains of the Cordillera Occidental. They made stops to bring merchandise to the small settlements along the route where peasants wore heavy woolen *ruanas* against the cold. They traveled down through the gorges along the Atrato River to the tropics and through the jungle to the swampy coastal plain.

The driver drove, Mono was silent, and my father talked. Though never a partisan of any political organization, he was always outspoken. "Look, this is one of the richest regions in Colombia: platinum, gold, gas, oil. And the people are the poorest. It's rich here in water and the people in the villages don't even have water safe to drink." Pedro's candid face changes, his lips curl to one side when he makes sarcastic remarks about the government. If these trips were intended to break Mono's connection to the revolution, they more likely fueled his commitment. They drove through torrential downpours and got stuck in the mud. They watched the foliage around them steam with mist as the sun came out again, though hidden from their sight by the forest canopy. The Chevy wasn't air-conditioned. With the windows down, swarms of flying insects came in, accompanied by suffocating humidity. On some trips, they traveled through areas where my grandfather had settled and resettled again, planting crops on a small piece of land here, panning for gold in the tributary of a river over there.

"Once he cleared a whole mountainside with just a machete," Pedro said. "A rich man hired him and he went up to the top and he was there, oh, a week, before he came down to town and the rich man said, 'You're wasting time. You haven't done a thing.' Your grandfather told him, 'Don't worry. Just tell people to head straight home after church on Sunday and stay out of the center of town.' See, what he'd done was to cut a notch in all the trees on the mountainside and, on Sunday, he began to push them over, starting from the top. It was a landslide of timber, all those trees knocking each other down the mountain all the way to the town."

True? I don't know. My father was proud of his father's ingenuity, but no longer thought clear-cutting such a good idea.

Much of Colombia is still inaccessible by road. Sometimes they left the car and traveled the rivers—the Atrato, the San Juan, the Baudó—along with fishermen in their simple boats, coming in at each landing to meet customers. They traveled mangrove swamps and coastal plains. "It's so rich here in Chocó," my father said as they traveled through land settled by people of African descent. "The richest in natural resources, and look at the misery. The government has never cared about Afro-Colombians. These people have been exploited and left abandoned."

Mono said nothing but envisioned a rebirth for Colombia, the original promise of the land restored. Rich in fertile land and a multitude of resources, a republic that for most of its history has been, at least nominally, under elected civilian rule, Colombia should have offered the Latin American Dream. Inequality wasn't present from the start and didn't just happen. In the Gabriel García Márquez novel *One Hundred Years of Solitude*—a very accurate if mythologized history—every house in the village of Macondo gets the same amount of sun and shade, and everyone has the same distance to travel to the river for water. At first. This primitive utopia doesn't last long in the fiction. It had little chance in real life.

La Violencia, the civil war that broke out between the Liberal and Conservative political parties in 1948, raged on and off till 1965 as a struggle of elites. Conservatives were closely identified with the Catholic Church but, aside from that, little if any difference existed between the parties in philosophy or practice. They fought over the spoils of patronage and land and economic power and, as people died, the killings gave rise to blood feuds that led to still more death.

The simple, rural people would pay the highest price as the frontier became wild. A small farmer would clear away jungle and plant his crops, only to be killed or driven off by armed men. Some of Colombia's biggest landowners accumulated their haciendas this way, letting simple people do the work and then taking the improved property by force. Some farmers died, some fled, some went to work on the plantations, which proved to be no refuge. Peasants who happened to work for Liberals fell victim to massacres by Conservative death squads. Survivors took to the wilds and formed the first guerrilla groups, which often transitioned to outright banditry from their origins in self-defense. In Colombia, we always claim self-defense. Plantation owners and ranchers couldn't rely on the government for protection, but when they understandably armed their peasants and workers, these private militias were soon turned loose to intimidate and kill. Corrupt police and right wing extremists executed community leaders, hardening a whole generation to violence. Pablo Escobar's mother, for example, was a schoolteacher in a small town. When death squads attacked, outraged at the idea of peasants being taught to read, the family huddled together in prayer, saved just in time by the army, which arrived too late, however, for the peasants whose cadavers were found in the schoolroom.

My brothers, sister, and I grew up in a world as hallucinatory as anything García Márquez has written. We'd see Pablo Escobar on TV, sometimes a public enemy, sometimes a benefactor. We'd take the bus through the most wretched neighborhoods and suddenly one day there would be new housing, or a soccer field with lights, and people would say, "Yes, Pablo made it." The guerrilla organization M-19 would hijack milk trucks and distribute the milk, free, to the poor. Through all this, the bullets kept flying, and the soundtrack was rock 'n' roll.

Guerrilla organizations split off from each other, representing different ideological tendencies and strategies, entering into a dizzying and shifting series of alliances and enmities. Most prominent was the Revolutionary Armed Forces of Colombia, or FARC (Fuerzas Armadas Revolucionarias de Colombia), which allied itself closely with the Communist Party. My brother's organization, the ELN, took its inspiration from the Cuban Revolution and now numbers fewer than five thousand fighters. The ELN condemns cocaine trafficking on moral grounds but doesn't hesitate to blow up oil pipelines and contaminate the environment or raise funds through kidnapping and extortion.

M-19, the organization that engineered Mono's release in 1982, was always more populist than Communist. Today, some of the social programs advocated by M-19 and the followers of the movement are still part of the political landscape, although M-19 no longer exists as a fighting force. But back in 1974, their movement captured the nation's imagination by pulling off an incredible symbolic heist: lifting the sword of South America's liberator Simon Bolívar right out of the National Museum, asserting, "The Spanish chains broken by Bolívar are replaced today by the gringo dollar." As they brought the struggle to the cities in one daring action after another, they gained many sympathizers, including me. In 1979 they managed to lift five thousand weapons right out of the army's main arsenal. The following year, they shocked the world by taking over the embassy of the Dominican Republic and holding ambassadors and special guests for ransom.

I was in Bogotá at the time, participating in a weeklong theater festival with my group, Mojiganga. In our play *There Was Once a King*, three street kids fight over a single cart. Who will push? Who will ride? In our comic way, we were talking about power and inequality, while at the same time, soldiers and police were mobilized because of the embassy takeover. There we were, political theater companies from all over the country, gathered together and afraid our festival would be raided and all of us taken into custody. The show went on and I even found time to fall briefly in love.

M-19 lost my sympathies as their actions began to have fatal consequences. The guerrillas tried to take over the Palace of Justice. The army, also miscalculating, stormed the building. More than a hundred people died, including twelve supreme court justices and the president of the court.

For us in Medellín the most lethal mistake by M-19 was the kidnapping of my university classmate, Martha Nieves Ochoa. As I mentioned earlier, the Ochoa brothers turned to Pablo Escobar for help in getting their sister back unharmed. He forged an alliance with the Castaño brothers, Carlos and Fidel, to create MAS, an anti-guerrilla terrorist movement that soon had official military allies as well. Once Martha was released, Pablo himself made peace with M-19 and, typical of the way alliances shift in Colombia, it's been reported he channeled money both to that organization and to FARC. MAS, however, went on killing. Pablo went on killing too, so indiscriminately he made enemies of his onetime allies. The Castaños and their men went over to the Cali cartel to bring him down. They also contracted with right wing businessmen and landowners to provide so-called "self-defense" by eliminating left wing activists and entire populations.

While all this raged, my father and brother traveled through a land where the central government had little or no power, through places unknown to the authorities but well mapped in the minds and memories of local people. Long before anyone talked about free-trade agreements, smugglers brought tax-free consumer goods to the coastline and across the border from Panama. For a time, the drug traffickers followed the same hidden smuggling routes through the jungle. As an ELN comandante, Mono crossed into Panama the same way to buy weapons.

Pedro likes to talk about the rivers of Chocó: the rio Atrato, "not that wide, but deep enough so ships can enter the port of Quibdó. We're fifty miles from the birthplace now," he told Mono, "where fifty rivers flow into the Atrato with all their waters." The Atrato flows parallel to the San Juan, which flows north to empty into the Caribbean Sea while the Atrato flows out to the Pacific. "This is unique in the world and it's all being polluted and destroyed."

Mono carried his flute on these trips and he would play a melody to signal Dad that he wanted a meal stop. The driver usually got hungry first. He'd interrupt Pedro's educational monologues: "Juan Fernando, play your flute!"

The paved highway was an obstacle course of potholes, sinkholes, and hairpin curves. Even today, a popular video game in Colombia has players navigating the lethal roads of Antioquia. The car was always breaking down. You could get stuck in the high mound of dirt that remained in the middle of an unpaved road after heavy trucks passed and cut deep ruts on either side. The tires kicked up rocks that damaged the undercarriage. At the swampy lower altitudes, you got bogged down in the mud.

The three travelers were on their way to Pueblo Nuevo when they got stuck overnight. The driver slept. Mono and my father stayed awake, keeping guard. "There are 577 bird species in this region," my father said, but he was more concerned with the fifty-two different kinds of snakes. They stayed in their seats, afraid to leave the car.

At dawn, a truck from a soft drinks distributor came skidding down the muddy road, stopped, and towed them free. They reached their destination, the pharmacy that served a settlement of twenty small houses for the men who were cutting down acres of rainforest for an American company. "They paid them fifty pesos to bring down a tree forty meters high. The forest was gone almost as far as you could see." The valuable hardwoods were for export; the cheap pulpwood was for domestic use. "They'd pull the timber with tractors and chains to the river and float it down to port." The Atrato may have been clogged with timber, but that was still better than the other great river, the Magdalena. Parents in those days kept their children from going near the riverbank, where they'd see hundreds of bodies floating, victims of right wing atrocities.

"The geographical coordinates of Quibdó are 5°41'41" North, 76°39'40" West," said Pedro, "and the city gets more rainfall each year than any other place on earth. More than 420 inches every year," making me think Ignacio got his penchant for hard work and hard facts from our father.

In Quibdó, Mono learned something else.

My father explains: "Most of the guerrilla fighters had very little education, maybe a year of primary school or two. They were rural people, peasants. But Juan Fernando had a special bond with a black man in the ELN who was from Quibdó and an educated professional. His father was rich. He owned the bus line Transportes de Quibdó, and he was a worried father like me." The friend went by the name of

Kunta Kinte, like the character in Alex Haley's book *Roots*. He warned Mono they could no longer trust their compañeros: "They are going to kill you. You know right from wrong and you haven't done the things they ordered you to do. They are going to kill me, too, and so I'm going to quit the movement. You should get out."

Some time later, my father returned alone on a sales trip to Quibdó. He was staying in a room on the second floor above the Farmacia San Vicente when he heard men asking where they could find Kunta Kinte. "They were disguised as civilians, but I knew." He went to the bus company to warn the young man's father. "They're looking for your son."

"They already have him."

As soon as you leave Quibdó, there's nothing but jungle. That's where the men took Kunta Kinte, and that's where they killed him.

MY FATHER TRIED so many times to talk to my brother. I tried, too, but Mono maintained his silence.

"How can you be part of that?" I asked. The ELN committed acts of sabotage on oil pipelines. Sure, that cost the gringos some of their profits, but it also led to contamination of our own environment. The ELN raised money by kidnapping civilians and holding them for ransom. "How can you say you're on the side of the people when you cause ordinary families so much pain?"

I wanted him to debate me. After all, didn't we share an ideology? I don't know what he thought of me. An artist? A bourgeois individualist? I hope he respected me, but he didn't engage in dialogue with me. My brother, the revolutionary, believed he'd found his calling and there was simply nothing to discuss.

After Mono stopped accompanying Pedro, he continued his clandestine travels. I was already living in the U.S. when he was arrested again after a civil disturbance in a small town. This time after his release, my mother had to do for the second time in her life one of the hardest things a mother can do. For the second time she had to tell a son to get out. "I love you, but as long as you live here, you're putting the rest of us in danger."

Mono didn't argue or try to justify himself. He recognized the truth in what she said and he left.

Recently, my mother told Diane how, after Mono left, she closed the windows and doors so no one would see and went through the rooms gathering up all the books and papers she could find. She burned everything—"I almost burned the house down!"—and almost died of asphyxiation from the smoke. For years, I'd tried to find my own papers, the journals I kept as Xicotico, my old scripts, everything I'd left behind, and for years, I couldn't figure out where I'd stored them. Now I finally knew where all of it had gone.

For years, Mono stayed in touch with the family, appearing at the house, always bearing a gift, for birthdays and occasions like Mother's Day. He left the guerrilla movement, but his life was still unsettled, a grown man with little formal education, a prison record, unable to get even a minimum wage job. No one wanted to hire someone known as an ex-guerrilla. That sort of association could get you targeted and killed.

My brother had joined the ELN as a young man. His only work experience came from years of making war. That was his identity. His mission, his relationships, every aspect of his daily life for years had been intimately connected to the movement. Once he was no longer a part of that, aside from the practical problems he faced, Mono lost what he'd seen for so long as the meaning of his life.

He tried his hand at many things. I know for a while he traveled back to the mountains and Chocó buying gold from the rural miners and taking it to the cities to sell, but the profits were low and he wasn't getting by. In 1994, he was arrested while trying to rob a bank. This was the heaviest blow to my parents' dignity. While I could glibly quote Bertolt Brecht to the effect that it's more of a crime to found a bank than to rob one, my mother and father are two of the most honest people on earth. They've never taken a crumb that didn't belong to them. I'm not even sure either one has ever told a lie, so it was bad enough when Juan Fernando got himself arrested for putting his political beliefs into action. *This* was to my parents the shame of real crime.

All over the world, countries are faced with crime waves when armies, whether official or insurgent, are demobilized. Thousands of unemployed people go back into societies that have no ready place for them. Even the killing of Pablo Escobar, shot dead on a rooftop in 1993, led to a local wave of terror as the army of *sicarios* lost their employer but still had their weapons. The children terrorized their neighborhoods. Their own parents formed self-defense groups that went out at night to kill their own children. On all the hillsides ringing Medellín, *sicarios*, ELN guerrillas, and paramilitaries battled for turf. The police entered the barrios now and then not to keep the peace but only to collect the bodies.

Mono at least could turn to our parents. They weren't rich, but had some resources and financial help from me. My brother served a two-year sentence and came out subdued, changed, and finally ready to listen when my father took him in hand. Pedro rented a small piece of land and taught my brother all he knew about raising poultry and rabbits. These were the years when Mono finally opened up to Dad. Sometimes, he reminisced about his life with the ELN, mostly stories that in retrospect were funny, like the time he was being pursued and hid the money he was carrying, a million pesos, by burying it in a box in the ground. When he returned to the jungle at last to retrieve the cash, it had all rotted away in the damp soil. But those days were far behind him. Now Mono took his chicks and rabbits to market every week, just a small farmer living a quiet and ordinary life with Laura, his daughter, and his girlfriend Margarita.

"He seemed content," said my father.

"I'd finally stopped worrying about him," said my mother.

I WENT TO THE MORGUE. A cold room. On the wall to the left was a crucifix with a tortured Christ; on the wall to the right, a medical diagram of a human body flayed to show its veins and arteries and organs. Mono was in a black bag with a zipper. They opened the bag.

I demanded an autopsy and I demanded that the pathologist let me stay and watch. I wanted to know exactly what they did to him. In front of me was a table—all cold, stained, white tile—and bars on which they laid my brother's body down. Under the bars, I saw the sink, and the drain to carry away the fluids that would come out of him.

I wanted to see with my own eyes and I brought my camera because I wanted the whole world to see. In the most recent photographs I had of him alive, he was smiling and laughing, and Laura, his young daughter in a pink bikini, was goofing around and sticking out her tongue. My parents still talk of what a fussy baby Laura was, always crying, and how Mono never lost patience with her. He was always very patient and very calm.

Now my brother's body was naked, and covered with blood and dirt. This could have happened to me. It happened every day. It happened to him. I touched and caressed him. The pathologist didn't try to stop me, but he pointed out the ligature marks and my brother's arms and legs and torso, covered with burns. The whites of his eyes were bloodied and red and the blood was crusted where it gushed out of his ears. The pathologist opened my brother's body. The brother who never let me know him could hide nothing from me now. He was so vulnerable as his tortured body was cut into pieces, butchered in front of me, so that I could see inside.

I took pictures, my fingers stiff with the mortuary cold.

"When he was found, his intestines were empty," the pathologist said. "How long did they have him?"

"Ten days," I said.

"Well, for ten days, they starved him."

Dead, like his hero Che. The tragedy was their deaths, and the pointless outcome of the revolution they dedicated their lives to. Perhaps most tragic of all was that they both grew up in a world where the finest and best of us could not imagine any way to contest injustice except through violence.

I don't have the words to describe what it is to see your brother dead and his body opened and his scalp lifted up and placed over his face like a mask while they take out his brains so that you can look. There it was, in plain sight in front of me, the trajectory of the bullet through his skull, but what I wanted to see was invisible—the thinking that went on there, in his brain full of ideology and the words of Marx, Lenin, Mao, and Che. My brother left school early, but he was always reading. He read the poetry of Pablo Neruda about the people's tree of freedom, nourished with the bodies of the naked, beaten, and wounded dead. He read García Márquez, whose fictionalized versions of Colombian history made our story part of the cultural patrimony of the entire world.

I looked at pieces of my brother. I saw his heart, but where was the place where he held Laura, and Margarita? My brother, with his nobility of soul. Pieces of his body went into a plastic bucket and parts went down the drain. The family was left with the remains, an empty shell.

No human being, no matter what he's done, deserves to die this way. The torn skin and abrasions on his throat and neck. The bloody mess at the back of his head where the bullet finally brought the torture to an end.

AT MY BROTHER'S FUNERAL, his former comrades-in-arms told me about Mono's trips through the jungle on old smuggling routes to Panama where he bought weapons. "We trusted him with millions of pesos," I was told. "He never kept a penny for himself." I learned he'd been expelled from the movement for his strong opposition to military executions of soldiers out of combat, the kidnappings, and the terrorist acts against oil pipelines: the same tactics I'd criticized.

Another compañero who'd returned to civilian life told me, "He was fingered by one of our own." He named a former guerrilla who'd gone over to the paramilitaries. "He's been pointing out everyone he ever knew. I know they're going to get me next."

"Then you've got to get out of here." I offered him money if that would help him escape.

"No," he said. "I'm staying."

Not long afterward, he was disappeared.

At Juan Fernando's funeral people said, "You're lucky. At least you found a body to bury."

WHAT HAPPENED TO JUAN FERNANDO ARISTIZÁBAL, known as Mono, happens to twenty people in Colombia every day. In this atmosphere of relentless, seemingly sociopathic violence, even some of our best-known writers and intellectuals have begun to suspect there is something deeply wrong with our character. You might say no one and nothing is pure in Colombia except the cocaine. But if the national character is so twisted and violent, then how do you explain my parents, who never raised their voices, never physically disciplined us, and who've always lived their lives with gentleness and scrupulous honesty and dignity? Mono and I never knew how to handle money. Whatever we had, we spent, a consequence I always said of growing up poor. How can you learn about saving when you've never had enough to make ends meet? It was Cindy who taught me about living within a budget, or tried to. But Ignacio always knew how. He's always been frugal and responsible. He and his wife save for retirement and think about the future. How can anyone claim there is a single and unalterable national character?

In spite of a system that sets the stage for helplessness, complicity, and atrocity, Colombians of immense creativity devote themselves to creating beauty, and thousands daily risk their lives doing their jobs with integrity and working for peaceful change.

Claudia Monsalve and Angel Quintero worked with a human rights organization called ASFADDES, a group made up of families and friends of the detained, the disappeared, the tortured, and killed. Right after Mono's funeral, Margarita and I went to see them and made a report that was sent to human rights groups around the world with the demand that the Colombian government investigate the crime and bring the perpetrators to justice.

The next day, the phone rang at my parents' home. It was a male voice, for me: "Your brother was hard. You motherfucker, didn't you see what happened to him? Do you want the same treatment? Just shut your big mouth and let it go. You know you are very easy to locate."

Margarita's sister, who is an attorney and a judge, also received a call. "It looks like his death affected you a lot," the man said. "Don't pursue this. We know where you take your son every day." She called me terrified. "It's like they were there observing us at the funeral, as if they know us intimately. Please, Hector. Drop the case or there will be more deaths."

My whole family agreed with her. "This is why we didn't want to call you."

They hadn't wanted me to return at all, not this time. I'd made visits back to Medellín since my exile, but always very quietly. I kept a low profile, saw family and friends, and stayed out of politics. I didn't entirely avoid controversial behavior. During one trip, Cindy and I accepted an invitation to the baptism of La Negra's first child. José Luis Ochoa was the godfather, though at that time he happened to be housed in Itagüí prison. In the deluxe suite of cells that the Ochoa brothers called their temporary home, the priest conducted the rite witnessed by sixty guests, who were then fed a splendid meal by the Ochoa family cook. During the mass, I didn't take communion, but the devout cartel bosses did. Ironically, it was during this visit, when my friends could detect no signs of narco-prosperity in the way I dressed and acted, that the rumors about me finally ceased.

Socializing with the Ochoas was fine. Seeking justice was another matter. I listened to reason and to Margarita. When Mono first disappeared, she had gone to La Procuradaría, an office like the District Attorney, to file a document requesting an investigation. Now she was so scared, she wanted to close the case and asked me to go with her.

As soon as we got on the Metro, I realized we were being followed.

I was paralyzed with terror until Margarita touched my arm. "Hector, those five men. . . ." She had seen them too, and swayed against me as her knees gave out from fear. That's what snapped me out of it. I was responsible for her safety and for my family. I had to do anything possible to save my parents from the horror of burying another son. In those days, death squads rarely came to your house—too many witnesses in the barrio and too many people with guns. The preferred method was to snatch people off the street, just as they'd done to my brother. And so somehow, we had to get home.

I started joking around, acting loud and unconcerned as though justice was the last thing on my mind. When the doors opened, I hustled Margarita off the train, but the men followed. I'd chosen this stop because it put us right by El Exito, one of the city's largest department stores, and I knew a taxi stand was just around the corner. "Walk like nothing's happening," I told Margarita, "but as soon as we turn the corner, *run.*" We did, as fast as gazelles followed by lions.

We threw ourselves into the back seat of a waiting cab. "Drive! Get us out of here, fast!"

The poor taxi driver was soon as terrified as we were and took off at high speed. During a twenty-minute ride that felt like hours, we made him an indirect victim of the reign of terror that hovered like a cloud over Medellín.

At ASFADDES, Claudia and Angel received so many threats they asked for government protection. They got none. About a year after they reported my brother's murder, these two brave human rights workers were abducted outside the office. Their bodies were never found.

FEAR, IMPOTENCE, OUTRAGE—a toxic mix. If my family wanted me to act rationally, well, I would free myself of my family. They alone were responsible for my cowardice. I sent my parents, my wife, and my children back to Pasadena so that I could flirt with death. I promised them I would follow right away, but instead, I managed to get to the airport so late that not just once, but three times, I missed my flight. I wasn't going to leave Colombia till I settled scores.

I convinced one of my best friends to take me to Santa Rosa de Osos, an enclave controlled by the paramilitary, the town where Mono's body had been found. In my delusional state, I wanted to find my brother's killers and kill them. So there we were, driving the crazy roads of Antioquia, headed into the lion's den: a clearly suicidal act. My friend was driving and we were drinking *aguardiente*. Halfway there, my friend stopped the car. He looked me directly in the eyes and said, "What are you doing? And what am I doing taking you there? I don't want to die with you this way."

I said nothing as he turned the car around and we returned to the city drinking *aguardiente* all the way. We ended up at a strip club. I kept drinking, now with one of the young dancers. She told me about her sick child at home whose father had been killed by the police for no apparent reason and how this was the only job she could find to support herself and her child. For the first and last time in my life, I paid someone for sex. My own despair took advantage of hers, and never before had I felt so ashamed. I'd touched bottom.

Chapter 9

The Terrorist Within

A rabbit one day was pounced on by a lion. "Please, Mr. Lion, give me a moment before you eat me." The lion agreed: "Go ahead and say your prayers." The rabbit lay down, rolled around and, thumping against the ground in great agitation, kicked up the dust.
"Now I'm going to eat you," said the Lion, "but first, satisfy my curiosity. What good did that do you?"
"Yes, I will be gone," said the rabbit, "but when people pass by, they will say, Look! A struggle happened here!"

—a story learned from
Nigerian author Chinua Achebe

Back home in Pasadena, I went through the motions at work and in front of Cindy and the kids, but I'd startle awake in the morning with the conviction that this was the day I would have to return to Colombia and track down Mono's killers.

In some of the worst moments of my adult life, looking into the eyes of my children has been enough to bring me back to my senses. Not this time. As I drove the freeways, I raged with hate against my fellow Americans, all commuting inside their little bubbles, paying taxes—

just as I did—that helped fund atrocities around the world. We were all guilty. We all deserved to die, and I fantasized making that happen. I saw myself with a high-powered weapon picking off strangers, blasting them to hell, one at a time. I dreamed at night of explosions and, against the screen of my dreaming, blood ran in torrents. Every night and sometimes during the most ordinary moments of the day, it appeared in front of me: a kaleidoscope of body parts. I wanted to kill, I wanted to die, anything to stop the pain.

I am not a killer. Having sex with the prostitute, which I consider an act of spiritual violence, is the only violent act I've committed in my life. And yet, a terrorist was being born inside me. I suspect that while I was in this thoroughly traumatized state, if someone had handed me a suicide vest and said *Go. You can have your revenge, and you can end it*, I might well have strapped that vest on and gone to kill and to die.

I was a psychotherapist and, though I knew that I desperately needed help, everything inside my being recoiled from the idea of turning to the sorts of treatment offered by my own profession. My brother had been brutally murdered and someone would have the nerve to put a label on me: posttraumatic stress disorder, PTSD. Someone would prescribe drugs to take the power away from my justified rage. The more I thought about this sort of help, the more I burned.

Some inner compass pointed the way. I picked up the phone and called mythologist and storyteller Michael Meade, the first person outside of books who talked to me of ancient and tribal wisdom, who said that every person on earth is born with an aimed soul along with the gifts that help the soul move in the direction it's meant to go. Meade uses these concepts in his work mentoring youth, he had influenced my own work with kids, but now I was the one who needed help. He invited me to join him at a weeklong conference he was about to hold in a beautiful wooded retreat outside Chicago. As he would say during that gathering, "Death is the teacher. All philosophy begins in death. You have to deal with it or it will deal with you."

THE PHOTOGRAPHS OF MY brother's cadaver had been developed and I kept them in a safe place, but I hadn't once looked at them. I didn't want to, or need to. The images played constantly in my mind's eye and my own body responded to the pain of every burn, every broken finger, and every broken rib. I took the photos with me to Chicago.

There I joined seventy men I'd never met before, of different ages and races and backgrounds. We were guided by Meade; Malidoma Somé, the shaman from Burkina Faso; Orland Bishop, the director of Shade Tree Mentoring; and Luis Rodriguez, the author and poet of East LA. They asked each of us what expectations we brought to the gathering. I talked about Juan Fernando, about everything he'd gone through, and how I needed to come to terms with his death. For the first time, I opened the envelope and made myself look at the pictures and I shared them. During the lunch break, some men who'd never met me before or known Mono asked if I would allow them to join me in building a memorial altar to him. At lunchtime and during breaks, we walked outside through the woods and gathered natural objects. Throughout the day, we carried in earth and shaped it into a mound to which men kept adding stones and branches and leaves. On it, I placed a single picture of my brother. Some men asked if it would be all right to add pictures of their own loved ones or objects representing people they had lost and mourned. As the evening went on, the small altar to my brother grew into a giant shrine of fascinating beauty.

That night, we were led in a ritual. We brought water, fire, and earth to the meeting room and Malidoma taught us ritual songs from the ancestors of his tribe. We lit hundreds of candles to symbolize the spirits and we all invited our own ancestors to join us. We invited the mothers, fathers, children, siblings, and friends who had entered the other world and left us. The room was filled with an astonishing radiance as the dancing lights seemed to be beckoning to each other in greeting.

This group of strangers turned into a sudden community and carried out a symbolic burial of my brother. They cried for me because I still couldn't cry. Months had passed and I was still in shock, but something was happening to me now in this world filled with candles and rocks and nature and the tears of men. At one moment, seventy men were behind me, some with their hands on my shoulders, and as I stood in front of my brother's picture at the altar, I felt the ground disappear. It was not the awful plunging into the abyss I'd known in the past, when the earth opened under my feet. Instead, I felt I was no longer a mass of muscles and bones but something else that was simply swept away, lifted up from the ground.

A young man placed an amulet on my hand. "This has protected me for years," he said. "Now I would like you to have it."

Orland then offered me the pictures of my brother, no longer in the envelope from the photo lab but covered in delicate fabric that looked like butterfly wings. I buried the package in Mother Earth and asked her to carry some of the pain for me and to receive my brother in her womb.

All around, many other men were crying, for their own wounds, I'm sure, but they were also crying for me. As they surrounded me with murmurs and prayers, I felt suspended in time as I looked at my brother's picture and felt the power of his presence. The moment lasted an eternity and its effects still resonate within me.

The gathering led by Michael Meade gave me access to a spirituality I had long gone without. His words resonated in my being, but
I was not healed. People I met that week continued to reach out to
me. One day, I received a call from Alan Cohen, who'd been unable
to stop thinking about my brother. He told me he'd asked an artist,
Ric Leichliter, to create a sculpture and embed a picture of Mono in
it. Alan had it sited in the middle of the woods on the ninety acres of
Ohio countryside where he lives with his wife Evie. "A place for Juan
Fernando's photograph," Alan told me, "and I hope for his spirit."

I went for a visit, and in addition to enjoying Alan and Evie's hospi-
tality I was able to spend time in the magical place in the woods where I
felt Mono was near me. I, always stubborn—someone who takes advice
from no one, looked to my brother's spirit as though it were the spirit
of the ancestors and asked him humbly for guidance.

I HAVE BEEN CLOSE to, even intimate with, death. My brothers and
friends have died. Bullets have just missed me. I've had a rifle shoved
into my mouth and told I was about to die. Like gang members who are
so willing to self-destruct they court suicide with every homicidal act,
I suspect I suffer from survivor's guilt. Somehow, I believe I should die
because I've seen so many others pay the ultimate price for doing the
same things I've done. Like many other survivors, I try to justify my
survival by bearing witness.

And I take risks. I feel life most intensely when I know how easy it
is to lose it. I have to fight against the attraction to death, to being on
the edge, to feeling most alive—the way many soldiers returning from
combat feel—when flirting with annihilation.

I've developed a strong connection to the two brothers who are dead while I have little to say to my brother and sister who are alive. Is it my fault, my psyche? I've little in common with Ignacio. When Estela and Ignacio went to identify Juan Fernando, they did it from police photos. Faced with his body, all they could bear to look at were his feet. Estela called my attendance at his autopsy sick and morbid.

Why did I do it? Did I think I would finally get to know him, after all the secrets he kept all his life? I told myself I was documenting the atrocities in order to seek justice. But was I like the apostle Doubting Thomas who couldn't believe what was before him until he plunged his hands deep into the wound? I still can't answer these questions. But after the ritual I joined in for Mono, I came to see death not as the opposite of life, but the opposite of birth, to be neither desired nor feared.

The abortions led me to work with pregnant teens; Hernán Darío's pain took me first to CENIT and then to the gay and transgendered Latinos at Bienestar; torture directed me to PTV. My life leads me to my work, and from my work I pull the threads that weave my life. After Mono's murder, I went to hospice.

Through hospice work, I've seen how the last stage of life can overflow with meaning among those who aren't dealt a sudden death, but are given the time to mature their souls as time grows short. Juan Fernando died alone, by which I mean without the company of anyone who loved him, surrounded only by those who inflicted pain. In this country, I see people dying alone, not because they've been abducted, but because they die in hospital beds surrounded by equipment and technicians. When I brought hospice services to the City of Hope cancer center, I found that embedded in the very word "Hope" was a refusal to acknowledge impending death. While family members met with doctors in the hallways to discuss test results, clinical trials, and scientific breakthroughs, terminal patients were sometimes left alone, with no one to hold their hands, to forgive or be forgiven.

A dying person shouldn't be rendered passive. You shouldn't merely be done *to*. The dying have a lot to do and not much time in which to do it. I see my role as helping people find long-delayed emotional satisfaction and release, to use the time of dying as an opening for whatever has remained unexpressed and unresolved.

Sometimes the issues are purely practical. It's amazing to me how many people diagnosed with terminal illnesses have never prepared a will or an advance directive. Preparing for the end feels to many people like giving up hope or even jinxing the possibility of remission or cure. So I tell them of the plans Cindy and I made when we went to Cuba. We were both young and in good health, but this was the first time we'd both be on an airplane without our children. We realized in case that plane went down, we needed to make provision for Camilla and Gabo. What would become of our kids if we were gone? My parents love them, but my parents are old. Cindy's family lives by values very different from ours. We decided the best possible parent for our kids would be our good friend Nancy. Much to our joy and relief, she said she'd be honored and we arranged for her to have a continuing role in our children's lives. As I explained to my dying clients, "And see? No jinx. Our plane landed safely."

Many of my clients are immigrants and this raises huge issues to be resolved. Some want to see once more the towns where they were born. They have to decide whether to be buried in the U.S. or in native soil. They want to say goodbye to family and friends thousands of miles away, separated by a border.

Justina had five grown children, two living in Los Angeles and three in Oaxaca, Mexico. She wasn't even dead yet and the children were squabbling over her body, as they all wanted a burial place they could visit. I suggested to Justina that she herself had to make the choice. Some of her children would inevitably be disappointed, but at least the decision would be her own and that would prevent animosity among the kids after she was gone. Though she'd never expressed her wish, she'd never had any doubt in her mind. She wanted to be laid to rest in Oaxaca near the graves of her own parents.

I adapted the concept of "wraparound," usually applied to child and family services, to my work with the dying. The idea behind wraparound is if you're treating a child, you need to work with the whole family and it should be the family that drives the process, not the professionals. We ask the family to agree on what they want and what they need: maybe it's family reunification; maybe they need transportation, a house, education, or a job. But they tell us; we don't tell them. The family also decides who should be on the support team, which means going beyond the therapist or social worker to engage anyone who's important in their lives: a probation officer, judge, teacher, the aunt who's the only one that a child really listens to, or the grandfather or a neighbor. Then everyone on the team works toward the family's stated goal. I have on occasion made the kid's drug dealer a part of the team. After all, a teenager with a history of running away from home may disappear again, but is likely to stay in contact with his or her drug dealer. If I have a relationship with the dealer, that person can call me when the runaway turns up. This turns out to be much faster and more effective than waiting for the police to find the kid.

In my work with the dying, I ask *What is your goal? Who is meaningful to you?* I try to create a village of support around the patient. *Who do you want to thank? Who do you want to say goodbye to? Who do you need to be reconciled with?* People ask for relatives, old friends, a priest or pastor, a teacher who once took an interest, a former neighbor, a lover. For patients whose loved ones are outside the borders of the U.S., when it's impossible to arrange visas and travel, we use technology and imagination. I set up phone calls and videotapings. For my brother Hernán Darío, the film we made together was his chance to tell his own story, to be sure that the truth of his life and his soul were finally seen. And so I don't just interview the dying person on tape. We create a short film in which they can show their distant friends and families what life here was like: *This is where I live, this is my neighborhood, these are my friends.* But what we do is always up to the person: *What do you want to accomplish when you think you're at the end of your life?*

I LEARNED OTHER LESSONS from my brothers.

In healing from torture and from Mono's death, I discovered I couldn't stay in the passive position of the victim. I had to take action and so I wanted my clients to begin to see themselves as powerful, too, capable of being agents of change. I understood that activism could be part of their therapy.

People in the United States seemed to me to live in isolation from their neighbors and I began to think this even influenced the way in which we practice psychotherapy. I became critical of the emphasis on the individual's problem and the individual's search for relief. When I saw a troubled child, I always went to see the family as well, even if that meant tracking a mother down in the laundromat or at the swap meet. But I soon understood even that was not enough. I was influenced by the public health approach of my mentor, Dr. Héctor Abad Gómez, who always said it didn't make sense to treat diphtheria patients one by one. You had to organize a vaccination drive and pressure the city to see it was done. So, if I saw many kids were having the same sorts of problems in school, I brought the parents together and encouraged them to write letters, organize, and pressure the public institution to be more responsive to their children's needs.

When Hernán Darío was dying, I'd taken a first faltering step in the direction of ceremony, and I'd hoped our little rite had helped ease him. Jerzy Grotowski had spoken to me of the origins of theater in ritual and the notion appealed to me but I remained in some fundamental way aloof. Leo Cabranes-Grant, the playwright and scholar from Puerto Rico, says that Latin American actors in their theatrical training learn to induce a state of trance. It's true that when I perform, I enter another world, and once I come out of an improvisation I rarely remember anything I've said or done. But "trance" sounds so primitive. As an educated Latin American, I resist being exoticized. So, I've always insisted on using psychoanalytic terms: I don't enter a trance; I tap the unconscious.

It was only during the symbolic burial of Juan Fernando that I felt the power of ritual in my own life. I believe that during the burial of my brother's pictures I didn't bury him but the part of me that had held itself apart, the great skeptic, without any connection to the spirit world. I still prefer to think of this other world as the symbolic world or my unconscious—to conceive of it in metaphorical terms rather than admit to belief in the overtly supernatural. But I can feel the power that comes from allowing myself communion with realities that go behind profane material life.

The Chicago gathering offered me the extraordinary coming together of the spirit world with the passionate support of a community that was not asked to subscribe to any dogma or be part of any particular ethnicity or race. This community didn't promise to cure me, but gave me a profound sense of connection. The solace, solidarity, and support gave me a base from which I could harness my own resources to move forward.

It was also Michael Meade who first gave me the idea of resignifying the time of my torture as an initiatory ordeal. The initiate, after all, is also separated from his accustomed world. He doesn't know where he's been taken. Naked and unprotected, he will face severe trials. He won't know what comes next. He must accept the unknown outcome. Afterwards, he returns to his society and is celebrated by it. But while traditional elders would have taught me to love and value life, the perpetrators tried to make me hate and lose faith in life. I came to understand it was now my work to defeat them and to own my wound and find its blessing.

A ritual doesn't have to be elaborate and sophisticated. It doesn't have to cost a lot of money, as it isn't created from material props but from the human imagination.

When I help young people develop a theatrical performance, I invite the parents, teachers, and people from the community so the kids can be seen by as many of them as possible. I invite them to bring food, and though they're very poor, these people feel honored that they were asked to contribute, and we always have more than we can eat. After sharing this communal meal, we do a ritual as simple as creating a tunnel with our hands for the kids to walk through as we say their names.

I don't make these rituals up alone, out of my own head. In one of the middle schools where I work with kids as part of a gang-prevention program, I ask parents and teachers to join with me in creating a graduation ceremony. Some of the kids won't graduate from school, or get passing grades, but I wish to acknowledge their participation in the program and salute what they *have* accomplished. We don't hand out one-size-fits-all certificates. I ask each parent and each teacher to identify specific gifts and accomplishments, so that each young person is recognized for his or her particular achievement, even if that achievement is merely one of having survived the mean streets.

Rituals can be rooted in ancient cultures and still build bridges. In April 2007, I was leading a workshop in Brattleboro, Vermont when a woman named Ellen Kaye approached me: "Since you're so interested in ritual," she said, "I'd like to invite you to a seder," the ritual meal commemorating the liberation of the Jewish people from slavery thousands of years ago in Egypt. It was at this Passover table that the Palestinian student Ziad Allas and I met again.

Ellen and Rupa Cousins had compiled their own version of the Haggadah, the book of prayers and readings that accompany the ritual meal. Nothing in their Haggadah deviates from Jewish learning and tradition, but their interpretation ties ancient history to their desire for peace and justice for both Israelis and Palestinians. It's a Haggadah with "two tellings: One that tells the story of our ancestors, and one that tells the conflict of our two peoples." After the lighting of the candles and the first prayer, the *Baruch atah Adonai, eloheinu . . .* , after the first cup of wine, we heard wisdom from the Talmud: "A person who does not own a piece of land is not a secure person." We passed parsley and salt water. We heard a blessing. A piece of matzoh was raised: "This is the bread of affliction. It is whole, and so long as it is whole, no one can eat from it." The matzoh was broken and I heard these words, "The bread of affliction becomes the bread of freedom when we share it. . . . So long as one people grasps the whole land, it is a land of affliction and no one is nourished by it. When each people can eat from part of the land, it will become a land of freedom."

The rite continued. We sang and talked and told stories for hours, and of course, we ate and ate and ate: a group of people drawn from different nations and different religions, learning that at least on this night different from other nights, we didn't have to be enemies. May the fellowship we learned on this different night prevail even after we leave the table.

AFTER CHICAGO, MY HEART was more at peace than it had been for many months but I was not a peaceful man. I gave angry speeches: "This country, the United States, funds what you call the war on Communism, the war on cocaine lords, the war on narcoterrorism; what your taxes buy is a war on the people. You provide the military aid, the weapons, planes, chemicals, and helicopters. The paramilitaries who terrorize the country are tied to the government. The weapons you provide end up in their hands. As my father always puts it: *The war will never end because after witnessing the atrocities committed against your own, all you are left with is the desire for revenge. If one gets the opportunity, one will use it.*" It had become my way to make fun of people who talked about an end to violence. "Without justice, there can be no peace. Without anger, there can be no peace. How can we have peace with all this oppression?"

I wanted to be, like my brother, a true warrior.

A few months later I met people who'd chosen a different path.

After a young photojournalist, Dan Eldon, was killed by an angry mob in Mogadishu, his mother Kathy and sister Amy devoted themselves to seeking alternatives to violence instead of seeking revenge. The Eldons and I shared a stage one night. I'd been asked to present a play about gang violence I'd developed with kids from East LA and the Eldons had been invited to show their documentary, *Soldiers of Peace: A Children's Crusade*, about Colombian children who'd pledged never to take up weapons. Before the film screened, Kathy and Amy asked me to speak about my country and to introduce a few representatives from the Colombian Children's Peace Movement who'd been able to travel to LA. I was still angry and cynical. What a sick joke this is, I thought, as if my country could ever know peace!

Then I watched the film. I saw kids who'd gone through situations similar to mine or worse: whose parents had been killed, kidnapped, or tortured; who'd witnessed massacres, or had their friends killed by gangs. But they pledged not to retaliate or take up weapons. None of them spoke in ideological terms, as my generation had, and I realized they had something I didn't. The generations that had come before them were destroying the country, and these children understood that none of these groups, right wing or left wing, would bring justice and peace to Colombia. They were behind the remarkable referendum that Colombia held in 1996—the Children's Mandate for Peace and Rights in which only children could vote—and millions of children came out and voted for peace.

The children—Farlys, an extremely focused and self-possessed young lady, and Wilfredo, a dancer and a clown and therefore the most like me in terms of personality—looked me in the eye and confronted me gently. They were kids, just thirteen and fourteen years old, and their actions and their hearts were in complete accord. There I was, forty years old, talking about violence and full of rage.

"Hector," they told me, "it's okay if you're not ready to forgive. Just pledge that you won't retaliate."

They put me to shame with their wisdom and allowed me to connect with my own compassion and my desire to create, not destroy; to love, not kill.

"What can I do to help you?" I asked and they, shocked by what they'd learned about conditions in East LA, told me to do more for the children in the U.S.

They asked nothing for themselves, but I started raising money to help them continue their educations. A few years later, I organized a fundraiser for the conscientious objectors of Red Juvenil, another organization of young peace activists in Colombia that offers kids alternatives to joining any of the four armies. I helped one family get political asylum after they were targeted for assassination.

My contribution is a very small act of recognition for these young people. Their initiatives aren't token gestures, but absolutely vital in a country where the ranks of armed combatants include as many as 14,000 children, some as young as eight years old. Some kids have been kidnapped or coerced by force into fighting; many have been driven to join the guerrillas or paramilitaries by hunger and homelessness, by payments made to their parents, or by the desire for revenge after the massacre of their families.

After I met Farlys and Wilfredo, I realized—almost in spite of myself—that I could continue my brother's struggle and take up his commitments, but I could do it through nonviolence. Juan Fernando's life had to be honored. It had to have meaning, and making that meaning was up to me. Continuing his struggle through nonviolent means would also give meaning to my exile. Maybe I could serve the land of my birth best from here, in a country where I can speak out about injustice in ways that in Colombia would likely cost me my life.

To honor my brother's sacrifice, I joined the Colombia Peace Project in Los Angeles, where we raise awareness by bringing Colombian issues to the attention of the public and of Congress. We help sponsor visits to the U.S. of grassroots leaders whose personal stories stand in contrast to the official versions presented by government officials and industry lobbyists. We have supported people like José Julio, whose entire town—homes, school, and church—was razed to the ground by a multinational corporation; the trade unionists facing death threats working at Coca-Cola subsidiaries; and Stella Orjuela, a union leader working in one of Dole's flower plantations in Bogotá. Stella told of attempts to suppress union organizing; of being poisoned by pesticides as chemicals that should be restricted to outdoor use are sprayed inside closed greenhouses; of safety equipment that isn't functional, such as respirators provided without the necessary filters.

Stella paid a high price for her activism. A year after her visit, she and her husband lost their jobs. With their three children they moved into her sister's one-room house outside of Bogotá. The last we heard, Stella had not found work and her husband was trying to make a living as a street vendor selling snacks. At least they're alive. It's dangerous to organize, or even join, a labor union in Colombia. The DAS, Colombia's FBI, has been exposed for providing paramilitary death squads with a hit-list of labor leaders to be eliminated.

We expose the fact that U.S. tax dollars pay for protection of Occidental Petroleum's oil pipelines. After U.S. pilots were involved in an anti-guerrilla action on behalf of the company that instead led to the massacre of civilians in the village of Santo Domingo, not only did we protest but we succeeded in arranging the relocation of the five surviving members of a village family. Our protests continued when three U'wa children were killed after Occidental Petroleum asked the military to put an end to the tribe's peaceful protest against an oil exploration project in their cloud forest. Though denying that protests had been a factor, the company backed off and dropped the project.

One of our major efforts has been to cooperate with the organization Drummond Watch, participating in a nationwide public relations campaign on behalf of the union and workers to shine a spotlight on Drummond Ltd., a family-owned business based in Alabama, that acquired the La Loma coal mines after the International Monetary Fund demanded that Colombia privatize the exploitation of natural resources. Drummond has contracted with paramilitaries for "security," and these men on the company payroll have repeatedly threatened and assassinated union leaders. U.S.-based Chiquita Brands International has also hired paramilitaries, one of whose most notorious leaders claims he used Chiquita boats to transport cocaine and weapons.

I've tried to rally the public and lobby Congress about the billions of tax dollars spent on misguided military assistance under Plan Colombia. This crazy initiative has thrown U.S. personnel into the middle of Colombia's conflict, ostensibly to fight the losing War on Drugs, but by extension, the guerrilla armies that tax drug production. It was supposed to eradicate the coca crops, but it's accomplished nothing. For all the toxic chemicals we spray over Colombia, for all the devastation our tax dollars have caused, the demand for the white powder has not gone down in the U.S. Nor has supply disappeared or the price gone up. In 2007, the United Nations found that coca cultivation had actually increased. Whereas it was once confined to a few of Colombia's thirty-two departments or provinces, coca was now grown in most of them.

Plan Colombia has been good for some American businesses. Dyncorp makes money providing the mercenaries who fly and service the helicopters. Monsanto makes the chemical sprays that are supposed to eradicate the coca fields. When the appropriations are debated in

Congress, no one debates whether military aid to Colombia is a good policy. It's all about whether the contract for helicopters should go to Sikorsky in Connecticut or Bell in Texas. So they compromise and split it. I shouldn't say "no one." Senator Patrick Leahy of Vermont has objected loud and clear to military assistance that always seems to find its way into the hands of units accused of the worst atrocities. But the aid keeps flowing.

SOMETIMES I THINK being a nonviolent activist is little different from being Chinua Achebe's rabbit. For years, I've been part of the mass movement to shut down the School of the Americas, where for decades the U.S. Army has trained Latin American military officers responsible for the worst atrocities in the hemisphere. One year, we succeed in getting Congress to cut off funding. The Department of Defense simply changed the school's name to WHINSEC (Western Hemisphere Institute for Security Cooperation) and found the money from another budget line.

We protested the war in Iraq and President Bush responded with the Surge. When President Barack Obama was elected, I actually found myself crying tears of joy, until he sent more troops to Afghanistan amd expanded the war to Pakistan, while more than two hundred prisoners—many of them cleared of all charges—remained locked up at Guantánamo. Now I hear that the U.S. plans to put seven military bases in Colombia.

In August 2008, Diane traveled with the nonprofit organization Witness for Peace to visit Putumayo, once the epicenter of coca cultivation. The humble farmers she met in the Amazon basin reminded her more of farm-workers in the California vineyards than of The Godfather. When Pablo Escobar's emissaries first encouraged people to plant coca back in the 1980s, it's likely that the campesinos who took great pride in their cultivations didn't even know they'd become part of a criminal enterprise.

Today, U.S. policy has an enormous impact on the lives of the people of Putumayo, but U.S. Embassy personnel aren't permitted to see the effects of these policies firsthand: the region is considered too dangerous for them to visit. After the implementation of Plan Colombia, Diane found that aerial fumigation had killed staple food crops and caused widespread hunger. Much of the Amazon jungle remains thick and green—though in some places, medicinal plants have died, but cultivated fields are left barren.

Through USAID, some campesinos have been encouraged to plant cacao, but it takes three years till the first harvest, with no provision for cash or food before then. The hardy coca plant, however, yields a harvest every three to four months. Base cocaine is not only profitable, but compact and easy to carry—an important consideration in a region without infrastructure and no way for most people to bring their goods to market. The only road Diane saw was the one that runs along the oil pipeline which, discolored and rusted, snakes along—sometimes half-buried, sometimes leaking, sometimes sabotaged by guerrillas, sometimes suspended from cables over rivers, and sometimes propped up on metal supports or even on bits of metal and rock.

Paramilitaries still control the towns and cities, leaving the jungle to the guerrillas. Authorities in Putumayo continue to discover mass graves, while much aid seems misdirected. Twenty demobilized killers were given cash benefits and one hundred hectares of productive land. Their victims, women whose husbands were murdered, were given nothing. One hundred widows scraped together enough pesos to purchase four hectares. They planted corn, yuca, and banana to feed their children, only to see their crops fumigated by the U.S. and destroyed.

Natural areas and wilderness are affected, too. Colombia, with its rich biodiversity, is a paradise of birds. The birds are being poisoned, something that would appall the seventy million bird-watchers in the U.S., if they knew.

When the administration of the Colombian president Álvaro Uribe sent eighty supporters to Washington to lobby in favor of the proposed Free Trade Agreement (FTA), we spoke out against it not only because of Colombia's human rights violations but because it was likely the treaty would destroy the livelihood of many small farmers, just as NAFTA did in Mexico. The FTA as written is "free trade" in name only, suitable for a sound-bite until you learn the details of a system tilted heavily toward U.S. business interests. The Colombian government would permanently lose the power to set any conditions on foreign investment: no environmental safeguards for the mining or oil-extraction industries; no means of requiring reinvestment of some profits in the country; and no ability to set standards for local hiring in a nation where sixty-five percent of the population lives in poverty and where only twenty-five of every hundred people seeking work has secure employment.

The introduction of generic drugs would be delayed in order to protect the profits of pharmaceutical companies. And while the U.S. would be allowed to bail out troubled banks and provide agricultural subsidies to U.S. farmers, no such programs would be permissible in Colombia. The proposed FTA would inevitably exacerbate the conditions that have already made the narcotics industry and armed conflict the two most reliable sources of employment in Colombia. That can't be good for either of our countries.

• • •

"WHEN WE KEPT SILENT, they killed us. When we spoke up, they killed us. So we decided it's better to be killed for speaking out." Because the speaker was an indigenous leader in Putumayo, these words about being killed were not a rhetorical device.

For its fight against the FARC, the Colombian military is establishing bases on sovereign *resguardo* (reservation) land. The army presence makes the indigenous communities vulnerable to retaliatory attacks by the guerrillas. But the main reason for military and paramilitary presence on Native territory is apparently to eliminate opposition to oil exploration. The existing wells no longer produce many barrels, and so a consortium—no one has seemed able to identify the actual companies involved, is moving onto indigenous land seeking new fields to exploit.

When the Witness for Peace delegation met with dozens of representatives of the Cofán, Embera, Nasa, Awa, Kichwa, and Pasto peoples, passionate words came pouring out: "We became military targets when we resisted oil extraction. We feel like a bunch of Indian rabbits, and everyone's just trying to see who can hunt us best."

"They present us with a Development Plan. We reject it. We want a Life Plan. We're not against development. But development must also consider human beings and nature."

"Extraction doesn't require the destruction of people and of memory."

"We want to share, but not in the way that leads to our extinction."

Many of Colombia's indigenous groups have indeed been officially classified as on the path to extinction. But, one man insisted, "We're still here. We'll always be here, even if it's only as the pebble in the shoe."

Another man warned, "The Amazon basin is the lungs of the world. If nature here is polluted, if the lungs fail, it's not only the Native people who will be brought down."

I think of my brother Hernán Darío, and how he taught me to cherish the natural world.

The delegation traveled to a reservation near the border with Ecuador. People used to live in the center of town and enjoy a rich community life. Now families live scattered in the jungle so they'll be harder to find and less vulnerable if the army sweeps in for a mass roundup. But crowds gathered for a crisis meeting—men, women, and children all wearing the black rubber boots that make foot travel safe in their difficult terrain. When the council concluded, they opened the door of the meetinghouse to the Americans.

An indigenous leader challenged the group: "We commit our message to you so you can make it travel. But what are you going to do to help us? And when?"

A young American activist, Candice Camargo, stood and tried to answer, but soon she burst into tears. A hush fell over the crowd until the leader spoke again: "We've heard gringos aren't like us. We've heard when there's a death in the family, gringos don't cry. We believed gringos don't feel things in the heart. Now we know that isn't true."

In this way, one young woman changed a false view of Americans. But what will it take to change U.S. policies that are both counterproductive and heartless?

GROWING UP, IT WAS HARD for me to imagine that the countries of Latin America could ever be free from U.S. domination and rule by the wealthy elite. The U.S. simply would not permit a government under the elected leadership of an Allende, an Arbenz of Guatemala, or a Juan Bosch of the Dominican Republic. But Néstor Kirchner, as president of Argentina, stood up to the International Monetary Fund, restructuring the foreign debt and refusing to sacrifice social welfare. Michelle Bachelet, a socialist who was tortured under the Pinochet regime, was elected president of Chile. Grassroots leaders like Luiz Inácio Lula da Silva in Brazil and Evo Morales in Bolivia have been elected to their nation's highest office. Rafael Correa, president of Ecuador, has a vision of a new "socialism for the twenty-first century." Tabaré Vázquez took office in Uruguay in 2005, the first time a left-leaning president was ever elected in that country. Paraguay suffered under the brutal regime of the late General Stroessner and then of his Colorado Party for decades until 2008, when Fernando Lugo Méndez, a former priest known as "bishop of the poor," triumphed at the polls. Twenty years ago, I would not have believed this possible. Chávez in Venezuela? The Farabundo Martí National Liberation Front (FMLN) winning an election in El Salvador, as did the Sandinistas in Nicaragua? Without being overthrown by the U.S.? These transformative changes in the Southern Hemisphere didn't just occur by magic. They are the result of years of risk and courage on the part of people who, in spite of all the evidence of repression, violence, and inequality all around them, never gave up.

IN THE SUMMER OF 2006, I took Gabo and Camilla with me to visit Colombia. On this trip, I vowed to do nothing that might bring danger to myself and those around me. I made up my mind to be a father, not a hero. I wanted my kids to see what was beautiful about the place I come from and that is part of their own heritage. I wanted to give them some entirely positive experiences to counteract all the terrible, bloody stories they had heard.

We went to the campus of Antioquia University and to the theater where so much began for me.

"Dad!" Gabo said. "You look happy."

They got to see a Medellín much different from the city I'd known. No more *sicarios* on motorcyles. Social scientist Alonso Salazar who, like me, interviewed *sicarios* and wrote acclaimed books about them and about Pablo Escobar, was poised to become the next mayor. Parque Berrío, where Xicotico once ran around the statue of *La Gorda*, is now the site of an extraordinary open-air museum. Fernando Botero has contributed an entire collection of sculptures to his native city: gigantic men and women and even a great big rotund cat. Crime still occurs in Medellín: there were 770 killings in 2005. But in 1991, there were six thousand. Today's murder rate is still too high, but it's lower than in many North American cities. Violence continues in rural areas, and four million Colombians remain dispossessed of their homes. Union leaders are still targeted for death. Twenty people are abducted and disappeared every day. Millions of citizens still live in poverty and dislocation and despair. But Medellín proves change is possible. People walk the streets without fear—streets where my kids played safely with their new Colombian friends. "They don't spend as much time with video games," Gabo noted. "No one's fat. And kids in Colombia don't use so many rude words."

We traveled. Camilla fell in love with the Caribbean Sea and wanted to stay in its warm waters till midnight. The military guards the nation's highways. The huge potholes are still infamous and the roads still dangerous, but not from armed attack. Every time we came to a military checkpoint, I stiffened inside, but the soldiers were friendly, helpful, and correct.

IT'S STILL EASIER for me to sit in a room with Israelis and Palestinians and imagine nonviolence than to conceive of peace in my own country. But I like to think the work I do now is preparing me to go back to Colombia one day and sit in the same room with a worker, a peasant, a military person whose institution tortured me, a paramilitary like the ones who killed my brother, a guerrilla who'd probably want to kill me because of how I criticized his movement, and a CEO from a big company that I've called evil, and we will talk about how we can all work together to rebuild our country.

Chapter 10

May 2006: The Wind Comes and Takes Away

The red light flicks on as my fingertip is scanned. I fill out a paper slip and get the alarm I'm supposed to wear or carry at all times. But once I'm past the control station, I always get rid of it as quickly as I can. The clinic stretches down the corridor to my right, but I have to walk left, past the California Youth Authority cells. It's not like the movies, where you see the men through the bars. Instead here are massive gray doors with complicated locks, like what you'd find in a bank vault. The difference is, money is valued and these kids are not. When I feel confused about the United States, about how such a generous and compassionate people can also be so heartless, perhaps nothing confuses me more than the juvenile (in)justice system.

I'm here each week to bring group therapy. At least once with every group I work with in the Youth Authority, I show *Juvies*, Leslie Neale's eye-opening documentary about kids tried as adults. I can't get one of the young people featured in the film out of my mind: Duc Ta, who was born in Los Angeles to parents who fled Vietnam as "boat people." Duc grew up in a neighborhood that was violent and gang-infested. His mother became disabled from her work in a sweatshop and, living on the father's income alone, the family was in constant danger of being evicted. Duc's father was so anxious for Duc to succeed that he became a harsh disciplinarian, beating the boy for bad grades and once even holding a gun to his head. Duc was briefly removed from the home and befriended by a police officer who soon tried to recruit him as an informant—a dangerous role that Duc quickly refused, a decision that ended the "friendship." On the streets and at school, he was a constant target for violence. Is it any wonder he was jumping out of his skin? But as is all too common, it was easier to diagnose Duc with ADHD than to address the conditions in which he had to live.

Duc had a rough adolescence. He ditched school often and he got into fights, fists only. He was never in trouble with the law and never joined a gang, but he traveled back and forth to high school with a couple of gang members who were the only other kids from his neighborhood enrolled there. In 1999, when Duc was sixteen, one of his passengers fired a gun out of the car window. No one was hit or injured, but Duc was arrested with the others, charged with two counts of first-degree attempted murder. In a city fed up with drive-by shootings, he was tried as an adult and sentenced thirty-five years to life.

The kids in lockup are shocked. Some of them tell me they've done much worse things than Duc, but they were lucky. Because they weren't charged as adults, they are getting a second chance.

I don't remember when Diane first learned of my interest in Duc's case or when I heard, to my surprise, that she and Duc are friends. She visits him whenever she can and that's why one morning in May, she joins me at 6:00 AM for the 180-mile drive up to Corcoran where I'll meet him for the first time. I've put together a gift package of books and CDs.

"We can't take those," she says. "It's maximum security. Nothing's allowed in."

"But books. . ."

"Nothing," she repeats.

I leave the package behind and figure I'll give him some money.

"*Nothing*." Diane is getting over laryngitis and I can't tell if it's her voice or her patience that sounds strained.

When I work in the juvenile lock-up, no one has ever stopped me from bringing in my djembe drum, laptop, videos, books, or sometimes a soccer ball. I've brought the kids pizzas and soda and have learned that gangbangers prefer Sprite. But this isn't the Youth Authority. This is prison.

It's taken months to get my visit approved. First, the prison ran out of visiting approval forms. When Duc was finally able to get his hands on one and mail it to me, someone at the prison removed it from the envelope. He tried again. Same thing. After three tries, he complained. The form arrived at last, I filled it out, returned it, but there was a problem with the signature and date, and a month later my request was denied. Now, at last, it's a go—assuming nothing happens while we're on the road that would put the whole place on lockdown.

The first time Diane drove to Corcoran State Prison, the guard told her she was in the wrong place. He sent her to the Substance Abuse Treatment Facility, which seemed weird. Duc wasn't a drinker, he didn't use drugs. It turned out the treatment center had been converted to a Level IV prison for men judged to be among California's most dangerous felons. The windows were painted black. Not a single ray of natural light enters the cells.

Not much light on the road today. The sun hasn't yet broken through the clouds. I'm used to the overcast weather Southern California calls June Gloom, but lately we've been experiencing an early May Gray.

Diane tells me the inmates are "cell-fed," as it's too dangerous to let them in the same room for meals. Prison jobs pay pennies an hour, but due to budget cuts even those jobs have mostly evaporated. When Duc finally did get work, at first there was no money to pay him, but he was happy to work for free just to get out of the two-man cell that measures about nine feet by ten. He's now making a kingly eighteen cents an hour. He's smart and good with paperwork and often works double shifts. "I didn't know anything about prison till I started visiting him," Diane says. "It's not something I wanted to know." A lot of people feel that way, which may explain why the system is permitted to go on the way it does. And even I, advocating on Duc's behalf, had very little idea.

I learn he's been assessed $5,000 in restitution. I always thought restitution was to compensate a victim. But there *was* no victim. Out of his eighteen cents an hour earnings and the little money his parents manage to scrape together to send to his account, the State automatically takes fifty-five percent.

During the 1990s, a political science professor and Brookings Institute fellow named John DiIulio predicted an impending crime wave driven by "super-predators": a new generation of monstrous, remorseless, even feral, youth. Around the same time, sensational media reports about young killers fueled fear and a public outcry. Legislators rushed to pass new laws to make it easier to try minors as adults and to focus on removing these offenders from society and punishing them rather than rehabilitating them. As a result, U.S. prisons house kids as young as thirteen with adults, where they are subject to physical violence, including rape. Children were sent to Death Row until the Supreme Court finally banned the practice in 2005. From the news, you could think kids are the carriers of a violent plague. But while a relatively few number of hardcore gang members can and do terrorize their communities, most violent crime is committed by adults, often against children.

Since my arrival in the U.S., the State of California has drastically cut funding for education and largely eliminated arts programs in the schools. However, it has opened fourteen new prisons. Even John DiIulio has expressed unease at the rate of new prison construction and has written that most inner city kids who get in trouble don't need incarceration. They need—in his words—"mentoring, monitoring, and ministering" to initiate them safely into culture and society. In 2001, according to a *New York Times* report, he no longer believed that violent juveniles were super-predators and should be put in prison. I'd call it a safe bet that even in DiIulio's most hardline days, he would never have considered Duc Ta any sort of predator, let alone a "super" one.

Prisons dot the California landscape. As we get off the Foothill Freeway, we head north on I-5 instead of branching off onto Route 14, which would take us to the prison at Lancaster and the prison at Tehachapi. Duc was locked up at Tehachapi for a while, but there was so much violence, he actually requested the transfer to Corcoran. He thought he'd stand a better chance of getting out alive. Racism was pervasive. He even got hassled by a guard for having white visitors.

We pass the turnoff for the Pitchess Detention Center at Castaic, infamous now for days of fatal racial violence and rioting. New housing developments—cookie-cutter houses squeezed along mountainsides—have been built for people who can't afford LA housing costs and are willing to spend hours a day commuting if only they can own a home. Then, Tejon Ranch, 426 squares miles owned by a company with interests in agribusiness, mining, oil, and real-estate development. The place is also available for film shoots, and so Tejon Ranch was my hallucinatory introduction to Southern California. I was paid very well for portraying a car thief in a Subaru commercial, after which I got to watch as nearby acres were populated with lions, giraffes, and zebras to create "Africa" for the silver screen.

Just before the highway crosses the Grapevine—the canyon where the grade is so steep, water is available at the side of the road for vehicles that overheat—we stop at a rest area and fight our way across the parking lot against the wind. In the bathroom, the mirrors are made of blurry sheet metal rather than glass, as though we've already entered prison.

The freeway splits. We leave the mountains behind and now it's the long flat road north to Bakersfield and up through the Central Valley on Route 99—the Gulag Highway. For a while, we drive beside a hay truck and smell its fresh perfume. The oleanders are blooming. Along with the white and pink flowers and vineyards and orchards and groves, it seems every town has a prison: Avenal, Wasco, Coalinga. In Delano—once the center of Cesar Chavez's farm-workers movement—there are two. Past Corcoran, there's Salinas, Chowchilla, Tracy, Jamestown, Solano, Mule Creek, Vacaville, Folsom, and more. In California, on the day we drive north, more than 400,000 people are in the so-called correctional system. We have seventeen youth prisons and thirty-three adult prisons which daily receive transfers from the youth facilities.

When new guys show up at Corcoran, Duc always asks how old they are. Most of them are eighteen, all with long sentences, many of them serving life. Few of them have any support on the outside, certainly not the community of support that Duc has. So I keep showing *Juvies* and I keep talking to community groups. I remind people how often we ask kids, "Are you looking for trouble?" The answer, of course, is *yes*, and there's a good reason for it. Adolescence is a time of second birth. It's when you grow into your self, into who you are. The trouble we get into can be an asset. "We don't learn through what we get right," I point out, "but rather through our mistakes." I keep hoping society will reconsider how we treat our kids when they make their adolescent mistakes. Change will come. I'm sure it will, but will it be too late to help Duc?

After he was sentenced, Duc was put on a bus to Pelican Bay, the notorious prison that uses the latest technology to create the twenty-first-century equivalent of a medieval dungeon. Who knows how these things happen? Someone intervened at the last minute and got him off that bus.

We pass McFarland and Earlimart, known for grape fields and for cancer clusters among farm-workers' children exposed to pesticides. I somehow managed to survive my environment. Will they?

I GREW UP IN a world that bred nihilism. I know what it's like when kids see violence and hypocrisy every day, when they learn that their families aren't strong enough to protect them, and that the government and social structures that should help them can only be trusted to lie and oppress.

In Medellín, a whole generation was destroyed in the poor neighborhoods as the civil war and the four armies—the Colombian military, the guerrilla movement, the paramilitaries, and the mafia—claimed my friends and plunged our city into violence. In California, I work with and witness another generation dying and killing in the inner city. For a long time, I couldn't understand. Why here? But here, too, I find the children of war. I learned that Mara Salvatrucha, the horrifically violent Salvadoran gang, was founded in 1990, one year after my arrival in the U.S. The young men who started it had served in the Salvadoran army in the counterinsurgency war of the 1980s, sponsored by the U.S. Sickened by the atrocities they took part in, they switched sides and joined the guerrilla fighters. Eventually fleeing the wreckage of their country, they reached the U.S. where, as the newest arrivals in poverty-stricken barrios, they were attacked by the more established but still struggling Mexicans. Their response was Mara Salvatrucha. As they saw it, they knew how to fight and they knew how to kill. After all, it's what they'd been trained for.

I see so many children who've been initiated by war into death instead of life: kids in Cambodian gangs, whose families somehow survived Pol Pot; Mayan families who escaped the genocidal violence in Guatemala, alive but cut off from their land and language and tradition, caught up in new destructive cycles of domestic violence. It all begins to look very familiar to me. I can hate the violence, but in these people I recognize the friends I once loved.

In Kern County, we drive past dairy cows penned close together in agribusiness feedlots, languishing in the dust and their own shit. There's a sign: *Not hiring/No se contrata*. A single egret stands in an overgrown field. The air stinks.

We pen up our children.

In the Youth Authority I see how the new arrivals, the youngest ones, show up all hyper and excited to be with their homies. They haven't realized yet they're in jail. Then you see them inarticulate, tongue-tied, or sullen, young men who mumble and can't meet your eye. Once they feel accepted and respected, you can get them thinking. There's an innocence to them—maybe not in the legal sense, but in the freshness of young people just starting to open up and express themselves in ways they haven't tried before.

I tell them that according to statistics, seventy-five percent of them will be arrested again, in and out of prison for the rest of their lives. They look at each other and figure the odds. "That's what the System expects. It's not what *I* expect." They all have my cell phone number and I ask them to call me when they get out. If they're going to make it on the outside, they'll need help and I want to hook them up with job training and placement and, if they're willing, to make it easier to get hired, with people who'll remove gang tattoos free of charge.

I never ask what they've done or why. If they want to tell, I listen, but I've grown disillusioned with traditional talk-therapy and so we often start our session by playing a game.

We arrange our chairs in a circle: twelve of us with only eleven chairs. I stand in the center and say, "The wind comes and takes away everyone who's wearing underwear."

Everyone the statement applies to, including me, has to scramble and change places and try to get a seat.

Alex is left standing. He goes to the center and says, "The wind comes and takes away everyone who's in jail for the first time."

Most, but not all, of the kids get up and run.

They run and bump into each other. This is one of the reasons— besides showing trust—that I won't wear the alarm. I don't sit back and observe. I run and participate. Any sudden movement can set off the alarm and bring guards in a hurry. Even though many of them are used to me and my ways by now, they may not understand when they see this commotion. Kids crash into each other; Ray falls backwards over a chair and Bobby gives him a hand to help him up. I don't know what they're like outside of group, but here where everyone is respected, I always see sportsmanship. The first couple of weeks, the fat kid got teased. Not anymore. There's a young man with severe developmental disability. I'm not sure how much he understands, but he enjoys being with us, and the others encourage him, go out of their way to include him, and make him feel like part of the team.

". . . everyone who's wearing a blue shirt."

They're all wearing blue shirts stenciled with the institution's initials, and white undershirts underneath.

". . . everyone who's ever smoked marijuana," I say.

They bump into each other. It's a contact sport, but friendly, and what always amazes me is that fast and wild as the scramble gets, they're all very careful with me. No one ever bumps into me or even brushes against my clothes. I don't know how they do it. It's as though these kids echolocate like bats.

". . . everyone who has a sister."

I run with them, and though we don't touch, I feel the wind of their passage.

We relax, we laugh. These kids aren't used to affection, acceptance, and respect. When they get it, they give you glimpses of the fine, bright human beings they're meant to be. And though I don't ask direct questions about their families, all of it begins to come out in the game.

Tony is in the middle. "The wind comes and takes away everyone who doesn't know his father."

They run.

DIANE AND I CROSS the railroad tracks. We're almost there. Just past the Kings County line we see the flat white blocks of buildings, guard towers, razor wire. More buildings, more blocks. The place is huge. Later, I will check the figures: more than 6,000 inmates, and more than 1,500 staff.

The prison environment impacts the people who work here, too.

There are guards who do their best in a tough job; guards who staged gladiatorial fights among inmates and then shot the losers dead; guards who joined the "Green Wall"—their own violent gang complete with initiations and gang signs; guards who stand by and choose not to intervene when prisoners are beaten and raped.

Duc's case got enough publicity—thanks to Leslie Neale's documentary and newspaper accounts by Kerry Madden—that his case was reopened. The gang "enhancement," one of those new laws that mandates extra years behind bars for defendants who belong to gangs, was thrown out. The sentence was reduced to eleven years to life, but as it's still an indeterminate sentence, there's no guarantee he'll ever be free. Adults who have killed people are returning home years before Duc will even have his first parole hearing. In the meantime, in the course of his long years in prison he's been beaten and stabbed and has spent a year in mind-destroying solitary confinement, most of that time for his own protection.

In the parking lot, my allergies kick up. The tears streaming down my face make me look like a father with a broken heart. Diane has advice. "Leave your handkerchief. When they make you turn your pockets inside-out, they'll say you have to throw it away." I've read but haven't memorized the double-sided, small-print sheet of paper the prison sent me listing all the colors and styles of clothing that are prohibited. "No car clicker. It's not allowed inside. Just one car key. Lock up without the clicker or we'll set off the alarm when we come back." She hands me a Ziploc bag with some dollar bills inside. "For the vending machines. You can carry in thirty dollars in singles or quarters. And put your drivers license in here for ID."

We cross paths with a young man wearing denim shorts. "No jeans," he says and shrugs. "Have to find something else to wear."

We go in, then to the back of the line where people are waiting for forms. It's a line so long it snakes out the back door into the cold morning air that smells of feedlot shit. The room is full of perfectly ordinary looking people: all ages, all races, all colors. It seems a perfect demographic sampling of California. In almost any other context, the diversity would lift my heart. There's a woman using a wheelchair, and several people with walkers and canes, and lots of children. The elderly woman behind us says it's difficult for her to stand this long. She comes twice a month to see her brother. She says once a guard denied her entrance "because he said my pants weren't white. He said they were the color of that wall." We look at the cream-colored wall. Cream isn't on the prohibited list. The woman nods. "I gave him a piece of my mind. But I still had to go out to the trailer and change."

We talk about dress code, about the woman who set off the metal detector from the hook at the back of her bra. They wouldn't let her wear the bra and they wouldn't let her go in braless. We discuss the young woman who was told to raise her arms way above her head, and was denied entry because her blouse rode up to reveal a glimpse of skin. Diane has brought a change of clothes in the car, just in case, and a volunteer organization has set up in the parking lot with a selection of used clothing.

I see a change machine and take the ten and two twenties from my pocket.

"Hector, what are you doing with all that money? You can't take that in."

I go to leave my excess cash in the car. On the way back, I stop to talk to a little boy. "Have you been here before?"

"Lots of times," he says. "My Daddy lives here because he hurts my Mommy."

In forty minutes, we're at the front of the line. We sign in, receive slips of paper and go to the back of the room to fill them out. Diane is carrying a note with Duc's inmate ID number and a reminder to use his English name, Michael, instead of Duc. After we copy the numbers, she throws the note in the trash. No paper is allowed inside.

Back at the front desk, we hand in our signed forms and drivers licenses, then wait for our names to be called. There aren't enough seats. People stand, lining the wall. We wait. How can it possibly take so long to process people? We've waited an hour. Just a taste of the patience you need to stay sane inside. We wait some more.

At last my name is called and I go up for inspection. When my brother Juan Fernando was in prison in Medellín, my modest, inhibited mother submitted to a strip search once a week in order to see him. Guards checked her vagina for contraband though drugs and weapons flowed into the prison freely, thanks to bribes. The prison was like a homeless encampment under armed guard. Prisoners were simply thrown into the yard and expected to scavenge up their own food and shelter. Men protected themselves from the elements with discarded pieces of wood, plastic sheeting, and oilcloth. And every weekend my father, who now keeps rabbits only as pets, would show up bringing his son a rabbit stew. By contrast, I can't bring anything to Duc, but my body cavities remain private.

I turn my pockets inside out and hand in my belt, my Ziploc bag, and my shoes. A guard inspects these belongings, and returns my pass and ID. I buy a couple of chits so we can get Polaroid photos taken with Duc. Another guard stamps my hand and gestures me to go through the metal detector. Diane follows, delayed a moment as she refastens the straps to her sandals—footwear without a back-strap is forbidden.

We enter a cage and wait to be released to the walkway. Above us, sparrows have built their springtime nests on metal crossbars. Birds perch on barbed wire in the safe spaces between spikes, but the grass below is littered with tiny bodies: sparrows that flew into the high voltage fence and razor wire.

INSIDE, WE WAIT.

In the room are thirty-five round tables, low enough so that hands are always visible. Each table seats about four people, this to accommodate visits for a thousand men. Today, the place isn't crowded. I watch two women carry on a lively conversation with each other at neighboring tables, ignoring the imprisoned sons they've come to see, and I have to control myself, the desire to intervene is that strong.

When I work with immigrant families, I hear it again and again: in the U.S., you're not allowed to beat your child so you have no way of guiding him. For native-born Americans, it's often the same story: U.S. culture has changed, and what was common practice a generation or two ago is no longer acceptable. My message is, when the old ways no longer work, don't give up. Learn new ones.

We live in a cruel world where parents have every reason to be frantic with worry: children are exposed to gangs, drugs, arrest, and risky sex. Parents cope with situations almost unimaginably dire. By the time families come to me, the problems between parent and child may be as big as mountains. I know the desire is to wave a wand and make the mountain disappear, or blow it up with dynamite, but we have to start with the smallest, most basic step: communicating, learning to listen. A mother and adolescent son sit facing one another. She tells him how she feels. He repeats back to her what he has heard. Has he misinterpreted? Left anything out? What does he want to say to her? What does she hear? I like doing this in a group setting, not to embarrass the troubled family in the center, but because the rest of the group identifies with the situation and wants to see them succeed. They can feel the support as other parents and kids silently cheer them on, buoy them up, giving them the strength to continue.

In this visiting room there are mountains so huge that though two mothers make the huge effort to be here, they can no longer hear their sons, or even see them.

Diane has told me Duc will look different from the tearful, frightened sixteen-year-old in *Juvies,* but he comes out the door and I recognize him immediately. We shake hands; he and Diane share a long hug. And he tells us that he's happy. Not only to see us, but that a week ago, on Mothers Day, he had a great visit with his parents. "They took a picture with me," he says. "They never want to do that. They don't like anything that shows me in prison. But last week, they took a picture."

We sit. Duc is required to take the seat facing the guard podium, so he'll always be in clear view. "Your throne," I say. I'm still thinking that this county is called Kings. "You know, man, every time I show that film, people fall in love with you. I tell them, hey, fall in love with *me*. I'm *here*. But no, all they're interested in is Duc."

"I've never seen it," he says. I think he's referring to so much love. "The film," he says. "There's no way for me to see it in here." But then he quickly changes the subject, enthusiastically, to what he *does* have. "I got black paper and put it around the locker so it's a nice border, and I covered it with wax so it shines. You go down past the cells and everyone's got pictures of women on the walls. I don't criticize that, but I wanted something different. Go against the grain. I have a poster of the Great Wall of China. You know back in school, it bothered me that I didn't fit in. Well, I don't fit in here either but that's okay. I just want to be myself."

He tells us he has a pet snake that wraps itself around his arm when he's relaxing in the cell. It's a gopher snake that a guard found in the yard and tossed over to Duc who was already known as an animal lover. He raised two baby sparrows fallen from their nest, feeding them with bits of bread from his own meals. He tells us, "When they started to fly, I'd let them go and then call them back to me and they'd come. Then I realized they had to be free." The sparrows flew off, but one day when he was out in the yard, they suddenly reappeared and landed briefly on his head. "That was the last time I saw them."

Now people call him "Snake Man." He says, "I know I'm going to have to let him go one day. He can grow to be five or six feet long and then the officers are going to think he's a weapon."

Duc tells us he had a dream. "The top of his box was off and I looked and looked and couldn't find him. Then I saw just his tail under the door of the cell. There was nothing I could do. He got away." In the dream, finally, a guy from A section brought the snake back. Duc hesitates, then tells us: "It really happened. He got loose and I couldn't find him, and that guy from A section—the one from my dream—found him and gave him back to me."

Dreams can be guides. "What's the meaning of a snake?" I ask, and Duc and Diane both answer, "Rebirth."

"Does he have a name?" I ask.

Duc says, "King."

PRISONERS CAN NO LONGER have fresh fruit with meals in their cells: "They're afraid we'll ferment it for alcohol," Duc says.

We notice people bringing back strawberries from the vending machines. Diane goes to buy us some, but the strawberries are all gone.

She manages to get us the last two avocados, something Duc has never eaten before. "Tastes like butter," he says.

It pleases him to tell me he's read a novel by a Colombian—*One Hundred Years of Solitude* by Gabriel García Márquez. "Trippy!" he says. He wasn't allowed to have books during his year in solitary, in the Security Housing Unit, the SHU. For twelve months, Leslie Neale helped keep Duc's mind and soul alive by photocopying whole novels and mailing them to him, pages at a time, in envelopes thin enough that they wouldn't be confiscated. "If I survived the SHU," Duc says, "I can survive anything." Now he's allowed to have books in his cell, but no more than ten at a time. To stay within the limit, he used to give books away to other prisoners. He tells us *The Kite Runner* by Khaled Hosseini was the one novel all the guys enjoyed. In a prison system infamous for racial violence, men of all races met in the yard to hold a book discussion group and talk about the themes of loyalty, class differences, betrayal. That doesn't happen anymore. "I'm not allowed to give a book to another inmate or even donate them to the prison library," he says. Books are taken away and he has no idea what becomes of them.

Duc has been told he needs to complete an anger management class before he goes before the parole board. But at Corcoran, only inmates on psychiatric meds are allowed into the program. I can't understand how he deals with so many Catch-22 situations without getting angry. I want to tell him not to manage his anger or to control it. It's the *violence* he wants to avert, not the anger. Anger is the heat in the blood that makes us capable of protecting ourselves and others. It makes a person stand up straight. It's the brightness that pushes ideas into the mind and out of the mouth. But I realize in prison it's not always safe to speak.

Duc tells us that in the privacy of his cell he's allowed to wear his own and not prison issue T-shirt, but not his own socks. He says he washes laundry in his cell in the sink. "When you put things in the prison laundry, you don't always get them back."

I ask about his relationship with his father.

"At first, he wouldn't visit," Duc says. "Then he started coming, but he'd just criticize and blame me for being here. Finally, I stood up and told him, 'I'm not going to listen to this. I need your support, not this.' I went to the guard podium and had them terminate the visit." And now? "We communicate better; we're getting to know each other. But I realize you can't teach an old dog new tricks. My mother has to put up with it." I offer to meet with them for counseling. "He won't go," says Duc. "I told him, 'You're my Dad, I love you. I'll always love you, but your temper, and the violence—there are things I just cannot accept."

Without anyone to show him the way, Duc has come to understand that his life, even behind bars, has meaning. "It's strange, but I feel sort of privileged and honored. Most guys my age? They're out there seeing what they can get and complaining they don't have enough. But because of *Juvies*, I've been getting mail from kids all over. Especially this one class in Denver, all these gangbangers, and they're confiding in me and asking for advice. I can't believe sometimes that I have this chance to reach out to kids, and hope I can encourage them to stay out of this kind of trouble."

"You're a mentor," I say, and he's embarrassed.

"I've grown up a lot in here. You wouldn't have liked me before. I didn't read books. I ditched school."

He's still caught up in the discourse of "good" and "bad."

"I didn't appreciate learning," he says. "I used to ditch school and go to Pasadena, to the arcades in Old Town and to that museum, the Norton Simon." He doesn't seem to get it that his trips to the museum constituted learning. "I wanted to see the Asian art, but they were doing construction on that part, so I never saw what I was looking for. But there were European paintings, like from the 1600s, and they were amazing. I mean, the 1600s—supposedly people weren't so advanced then, but they created this art I couldn't believe. I found out the best time to go was in the morning, before noon, because then there were no people there and I could be alone with the paintings."

I want to know how he first discovered the place.

"School field trip. We walked in there and I just couldn't believe what I was seeing."

That's what a field trip ought to do, awaken the person it was meant to awaken. Most of his classmates probably just dragged along, bored, and that's okay. What's sad is that the teacher didn't notice Duc's reaction, how transfixed he was. Building on that passionate interest was just the thing that might have kept him interested in school. Instead, he was left to find his own way, and I think of Hernán Darío, and how his life would have been so different if we who loved him had recognized his gifts, if we'd really *seen* him.

"Do you know how I found out Duc is interested in art?" Diane asks me later. "One day, I mentioned I lived near the La Brea tar pits, and he told me he used to go there all the time. 'Whatever for?' I asked. He said it was because it was where those big buildings are with all the paintings." He didn't know "those buildings" were the Los Angeles County Museum of Art. He only knew they contained wonders that pulled him in again and again.

In youth prison, Duc's capacities were brought out. Though the Department of Corrections offered little, outside organizations and individuals reached him. He was introduced to videography by Leslie Neale. Brent Blair cast him as Claudius (another king) in *Hamlet*, though Duc was transferred the day before the scheduled performance and never got to play the role. Mark Salzman taught a writing workshop and Duc, who'd never tried to express himself on the page before, brought in a dozen poems and essays every week. His incarceration was opening new pathways for him, but the journey was cut short. He was transferred to adult prison where there are no creative programs and where, for several years and for reasons unknown, the authorities repeatedly blocked his attempts to take the high school equivalency exam. When he finally maneuvered his way around the obstacles, he passed with flying colors.

No programs exist to assist prisoners like Duc with higher education. Friends and supporters on the outside raise money to pay his tuition for a college correspondence course. "What I really want to do is computers," he says. "I'm good at that, but we don't have access to computers in here."

He encourages others to study. "There's this one big guy, covered with tattoos. People always had high expectations of me and I let them down. But this guy, all his life people have been telling him he'll never amount to anything. I kept telling him to take college classes and he's like, *I can't*. I told him, 'Don't listen to all those people. Give it a try.' He's taking classes now and it's wild! Whenever I see him, he's got his face in a book."

Though Duc gets along with inmates of all colors, he's worried about the court decision that will desegregate California prisons. He thinks people are going to get hurt once men of different races share cells. "When a fight breaks out in prison, you have to side with your own race," he says. "That's the prison code. It can cost you your life to break it." He adds, "Sometimes in here you have to do things you aren't proud of."

Getting along with people is different from having friends. Duc says, "There's really no one to talk to. Guys just stay high. I don't blame them. They don't see a future."

I tell him to look for the spark inside people, but as I look at the other prisoners in the visiting room, men who don't expect to ever walk free, what I see are many pairs of dead eyes, spirits without hope.

EVERY CULTURE ON EARTH has a drum. Every human being has a drum beating inside the chest, carrying the rhythm of life. So when I tell stories, I accompany the words with my djembe drum.

I tell the young men in the Youth Authority a story I learned from Michael Meade. It's a morally ambiguous "dilemma tale," from the African tradition in which stories are used to provoke discussion. It's about how a father tries to teach his son to hunt and punishes the boy's thoughtlessness by hitting him with an ax. The son runs away and is adopted by a king who, after various tests, presents the young man with a choice: If he kills his father, he can inherit the kingdom. Or he can take the king's gold and go home with his father, if he kills the king.

"So," I ask my group. "What would you do? Kill your father? Or kill the king?"

"Awwww." The first sounds are of dismay. No one wants to answer.

Then Joey has to show how bad he is: "I'd take the gold and kill them both."

"I'd leave," says Mark. "I wouldn't kill anyone."

"But you have to choose," I say. "King or father. In this story, those are the only choices."

When people talk about imaginary situations, there's no internal censor and the defenses come down. I listen as the boys talk without hesitation about stepfathers who raised them when biological fathers were absent; about drug dealers in big cars who promised them money and more; about people who tempt you into doing wrong and then turn on you.

Ray says he'd choose his father. Bobby says he would kill him.

"Man, no one's really getting killed," says Tony. "It's a story. It's *symbolic*."

They talk about physical abuse, though Alex is quick to add, "There are other things, personal things, that hurt more."

Sometimes the longing for a father—a caring father—is almost palpable. I think of Duc's father, holding a gun to the frightened boy's head. I look at the young men now in this circle and think of all the wounds they bear—from absence, rejection, the violence they've done and the violence done to them.

I tell them that I "killed" my own father many times when I was a teen, looking down on him, not listening to him, thinking I was so much better and smarter. I suggest that even if you've got the best father in the world, you still need to "kill" him to leave home and move into your own adult life. I tell them as many interpretations of the story exist as there are people. All of their answers are right.

In spite of this, I can't resist continuing with my own interpretation. I want them to think and to imagine. They have to see beyond the world they've always lived in with its limited horizons, the culture of the street. "The king is saying you can have something better than what you're used to, but you have to take a chance," I tell them. "You have to leave what you know behind and move forward, even though the outcome is uncertain. Can you do that?"

They're all quiet a while.

"So how does the story end?" Tony asks.

I tell them that as long as people keep talking and thinking, it doesn't.

BECAUSE I SPEND so much time with homies, it's easy for me to slip into street talk. In the visiting room, I do, curious to see if Duc will relax enough to use profanity. His speech remains careful and proper. Diane tells me later, "He's very careful not to pick up prison slang. He doesn't want the kind of habits that could limit his prospects if he ever gets out of there."

He says, "You probably won't believe me, but I'm kind of glad I got sent to prison. What never made sense to me was this thirty-five-to-life. But I've grown up a lot. On the outside, I never would have met people like Leslie and Kerry. I keep asking myself, *would I be so kind to a stranger, the way they—and you—have been to me?* I hope so. You've all shown me a beautiful side of human nature, something I never saw before. I feel lucky."

People start sneaking glances at the clock. Time is running down. Goodbyes are hard, so it's almost a relief when the guard at the podium tells us it's over.

As people walk out the door, no one looks back. Down the paved area we go, staying inside the painted lines. We wait in the cage for the buzzer. The sky is blue now, with high cirrus clouds. There are nests above us, and dead birds on the grass.

"He's got to get out of there," Diane says. "If he were released tomorrow, he'd do great, but how long can a person hold onto his integrity in that place?"

We drive. The wind blows dust.

• • •

TWO YEARS AFTER OUR VISIT, Duc was transferred to another prison, one where Valley Fever is endemic. Almost everyone gets it: prisoners, guards, even some visitors. Once you contract it, you either develop immunity, permanent organ damage, or you die. Duc spent three months shackled to a hospital bed undergoing lung surgery and a toxic regimen of drugs that left his immune system permanently compromised. His parole hearing was canceled because he was hospitalized and couldn't attend. A second parole hearing, scheduled for six months later, was also canceled for administrative reasons. As of this writing, Duc is still waiting to present his case for release.

Chapter 11

Crossing Psychic Frontiers

I could be anyone. I could be one of my enemies.
Imagining this is always a helpful practice.

—Israeli author Amos Oz,
from "How to cure a fanatic"

Every January in Pasadena, crowds turn out to see the floats in the Tournament of Roses parade, for which corporate sponsors have paid a quarter of a million dollars each. I can't help but think of the people of Santa Elena, a mountain village about ten miles from my former home in Medellín. By tradition, families create beautiful designs made of flowers and weave them into bamboo and reed structures. The men come down from the mountains carrying on their shoulders these *silletas*, which weigh almost forty pounds, and parade their floral art through the streets. As an artist, creative expression is my practice and central to my identity, but it's everyone's birthright. Now I have to wonder how much is lost in a culture when the sheer joy and pride in creativity become instead a stunningly expensive opportunity to advertise.

• • •

IT'S 4:00 P.M. IN the spacious open room where we meet. The walls are decorated with the poems the kids wrote, the paintings they created with visual artist Susan Hill, the harps they made with Enzo Fina: decorated paper plates to which they've attached rubber bands to pluck and twang. Some kids discover a real passion or talent in our workshops, but all of them benefit as they access feelings and capacities that are struggling for expression. Regardless of what art critics might say about much of the work, it all has value because you cannot create art without being emotionally engaged.

Here I've worked with Bob Brodhead to combine methods of art therapy with council circle and rituals. We hoped to create an antidote to what we saw as mental health and educational systems that too often destroyed the spirit. With ten to fifteen kids at a session and at least four adults, we are able to combine group activities with opportunities for individual attention. Occasionally the parents join us for the full three-hour session. We let people know we aren't trying to "fix" them. Our goal is to help them access what they carry inside and bring it outside into the light to be seen.

One of my favorite techniques is to tap the power of narrative. I open up my laptop and encourage a kid to tell his own story. These young people aren't used to anyone asking, so I begin with simple questions: *Where were you born? Where are your parents from?* And I offer prompts: *One night I dreamed . . . I'm happy when . . .* and I type whatever they say. Later, if they give permission, I read their stories back to the whole group. I also print out their words so they can have an official-looking copy. They learn that what they have inside their heads can be transferred to the page and to the world, that it can be shared, and that it matters to others. That's where the poems come from. The kids select sentences from their own words to hang on the walls:

I dreamed I was flying.
I'm happy when someone loves me.
I'm happy when my Mom isn't sad.

When I first met Edgar, at seven years of age he made sounds—*ur blah arg*—instead of using words. He had no physical impediment to speech, nor was he hearing impaired. He'd been given a psychiatric diagnosis but that didn't interest me. I always believe a child is capable of doing more than a diagnosis suggests. My approach is to work with the child without preconceptions, so that we discover together what she or he *can* do and can become.

At home, it was as if Edgar and his mother shared a secret language all their own. She was constantly attentive, responding to every sound, every perceived need. I see this sometimes in immigrant families. A mother who's set adrift, confused in a culture that's strange to her, may need a bilingual child to serve as her ambassador to the outside world. But she may also fill her need to be useful and needed by keeping one child tied to her in a state of dependency. I explained to Edgar's mother: "If he's not learning to speak, it's because he doesn't need to." In his interactions with me, she saw that if he pointed to water and said *ur ur ur*, he got nothing. To get water, he had to say *water*.

But in our narrative sessions, though I encouraged the use of words, I wrote down whatever Edgar said, exactly as he said it. A typical story might go like this: *urg urg blah fell down ah ar ur Mom*. When I read Edgar's story to the whole group, I did it dramatically, clowning around to make the kids pay attention, and with emphasis on the words. The boys listened intently and they laughed: not at Edgar, but at my performance, and Edgar laughed, too. He began to see that his words could create a reaction in others and that what he said meant something. Over the weeks, we worked to transform his language of manipulation, which included hair pulling, kicking, and tantrums, into a language of communication.

His is an extreme example. The other kids had words, but in some ways they were in the same boat. No one had ever really listened to them. It had never occurred to them before that their own stories were important, but I recorded those stories and took them seriously. Kids who'd never before tried to put their thoughts into words and their words onto a page began to write. Edgar began to talk.

I've never met a human being who has never created art. We tend to seek these heightened and symbolic forms of expression at times of powerful emotion. High-school football players write love poems. So do incarcerated teens.

WHEN MY COLLEAGUE Miles Mosely works with boys on lyrics for the songs they're composing, he starts the three-hour session with physical activity: soccer or theater games. Kids have energy they need to expend, and I also want to expand our notions about thinking.

We're indoctrinated into a culture that says we're supposed to sit still. Students sit in class hour after hour; white-collar workers sit at their desks; managers sit around conference tables. Activists, who should be *active*, instead sit through endless, often pointless meetings, as if talking about a problem is the same as working to solve it. Then we sit in our cars or on buses or trains to go home and sit in front of the TV, video game, or computer screen. You know the clichéd image of the scientist pacing until the light bulb goes on over his head? It's based on something very real: our minds work in different ways when our bodies are engaged, when we shift gears, and *move* instead of sitting still. When we remain seated, our blood flows to our butts, not our brains. Our thinking tends to follow the well-worn path and simply repeats familiar patterns.

The brain thinks in rhythm. Enzo brought the traditional *pizzica tarantata* music of his native Lecce, Italy, to America. In Southern Italy, people bitten by the tarantula or afflicted with poison to the body or soul would dance to this music, entranced, for hours or days until collapsing, and would often come out of the dance cured. It's a treatment worth studying: Enzo and Roberto Catalano (the other half of the folk duo Musicàntica), were invited to play *pizzica* at Stanford University for an investigation of "brainwave entrainment to external rhythmic stimulation."

For Enzo, the healing power of music is not just theoretical. He, himself, was left comatose in 1982 following a motorcycle accident. Enzo emerged from the coma a week later with limited use of his hands and obsessed with the memory of someone playing an African thumb piano. He overcame his new awkwardness to build a larger version of the instrument, one he was able to handle. He named it the fina, after himself, and began trying to play. Today, his fingers move quickly and expertly as he plays tarantellas on a wide range of stringed instruments, amazing his doctors who said they'd never seen so complete a recovery.

And so in our group we dance and drum and I get the kids to move. But this afternoon when I bring out the soccer ball, Ray grabs it from me and slams it against the wall and then starts kicking not the ball, but our new mural.

"If you're upset about something, that's okay," I say. I would never suggest a kid's feelings should be suppressed or denied. "But don't damage our mural. Stomp on the floor if you have to stomp on something."

He stomps around. "I don't want to play another stupid game."

"Okay. But you can't sabotage it for everyone else."

Case manager Bobbybee Blanquez takes Ray to a table in the corner. Ray always enjoys talking with Bobbybee, who's generous in sharing his own Apache traditions, and so they talk and work together on a drawing while the rest of us play.

The kids are very competitive today, so after soccer I want to spend some time with theater games. As is my way, I don't use the word "theater," since some kids might object. They don't like *theater*; they don't know how to act. I just say "game." I like to start in a circle sending exaggerated sounds and gestures around and across, creating a sense of community. Sometimes we'll break up into pairs. Martin and Joey, for example, stand and face each other. This in itself can be an accomplishment for children who aren't used to looking and being looked in the eye in a way that isn't critical or hostile. Now they take turns counting to three.

Martin: *One.*

Joey: *Two.*

Martin: *Three.*

Joey: *One.*

Martin: *Two.*

Joey: *Three.*

And so forth. Then Martin replaces the word *Three* with a sound and a gesture and, from that point on, each of them must substitute the action whenever it comes time to say the word. When I give the signal, Joey comes up with a sound and gesture for *Two*. Next, *One* is also replaced. Now every pair in the room is coming up with their own set of substitutions. The room is full of kids flailing, shrieking, hopping, jumping, beeping, and honking. Of course, no one manages to keep all the numbers and substitutions straight. That's great. After all, if you're afraid of being wrong, you have little chance to be creative. Our educational system stigmatizes mistakes as though getting something wrong is the worst thing you can possibly do. Unfortunately, this approach educates people out of their creative capacities. So I make sure everyone gets it wrong. I urge the kids to speak and move faster and faster and faster. Now everyone is making glorious mistakes and the only penalty is shared laughter.

Michael Meade has said that a young person is like a landscape waiting to be hit by lightning so that what is hidden suddenly becomes visible. I've found theater can be that lightning as it's an art that engages the whole person. While rich with ideas, it works through the actor's body with movement and rhythm, and incorporates images, emotions, and words. The stage provides a safe container for the release of memory and feeling.

My approach has been profoundly influenced by the work of the late Brazilian theater director Augusto Boal. The techniques he pioneered have become known as Theater of the Oppressed (TO). TO traces its origins back to one day in the 1970s, during the military dictatorship in Brazil, when Boal and his theater company performed an agitprop drama for peasants whose land had been taken. The performance ended with actors raising their rifles—just props, of course—and calling on the audience to "spill our blood for the land." When the peasant leaders responded with enthusiasm—"Let's do it! Come with us!"—Boal realized he had no right to impose a course of action or tell people to run risks he wasn't willing to share. He began to explore ways of using theater to help people articulate their own goals and strategies, inviting them to build on their own knowledge of their own realities.

Boal's troupe would then arrive in a community and spend days listening to people talk about the problems and challenges they faced. People might express grievance against an employer or the police. They might talk about family issues, such as domestic violence. The actors would then create and perform a play portraying the problem. Audience members were invited to suggest changes to the script and explore how, with different words or actions from the actors, the outcome might be changed. Through imagination, people could consider alternatives to the existing dynamic, test ideas and tactics, and see what the results might look like. Without real risk to themselves or committing prematurely to action, they could role-play in search of workable solutions. Some problems aren't easily solved, but at the very least, participants learned that the mind can envision many possibilities, that reality isn't frozen or carved in stone.

During one performance in Peru, a woman grew dissatisfied with how the actors interpreted her instructions. She got up on stage, pushed the actor out of the way, and let everyone see how she herself would like to treat her cheating husband. This was a revelation to Boal. Passive audience members can transform from spectators to "spect-actors." From that point on, Boal's Forum Theater invited audience members to intervene, to interrupt the action of the play, get up on stage, replace an actor, and rehearse in public their imagined new approaches to problems in their lives.

Due to such subversive activities, Boal was arrested and tortured by the military regime. Most likely because of his international reputation, the dictatorship didn't dare kill him. Instead, they told him to get out of the country and, as he puts it, "That was the only advice I accepted from the dictatorship."

In exile in Europe, Boal found people who didn't fear the real police but still experienced anxiety and emptiness. He began to theorize they were oppressed by "the cop in the head," the internalized voices of parents and societal authority, and so he developed new techniques to help people get in touch with their authentic selves and desires and identify the obstacles that stood in the way of their realization.

With the fall of the military dictatorship, Boal returned to Brazil in 1986, a living legend, and even for a while served as a legislator in Rio. For one of his theater projects, he went to a prison and got the prisoners to play guards and the guards to take on the roles of prisoners, allowing all to see and feel the other's experience. They created a play and performed in the open air in the town. Local people watched and were moved enough that some began to bring food and services to the inmates.

Wherever you go in the world, prisoners are among the most invisible and stereotyped members of society. I love the way theater gives them a chance to make themselves truly seen. I thought of Boal's experiment when I led a TO workshop at one at the largest men's prisons in Pune, India. The superintendent was the archetype of a despot, and he had barred the way to every organization that wanted to bring services to the men under his thumb. For some reason, he allowed the Indian actress Sushama Deshpande and this crazy Colombian to come in and work with forty men. For three hours, they created images of the oppression they felt in their lives, and then imagined what liberation from this oppression would look like. The superintendent watched us, and afterward he asked me to his office. I expected disapproval. To my amazement, he invited me back to work with all four thousand of his inmates. I believe what had happened was, for the first time, he'd truly *seen* the prisoners. When he'd recognized their humanity, he himself had become humanized.

In Los Angeles, I joined with theater artists, teachers, therapists, and activists to start our own Center for Theater of the Oppressed in 2001. For several years in a row, until his death in May 2009, we were able to bring Boal to LA to spend time with us, to lecture, and to teach, and I learned to use the following very short play from him.

I stand before a group of students and ask who wants to come up and join me. A girl volunteers. As she approaches, I reach out as if I want to shake hands but when she extends her own hand I turn my back and stand with my arms folded. The girl stops short, startled, and rolls her eyes.

"Okay," I ask the group. "What did she do? What else could she do?"

We replay the scene over and over. Another student sticks her tongue out at my back. The third takes hold of my shoulders and turns me around very aggressively. The next walks around me and sticks out her hand again. The fifth walks past me, turns his own back and folds his own arms. The teacher walks past me and shakes hands with someone else. The alternatives—how to respond to disrespect and hurt—are almost endless. We see we may not be able to change the other person's behavior, but we learn that we can at least choose our own.

From my point-of-view as a clinician, seeing the choices people make also serves a diagnostic function. I've used Boal's short play lots of times. With groups of teachers, someone—usually by the fifth replay—chooses to hug me. With troubled kids, the first responses are always violent. We may have to repeat the scene over and over until someone thinks of trying a hug.

I recently created a piece of Forum Theater with students and parents from a Pasadena middle school. We were all concerned that the growing tension between cops and kids—even as young as middle schoolers—might erupt. Some kids felt caught in the middle between gang violence on the one hand and the racial profiling and violence of the police on the other. An incident occurred, for example, a few blocks away from my home. Gang members who realized they were being followed thought a rival gang was hunting them down and didn't realize that the vehicle that tailed them was an unmarked police car. A gang member fired one shot in the direction of the vehicle. The police responded with a massive volley that left a community center pock-marked with bullets. Fortunately, no one was hit in this incident, but the community could rightfully wonder if the police might not be the more dangerous armed gang and the more likely shooters in a poten-tially lethal drive-by.

I've worked with Pasadena's chief of police and always found him to be dedicated, responsible, and responsive to the community. He agreed that he and his officers would participate once we had a play to perform for them.

During a full day of exercises and preparation, students came up with a situation in which the cops, going after drug-using students, picked up a girl who'd just made a purchase but also the boy nearby who was innocent. We created a script including a follow-up scene in which the principal calls in the boy's mother, expels the boy due to the zero-tolerance policy, and turns him over to the police.

We presented this short play in the school auditorium with students, teachers, parents, and local police officers, including the chief, in atten-dance. What was immediately apparent was that the mother—played by a real-life mother who spoke no English—had no idea what was happening with her son, as no one bothered to interpret or explain. She panicked and tried to hold onto her child as he was being led away, then began struggling with the principal and the police. We also became aware of who was missing from the discussion: kids in the audience wanted to know, *Where are the campus security guards?*

We asked audience members to replace any character and see if they could find a way to change the unjust outcome. As we played the scene over and over, not one person ever asked the boy his side of the story. A sympathetic police officer took over the role of the arresting cop, assessed the boy as "not really a bad kid," and said she would get him supportive services, but even she never spoke to him directly. Even more shocking, one girl after another enthusiastically ran up to the stage to take the role of the innocent boy and tried to change the outcome. In each case, her "solution" was to resist arrest in progressively more violent ways. By now, we had real police officers on stage in different roles, and we had real students—all female, as it turned out—hitting and kicking them.

We were seeing evidence of what has become a disturbing trend: girls in our society increasingly apt to use violence. Admittedly, because we were in a safe space—the theater, the kids may have felt particularly secure, free to act with impunity. We can hope they might show better judgment on the street. Still, they seemed so confident there'd be no consequences that Diane was actually afraid one of them would try to grab an officer's gun. Fortunately, that didn't happen, but the kicking and hitting made it clear these kids had no respect for the police or fear, or even a realistic sense of how dangerous it is to behave aggressively or violently when faced with an officer of the law. That day, we came up with no solutions, but deep-seated problems that would have to be addressed became obvious. They couldn't be denied as they played out live before our eyes.

In part because he's worked in so many cultures, with people speaking so many languages, Boal often bypasses words and invites people to express their deepest feelings by using their bodies to create visual images. His work has reinforced my own respect for the power of the image. I can give a discourse about imperialism, or I can just get up on a chair and stand above someone, in a posture that's commanding, enveloping, grasping, and crushing.

Just as the folktale about the hunter's son had no correct answer, images are polysemic— open to multiple, almost limitless interpretation. If I take a rigid stance with a single-minded, demanding look on my face and I stare right at you while jabbing my index finger, some people will say I look like a dictator, parent, or angry authority figure, or even that I look like a person in fear. But the image reminds me of Gabo when he was two years old. These multiple interpretations might lead us to reflect: what might a two-year-old and a dictator have in common?

When we create images in a spontaneous way, we can shed new light on reality. In recent years, I've been invited to perform and lead workshops at some of the most prestigious universities in the U.S. where I've met young people who've grown up with supposed privilege, in circumstances very different from the kids I work with most. On these campuses with beautiful landscaping and the most up-to-date facilities, I invite the students to create the machine that represents their college. Again and again, the young people stand separated, in isolation, or act out scenes of sports, cheerleaders, drinking, drug taking, and sex. "What about learning?" I ask, and they laugh. When I ask them to show me what learning looks like, some pull out their hair to express frustration and stress, some show themselves at a computer. "Wait. Where are the teachers?" And they show someone dictating information or on a screen or simply absent. "Do you like what you see?"

I don't get it. Reading Freud and Lacan used to get me high. I

couldn't get enough. "Getting high is why it's called higher education," I say. If students aren't turned on by learning, it's no wonder
they turn on with substances. "If you're not having orgasms from your
reading," I say, "you're not reading the right books." Sometimes I meet
students who absolutely pulse with excitement over their studies, but
for the most part I see kids who supposedly have everything, but are
merely marking time until they can enter the workforce and take jobs
that pay well but don't connect with their spirits as they struggle to pay
back a mountain of student-loan debt.

"Who are you?" I ask. "Who do you imagine you want to be? Are
you following the course that will take you there?"

THROUGH THEATER GAMES we gain knowledge of ourselves, but
we also learn about people we've considered antagonists or enemies.
We discover that we all harbor demons, but that we also harbor angels.
On the West Bank, our theater exercise showed we are capable of love
as well as hate. Onstage, we're invited to be someone else. Empathy—
understanding another person's subjective experience—is ours only
through the imagination. Without imagination, we may lose it.

In 2007, my own capacity for empathy was challenged through the
good offices of social psychologist Jean Marie Arrigo. In the course
of more than a decade studying the ethics of military intelligence and
the impact of covert work on human subjects, Dr. Arrigo accumulated
an extraordinary archive of correspondence with an American man
whose recent mission was to conduct interrogations in Afghanistan and
Iraq. She asked if I would be interested in exploring his personality by
portraying him on stage.

My nemesis wasn't a mindless brute or a just-following-orders drone. Neither was he in the least plagued by guilt or self-doubt. Instead I found a sophisticated, highly intelligent, culturally sensitive man who claims he'd never himself physically abused a suspect. "That damages the subject and produces trash," he said. He befriends people, patiently engages in conversation seeking bits and pieces of information, provided willingly or inadvertently, that he can fit into the mosaic of the big picture.

"That's my dream job," said Diane, surprising us both. But it made sense. She enjoys immersing herself in languages and cultures, research, and interviews. "I'd get to do everything I love to do, and for really high stakes."

The interrogator whose words I came to know through Dr. Arrigo is a man who takes great pride in professionalism, in getting the job done and done well. However, while Abu Ghraib horrified me because human beings were abused, his horror at Abu Ghraib was that untrained, unsupervised, and unprofessional personnel could have been entrusted with such important work and allowed to screw it up in such a way that no valuable intelligence could possibly have come out of that place. He is tolerant of violent, even lethal methods used by others, as long as they don't interfere with his own interrogations. He has no use for human rights organizations, like the one that saved me.

But as I memorized the interrogator's own words and explored his motivation, as I "became" him, my initial resistance turned to curiosity, then respect and admiration. Today, if I could wave a wand and have dinner with anyone in the world, I think this man is the one I would choose to meet. It's been enlightening and, in a way, a privilege to portray him. In this way, art cuts through preconceived ideas and stereotypes to reach the heart. It can slip past borders and psychic frontiers.

When I perform *Nightwind*, which includes my own arrest and torture, I try to involve the audience. Early on in the performance, I kick a balloon representing a soccer ball into the seats and encourage people to hit it back, and so I am very aware of the people seated before me. One night, there was a man in the front row who definitely looked Latin American. As the show started, I saw him exchange glances with the woman beside him. A while later, I realized he was crying.

After the performance, this man stood and addressed the audience. "Everything you have just seen is true. I know that, even though I was on the other side." He told us he was in the Colombian military; his father had been a high-ranking officer. It was a family tradition. For generations they'd been committed to protecting the nation in the way they thought best. "Hector protested at the School of the Americas," he said. "I studied there." He swallowed hard. "What's happening in Colombia is wrong," he said. "Hector and I can both agree it has to change." Then he asked if I would allow him to hug me. We embraced. This wouldn't have happened at a protest march or rally. It happened in a theater.

Chapter 12
The Wounded Healer

If some are still dominated by their former bad habits,
and yet can teach by mere words, let them teach. . . . For
perhaps, by being put to shame by their own words, they
will eventually begin to practice what they teach.

—John of the Ladder, seventh-century ascetic

For years, I invited other people to use the arts as a healing path; but when I needed help, it was many months before I took my own prescription. In 2003, the time came when I could no longer imagine a future for myself. I was a marriage and family therapist, and yet my own married life was a mess.

I loved Cindy, I couldn't imagine life without her, but unless I changed my ways, I was going to lose her. Yes, I had women on the side, but that was only one small part of what had gone wrong. I knew I spread myself too thin. By committing to every cause, I committed to nothing. A sense of urgency kept driving me, or maybe it was my demons. If I stopped for a moment to catch my breath, they would catch up. I was still fighting to hold my own against the torturer. Everyone around me became his stand-in, and I kept even those I loved at bay. I would not let anyone possess me.

No wonder Cindy wasn't happy. She grew cold to me, which caused great pain, but also gave me new justification for my affairs. I went without her to my talks and performances. Once, being around me had been exciting to her or at least interesting. Now she hated showing up at events, where I'd walk in with my arm around her and then ignore her. After displaying my trophy, I couldn't be bothered to introduce her to people. I took it for granted that if I needed someone to clean up after me or fix things, she would be there, constant and unacknowledged. I couldn't be bothered to change the oil in my car no matter how many times she reminded me. I'd drive it till I damaged the engine. Then I'd smile and charm and expect to be forgiven.

"Don't *mi amor* me," Cindy would say.

We were probably the only people in pre-meltdown 1990s who lost money on Southern California real estate. We invested in rental property, but when I'd go to collect the rent, I'd listen to the tenants' hard-luck stories. How could I take money from them? Sometimes, instead, I lent it.

Cindy gave up painting and took a part-time job. Most of her energy and devotion went into raising Camilla and Gabo while, the way she saw it, I used our children as ornaments or took solace from them when I was in need. I invited my parents to live with us, to help with the kids, and now there was no privacy in the house, while, like all good grandparents, Pedro and Nidia spoiled their grandchildren. Whatever limits Cindy tried to enforce, the kids could always turn to their grandparents who would never say no.

I was the one who worked all the time. Why was she so exhausted? I went out almost every night and every weekend without her on behalf of one cause or another. I missed Cindy's body. I missed having her pegged to me like a shadow as I sought the admiration of the crowd and took center stage. Why wasn't that fulfilling enough for her?

Fourteen years earlier, a young woman had been daring enough to take off for California with a man she hardly knew and with whom she had no language in common. Now she hardly recognized herself. Recently she told Diane,: "When we met, an adventurous spirit was waking in me and I had a burning desire to be out in the world. I met Hector and I knew I wasn't meant to let go of him. I felt trusting of him but also of myself."

Our road trip sealed our commitment. I think Cindy saw the best of me then, because whatever challenges we faced—the car breaking down, stepping out into the unknown—I was easygoing. I don't get upset. I get mad at injustice, yes, but I never make a woman my scapegoat. Many women have complained to me that men turn on them in anger when things go wrong. I've never been that way, and that's part of why women often trust me.

Cindy saved me. My life in the U.S. worked out well because I'd had her by my side. She was the brains of the household, the one who managed our finances and made most decisions. I'd learned to defer to her judgment for the simple reason that she was usually right. Cindy was one of the strongest people I knew, but as the years passed, I lost her trust, and the deep love and respect a partnership needs.

Now she says, "I started to realize there was more to me, that I'm also a person with capacities that ought to be honored." Instead, she felt disrespected and erased. In some way, I understood this, but at the same time I pushed it away and out of consciousness. By December 2002, however, Cindy's unhappiness couldn't be ignored.

I was playing the lead in a staged reading of Diane's play about a transgendered Cuban, but I warned her I could not continue with the project if it went on to a full production because I had to be home with Cindy and the kids. I said that I needed to save my marriage.

"I really respected you for making that your priority," Diane recalls.

Today, I don't even remember saying that. I don't remember realizing my relationship with Cindy was in deep trouble.

I asked Diane to draw up a production budget, find a venue to rent, and come to a meeting with my colleagues at Theater of the Oppressed. Though I wouldn't take an active part, I would help find producers to get a production off the ground. But in the meantime, the Bush administration had begun beating the drums for war. I went posttraumatic: intrusive thoughts, echoing screams, visual flashes of explosions, faces distorted by terror, cadavers, and dead children filled my head. It couldn't happen; I couldn't *let* it happen. All my passion channeled itself into trying to stop something I had no power to stop.

I stormed into that meeting. "This is no time for theater. Forget it. We should be out in the street."

I dropped Diane's project and, much, much worse, as months went by in this haze of fear and rage, I forgot all my good intentions about Cindy. In March, the U.S. invaded Iraq. I watched the news, sickened. I stayed up all night sending enraged e-mails to people who only had to see my address on the screen to hit the delete key. At home, the new life and identity I'd so painstakingly constructed in exile was about to self-destruct.

It would happen in a way I could not have predicted.

By July 2003, the war I couldn't stop was raging, but I was taking a break from politics so that Cindy and I could visit India. After years of serious yoga practice and teaching, she had finally been admitted to study with the masters at the Iyengar Institute in Pune. I arranged to lead some Theater of the Oppressed workshops for local non-govern-mental organizations during our stay, but underlying the trip was an important goal: to spend time together trying to repair the damage that had been done to our relationship over the years.

Once we reached Pune, someone told us about a teacher named Osho at a nearby ashram. We were curious and went to this place Cindy immediately described as "a Disneyland of spirituality." A complex of black pyramids made me think at once of Vegas and I later saw promotional materials that called the ashram a "meditation resort." All the same, the site was beautiful, a paradise in the hills with trees and pools, running water and lush gardens that kept the grounds refreshing and cool. We were welcomed, our names processed and put into the computer, and given HIV tests with immediate results—interesting, I thought, for a spiritual retreat—and issued maroon robes.

I didn't know that Osho had once been called Bhagwan Shree Rajneesh, and that he'd left Pune in 1981 to establish an ashram based on communal living principles just outside Antelope, Oregon. By the time the U.S. expelled him in 1987 and forced him return to India where he changed his name to Osho, his followers in Oregon had been accused of crimes including arson and bioterrorism and some of his closest associates served prison terms for conspiracy to commit murder. Though to a rationalist skeptic like me Osho had died in 1990, to his followers he was "never born and never died," but merely visited the earth for about sixty years and now speaks every night in Pune from a gigantic video screen.

Our maroon robes exchanged for white ones, we heard his invitation to rebirth.

Drop dead!

Come back to life!

Hundreds of people, maybe thousands, fell to the ground and rose again on command inside a great room, our bodies and robes reflected in the polished floor.

I wasn't even in the U.S. during the years the Rajneeshis were derided as a dangerous cult. With no preconceptions, I was immediately impressed with Osho's extraordinary sense of theatricality. Light emanated from below us, from the walls, and from the ceiling, turning the world around us opalescent while the air changed from crystalline to full of shadows.

Drop dead!

Come back to life!

Lights dyed our white robes green and then red, then made us all glow until we seemed to be in flames. Later at night, robes gone, we dressed for vacation and everyone danced, and danced, and danced.

I was observing and learning, impressed with Osho's method of dynamic meditation and I remain impressed with it still. Traditional meditation doesn't work for me. *El potro* and the stress positions of torture caused permanent injury to my back and it's painful for me to sit in one position. When I try to empty my mind of thought, all the intrusive thoughts rush in. But Osho's technique—chaotic breathing followed by shaking and free physical movement and dance—felt just right, and I have incorporated it into my own workshops.

Osho advised people to shun authoritarian systems. I certainly agreed with that. He spoke of the divine primal energy of sex, how its repression is the source of most problems. As a teenager, wasn't that the message I'd taken from Wilhelm Reich? At the ashram, people behaved as the spirit moved them. Lots of people regressed to childhood and wandered about clutching dolls. Some uttered no sound except laughter for a whole week; or they might only cry, or stay silent. Someone pointed out a girl who had danced, constantly, for a month. People hugged and held each other. This all seemed nurturing and liberating, but it was also disturbing. Feelings were being released without any way to process the emotions and behavior psychologically, and I sensed how dangerous this could be.

Osho said, "Celebrate the divinity of your own life," and Cindy did. My wife danced among strangers, vibrant and sensual. She felt free in her movements and her face displayed a radiant happiness. Then I would come into her line of sight and her joy would turn to a look of faint disgust. Life with me, she said, had left her dead inside. Then India: "This call to beauty and awakening of the heart," she said. "It allowed me to completely open—open—open."

Cindy emerged like a butterfly, while I became a worm.

"Our marriage is a prison for me," she said. "You've been my jailer for fourteen years." She accused me: I was macho, chauvinistic; I had no self-control. My unending demands for attention from everyone and everywhere had crushed her. And I could deny none of it. I lived unconsciously, impulsively. I was dishonest with everyone in my life, starting with myself.

She tortured me, not only by leaving me but by forcing me to see that she had always been a joyful woman, ready to flourish, filled with laughter, sensuality, and the love of life; but that I'd made it impossible for her to be anything other than cold and depleted as long as she lived with me. I wanted her to look at me, consider me. But it was as though she'd already consigned me to the past, as though for her I could no longer exist. She erased me from her consciousness as thoroughly and easily as I had over and over again in our lives erased her.

I felt more pain and despair than I'd known in that chamber in 1982. Then I was at least free to hate the soldiers with all my passion and I could destroy them in my imagination. But now it was Cindy and I loved her. I couldn't imagine destroying her. The damage I'd done to her was real, not imaginary, and had already been done.

I always claimed to love her more than anything else in the world, but I abandoned her at any opportunity to fill up on the admiration of strangers, which was such an inadequate substitute for her love. Then I returned home each night expecting to be taken care of, only to find myself shrinking under Cindy's cold assessing gaze. We fell right back into that pattern in India. I left her at the ashram and led workshops in Mumbai where I was seen, once again, as successful and triumphant, until I traveled back to the ashram where the disappointment on Cindy's face was easy to read: *You? Back already?*

She wanted me to leave her alone. When I wasn't with her, I imagined her in the throes of orgasm in some other man's arms. This was part of Osho's philosophy after all: an end to institutions like marriage, freedom always over love. Cindy was experiencing a sexual and spiritual awakening. The psychologist in me saw it as a mental breakdown. She danced hour after hour, her eyes closed in bliss, oblivious to the world and certainly to me. I was frightened for her, and the more worried I became, the more I blamed myself. I'd made her prison so escape-proof, it was only in the most extreme fashion that she could find a way out.

She tried to explain what she was experiencing. I grew angry, and she gave up in fear and disgust. Later she would say, "We were speaking two different languages. When I knew no Spanish and Hector knew no English, we were able to communicate. But when I tried to talk about spirituality, there was no way to make him understand."

For me, her new language was nothing but psychobabble. She was the one who had called the ashram a Disneyland of spirituality and now she wanted to stay there. I wanted to shake her: "Wake up, goddammit! Disneyland isn't a real place!"

In the free environment of Osho's ashram, beautiful women approached me, offering the solace of their bodies, but I was emasculated. My body, once a source of pleasure, had become only a site of pain. No one could reach me. Like Hernán Darío before me, I took my grief away from the crowd of humanity. I broke down crying in a grove of trees. My brother had told me that trees feel pain at the destruction of their brothers and sisters in forests all over the world and now I confessed to them: *I'm guilty*. I killed the spirit of the most precious flower entrusted to me by life.

"No, the garden is truly inside me," Cindy said. "You start to die as a spirit when you start living for everything outside of you instead of what matters in your heart. There will be so much beauty in my life externally now because, my God, that's how I feel inside. It manifests because you tend the garden inside first. You clear out all the crap."

I was the crap.

CINDY REMAINED IN INDIA. I returned to Pasadena alone. What was I going to tell the children? Their mother was gone and their father was a broken man. And what would our relationship be like without Cindy to mediate it? She was right, I saw that now. I always said my kids were my reason for living, but for the last two years I'd spent too much time away from them. I'd been busy with activism and endless projects and now I realized how much I'd missed. I didn't know what they were thinking or feeling. I didn't even know where in the house Cindy kept their school supplies.

Day after day, I cried for Cindy and all my other losses. Though I'd mourned hard for both my brothers, now the tears came at last. Every morning at 10:30, acid would run through my veins. I would be burning, torn apart, and then realized that, with the time difference, this was exactly the hour when the dancing would end at the ashram and

Cindy would be spending the night in someone else's bed. I was a U.S. citizen by now, but my real home was Cindy. I'd made a woman my country. My rootedness in this world was through my marriage and now all identity dissolved again. I wasn't pulled up by the roots; rather the earth beneath me opened and refused to hold me.

People had always seen me as strong and courageous. I hadn't been in LA for very long when a new friend said, "You don't seem to fear anything." But I was afraid of the inner wilderness, of being abandoned, of being alone. I'd always relied on others to prop me up, to take care of me, to define my identity for me. Now there was nothing to hold on to. I tried to grasp my children, but even they couldn't keep me and I feared pulling them down with me in the sickening plunge into nothingness. I'd been in that abyss before, but this time I feared there was no bottom. All the old wounds were reopened. I was in a place where no one cared for me, or even if they did, they couldn't find me or free me. I was abandoned, annihilated.

Cindy's old wounds were reactivated too, she said, old patterns from childhood, from growing up in what she described as a very narrow background and place. She was breaking free of being the perfect little girl, of always doing things the "right" way, the only way. She returned to California briefly to tell the children she was no longer Cindy, she was Shakti. She put on headphones to listen to Indian music and the words of Osho. She closed her eyes and swayed and it was as if the children weren't even there beside her. She told them they could join her in India if they wanted. She knew she was compelled to return within a very short time.

How could she treat our children that way, and how could she do it using words like *compassion* and *love*? The girl who couldn't express anger when she was a child, who couldn't express her anger (which she'd every right to feel) during her unhappy marriage to me, was now too spiritual to admit her long-suppressed rage.

Cindy would eventually return to California and find a way to integrate her awakening with a renewal of her loving maternal commitment to Camilla and Gabo. Even during the worst times, I was amazed that Cindy always spoke of me kindly. Eventually, we'd both appreciate that our fourteen years together had included much growth, shared adventure, real partnership, and joy. Even during the months when I understood our marriage was in trouble, that knowledge was often easy to forget. Maybe I was in denial, but neither of us would now deny that we had days and nights when we were happy together. And if Gabo or Camilla was sick, Cindy and I were absolutely united caring for our child. It took time for me to realize that the accusations we hurled and the explanations we gave each other when our marriage fell apart were only partial truths, the rationalizations and stereotypes people revert to so easily in pain and anger. Today, she is a loving mother and we are once more close friends.

At the time, though—that terrible time in my life—sometimes I hated Cindy and sometimes I hated myself. Either way, it was an impotent anger, one that left me unable to act, but stuck in narcissistic misery. I told myself the greater the capacity for sorrow, the greater the capacity for joy; but I couldn't imagine ever feeling joy again. I couldn't even imagine relief from this all-encompassing pain. Though I continued using art to help others, I didn't apply the lesson to myself. I talked to others about Navajo healing, how a sand painting is created around a sick person while the healer sings the afflicted back to the beginning of their lives and back to the beginning of creation. When you are lost, return to the origins and there you can reignite the potential of life once again. Was there any potential left in me?

I tried to understand that by leaving me, Cindy was giving me a challenge and gift. For the first time in my life, I would have to find my way alone. I would have to stand on my own two feet. At the age of forty-three, maybe it was my time to grow up.

Still, there was nothing in the universe but Hector, and Hector was nothing but his treasured pain. Until Abu Ghraib.

The photographs seared themselves into the nation's consciousness and even penetrated mine. When the images emerged from that hellhole, I felt myself on the verge of going posttraumatic. It came back, the same despair I felt in that chamber. The questions tortured me again: *Where is everybody? How can this be happening? Why don't people care enough to make it stop?* Then Michael Nutkiewicz at Program for Torture Victims suggested I take my personal experience and portray it theatrically at an event to commemorate the United Nations International Day in Support of Victims of Torture. It was Michael who'd once said, "If a survivor cannot rebuild relationships, he is condemned to live alone in the anguish of his inner wilderness." Now I was reminded that I needed to rebuild my connections to others and this could be the way.

Instead of preparing a speech, I asked Enzo Fina to accompany me on the stage, to improvise music while I improvised comments on Abu Ghraib and a reenactment of my own experience. Diane told me later that she and Enzo, both of whom had known me for years, turned to each other after the improvisation with a single question: "Did you ever know that had happened to him?" I'd spoken out about torture so many times, I wasn't even aware of how guarded I'd been about revealing my own experience—how, until Abu Ghraib, I just wasn't ready.

I have always said torture was just one of many things that have happened to me, that it wasn't my identity and didn't define me. But I realized that what I survived *does* give me a special authority. Suddenly, there was meaning in my life again: by revealing my own story, I hoped to mobilize public opinion against these horrific practices. When I stood on stage, improvising scenes from some of the worst moments in my life, for the first time since Cindy left me, I was focused, my mind and heart and body somehow functioning once again in accord.

I'd remained mired in my own anguish. But now, as the audience responded, I realized that as a torture survivor who was also a therapist and actor, I had a unique way of reaching people. This was my gift and I had to reclaim it and use it.

One afternoon I improvised scenes in which I portrayed my mother and also some of the women who had participated in the ritual for Hernán Darío. My friend BJ Dodge, who was directing, asked what it had felt like to take on the personae of women.

"I felt myself slow down," I said.

"And what was that like?"

"I could *feel*," I said. In my own life I came to realize I was always in flight, not staying in one place long enough for anything to penetrate my soul or stick to me. I was always aimed at the next adventure, avoiding the experience of the moment, not allowing anything—even my pain—to affect me. "As a woman," I repeated, "I could feel."

WHEN I PERFORM, someone always asks how it affects me to relive the trauma. The truth is, I'm not sure, though I have many answers. Turning the experience into art, into an aesthetic object, gives me a sense of control and, I hope, creates beauty where once there was only pain. And that very pain becomes a means of mobilizing people to take action against such horrendous practices. Every performance is different as new ideas come to me even as I move and speak. Whether on stage or in daily life, I try to tap the power of improvisation. For me, imagination isn't about creating something from nothing. It's the capacity that moves us forward as we take what we've already known and see it fresh, re-envisioned in new ways. If you can change the script—the one imposed by society or the one that runs in a seemingly endless loop inside your own head—maybe you can change your life.

When I asked Diane to work with me on developing the play, I told her my goals were aesthetic and political, but beyond that, I had to use the theatrical work to heal my wounds so that my children, Gabo and Camilla, would not be further damaged by me. I understood that I myself might be healed only through using my gift. I'd continued to carry a torture chamber around with me; I replicated its conditions over and over. How could I break the cycle? How could I find the key to unlock the chamber door? I used to think I needed to unlock that door in order to get out. Now it occurred to me an open door also serves to invite people in. Torture happens in isolation, in secret. When I bring an audience into the experience with me, not only am I supported by their witnessing, but the space can no longer be a torture chamber. The space itself is transformed.

MANY HEALERS ARE WOUNDED. I recognize that I seek to heal others not only because of the insight and empathy I've gained from my own experiences, but as a way to process my own wounds. In my work, I must stay alert and aware so that the unhealed part of me does no harm. What makes me dangerous? I feel impatient and anxious when working with a person who seems stuck in the role of victim or addicted to the wound. Maybe because I've moved past that, or maybe because I fear I haven't, at times I feel myself ready to erupt.

One day, I showed some middle school kids the documentary *The Ground Truth* about Iraq War soldiers and veterans. At the beginning, the children were taking it in, but then some of the kids pretended to be sleeping and were talking to each other. During the film, when soldiers blew things up and the kids started to cheer, I found myself wanting to vomit all over them, thinking that they were beyond recovery. *I'm done with this work*, I thought. *I don't have one more inch left in me that's willing to come back here and do this.* I even walked out of the room and left them with the case managers.

Outside I crossed paths with other kids in the playground, kids I didn't even know, and I looked at them with the same disdain and anger. *You guys are lost*, I thought. I saw their gestures and smiles and what seemed to me to be their stupid, empty eyes and I had no idea why I was so angry. So I questioned myself: *What is making me feel this way? My fear that I may not be able to reach these kids' hearts? What led me to feel that these kids were beyond redemption?*

For years, I'd worked to fight against our cultural disconnect. I know these kids watch thousands of hours of television in which the actor gets shot and later takes off his shirt and his body is still perfect, and so I've taken kids to the hospital to visit homies who've survived a shooting and I've made the kids look at the horrific wounds and scars. "This is what it looks like when you're shot. This is real." Suddenly, I flashed back to my early days working in this country when I struggled even more with my English. I'd have kids with me, connected, playing games, but always a moment would come when they would just stare back at me because of my English, not understanding and not even wanting to understand. They dismissed me, just like that, and I'd find myself falling again into a void where I was no one and had nowhere to stand and nothing to hold onto.

The other day, in that classroom, when this one kid started laughing and going BOOM BOOM BOOM at the sight of people being blown up, it's as though I was threatened again with annihilation. "This isn't a game," I said. "Look at these weapons, look at those wounds, look at those soldiers," and I felt I was talking to an empty head and a heart that no longer felt anything. I felt that if I'd had a machine gun I could easily have killed them all—in my imagination, of course.

I understood I was capable of causing damage, so I left the room before I could lash out at them. I can understand why some teachers end up putting on armor, but we can't stay in that position. I took care of myself and my emotions, and then I went back: "Listen," I said. "I was very disturbed and I showed it. It seemed like you guys didn't care. Did I read you wrong? Was the film too much so you couldn't handle it? Did I overwhelm you, or is it that you really don't give a damn about these people being killed?" I invited them to talk about it. It had inflamed my wounds to think they didn't care, but I couldn't let them know that, for that moment, I was unable to care about *them*.

When I worked at CENIT, our regular staff meetings gave me a chance to work through my feelings of anger and despair. In California, it seemed I had to deal with the pain and frustration alone. Again and again I found myself asking what good a moment of individual transformation was if a child had to return to the same world of competitive consumerism or the same mean streets. I see the light inside a child and do what I can to encourage and nurture it, but then the child goes back to the same crushing environment, and sooner or later I hear he's in prison, he's killed someone, or been killed.

Aidan and Johnathan were identical twins whose paths kept crossing mine from the time they were in a local elementary school. There were problems at home—an absent father, a mother with health problems. The boys were handsome, very tall and strong, and this made them a target. Gangs tried to recruit them and, failing that, attacked them. They were great kids and I was very concerned about their safety. I tried to talk their mother into moving to a different neighborhood. I brought the boys into my theater company and for three years they were a big hit—singing, dancing, and usually stealing the show.

At age fifteen, though, Johnathan stopped coming around regularly. Aidan talked about becoming a police officer someday, but clammed up about his twin. I was worried and that's when I invited them both to a ceremony in the sweat lodge that a men's group had built in Sierra Madre. Aidan showed up alone. Sitting in the dark with eight men and three other kids, this boy who'd never shown any vulnerability before began to cry. He opened up in a way I'd never seen him do in talk-therapy and his words came uncensored from the heart as he admitted how frightened he was for Johnathan. *What can we do for you? How can we help?* people asked. We knew we might not be able to do anything for his twin, but at least Aidan knew he was supported, that he'd been able to open up his deepest fears in a safe place.

Moments like these offer an opening into the richness of life, but too often, the glimmer of possibility dies. Shortly after the sweatlodge, Aidan was gunned down by the Villa Boys, who'd been looking for Johnathan. Was it mistaken identity or, as often happens, when a gang can't find the person they're looking for, they go after someone who's near and dear? This death came close to breaking my heart.

IN JANUARY 2007, my license to practice psychotherapy expired. For years, I'd intended to take the final licensing exam. It would mean a higher billing rate for my work, and I always needed money, but somehow I kept putting it off. I forgot I was practicing under an intern's license. Just another detail I couldn't be bothered with. No license? I shrugged it off. My academic and professional credentials had been part of my identity for a long time; they had helped lift me out of poverty. But for the last few years I'd grown disenchanted with the mental-health field. I was more interested in facilitating groups and workshops and strengthening community. Still, I never actually decided to stop providing individual psychotherapy. Apparently I'd left it to my unconscious to make the decision for me.

In the pain of the divorce I'd promised myself to start living more consciously, but I was back on my feet, the pain had abated, and clearly I was back to my old tricks. In February, I drove up to Santa Barbara for a performance with Diane and Enzo. Going eighty miles an hour on the freeway, I decided to take off my sweater and it got stuck over my face. I squirmed in the driver's seat pulling at the sweater with both hands as the car drifted into the next lane and, until Diane grabbed the wheel, right at an SUV. Had I always been so reckless? Or was this the survivor of torture and war, once again flirting with death? We continued on our way to Santa Barbara and no one was hurt. Why was Diane so upset with me?

I organized the welcome ritual for my Zimbabwean friend Meluleki and told stories and played my drum and said his name over and over again, each time getting it wrong. What was the matter with me? Intractable narcissism, or had torture affected me the way I've seen it affect others, creating long-term havoc with short-term memory? Perhaps I'd rather have people think me selfish than admit I haven't overcome what was done to me.

I can't blame it all on torture. Wasn't I always impulsive? My feelings of abandonment and need go all the way back to the birth of my brother Ignacio—sibling rivalry taken to an extreme. I sometimes think the guilt I feel at surviving Hernán Darío and Juan Fernando comes from the unconscious wish to get them out of the way so I wouldn't have to share Nidia with them.

Through intuition, I recognize the spirit in people and what they need, but I often can't keep track of simple facts. I make commitments and forget them five minutes later; my solemn word lasts only until my next breath. I say *yes* to everyone and everything, which in practice turns out to be the same as saying *no*. Yet I know I can do better than that: I'm never late for a performance; I never miss a show. I hurl many accusations at myself in my darker moments, and many are hurled at me. Fortunately, they're not the whole truth. And fortunately, though my way of living and doing things gets me into a lot of trouble, it also gets me out of it. So far.

I admit: I'm always working, putting out lots of energy rather than effort. I still spread myself too thin, because I'm so passionate about so many things, though if I really felt passion, would it be so quickly replaced and so thinly spread? Needy? Greedy? I plead guilty. Taking care of Hector? I've been told it takes a village.

I kept saying I wanted an independent life separate from my parents, but they lived with me as I relied on them to cook and clean and care for my kids. I complained I had no real home. Yet I owned a house and paid the bills and as much as I could I avoided sleeping there. I said I wanted roots and a community to belong to, but when I talked about moving to an intentional community made up of people who choose to share their lives based on shared values, I'd quickly add I planned to spend half the year traveling. The community I claimed to want would be a place to leave my kids while I could avoid being a fulltime, true part of anything.

Attending a workshop in Costa Rica, I suddenly feel old. I say I want to become an elder; instead I fall in love with a woman half my age. I say I want a loving, intimate partnership and I have fallen in love with wonderful women who were, yes, partners to me, but a part of me always remained evasive, as though I held myself outside the border of my own life, unable to fully trust or share my full self. I wasn't just unfaithful, but worse: it's as though again and again I replicate the conditions of the torture chamber. But this time I'm dominant, in complete control. I want to have my lover's undivided attention while I show only a part of myself. I play the roles that keep me safe, and the real me—whoever he is—out of reach. No one can really know me or possess me and I remain still, always, lonely.

Bob Brodhead, with whom I developed the therapeutic arts program, is fed up with me. I'm disrespectful of agency rules. What's worse, he says, I win the trust of kids and then disappear. I want to do better than that, but maybe it's what I'm really good at. I show up, I impress and inspire, and then I move on, gone before anyone can see past the performance. I loved creating our program, but once it was in full operation, I couldn't wait to move on. New challenges, new adventures: I plant the seeds but I won't stick around to tend them.

Maybe Gbanabom Hallowell would understand. He's back in Sierra Leone at last, but he doubts he'll ever stay put again in any one place. I read his recent email: "As you very well know, exile has a way of making one a perpetual hunter and gatherer of all global fruits." Yes! Isn't that me?

But everyone's mad at me. Don't they see I'm leading dozens of therapy groups a week, providing financial support to an extended family in Colombia and asylum-seekers in the U.S.? Don't they understand I'm burning out, that my life is now as impossible and self-destructive as it was when I fled Medellín? Don't they see how much I want to live in accord with my words, hoping that someday it will be possible?

TODAY, MY PARENTS are back Medellín, living in their own place near Ignacio. I sold the house in Pasadena. Freed from the mortgage and with the equity as a cushion, I took time to think about what I want to do, how I want to live. I've stopped practicing psychotherapy. Inspired by the public health model I learned from Héctor Abad Gómez, I want to see communities and not just individuals grow healthier. With my new non-profit, ImaginAction, and my partner Vivien Sansour, I've been taking my arts-based therapeutic model around the country and the world to train community workers in the techniques. I may move on, but the people I train will stay. I still hear the accusation inside my head, *You start things and don't finish them*, but every now and then I revisit a city or a grassroots organization and someone thanks me: *Look, the seed you planted has grown into a tree.* I think of my kindergarten teacher, the wonderful Doña Lucila, who encouraged me to sing and dance and never knew she'd planted the seed that would grow me into my life.

When I turned forty-nine, Cindy threw a party for me—at Cindy's house, and for the first time I allowed friends to gather around me and I celebrated my life with them instead of feeling I should apologize for still being alive. Vivien has helped me see that my brother Ignacio is a good and loving man, happy with the choices he's made, though these are different from the choices I would have made for him and that I tried to impose on him.

Step by small step, I'm becoming more like the person I want to be, though more often than not, I still go wrong. I'm still trying to find my own style of living and working and loving, and hoping to do it with some beauty and grace. Accepting myself as a whole person with my many limitations as well as my gifts, my challenge is to find how best I can contribute to the weaving of life.

So I dance and I stumble; but there's no such thing as a bad dance. The only thing that's bad is not to dance at all.

Afterword

FOR YEARS, I'VE PARTICIPATED in a solemn ritual just outside the gates of the School of the Americas at Fort Benning, Georgia, drawn there by a Maryknoll priest, Father Roy Bourgeois.

Father Roy entered the priesthood after his military service in Vietnam led to a crisis of conscience. The Catholic Church then sent him to El Salvador and Bolivia, where he witnessed poverty and government repression firsthand and was himself detained and interrogated. One summer night in 1983, he and a few friends trespassed onto the grounds of Fort Benning and he climbed a tree just outside the barracks which housed soldiers from El Salvador.

Father Roy set up a portable stereo and waited for lights out. Suddenly the nighttime quiet was broken by the recorded voice of El Salvador's Archbishop Oscar Romero: *When you hear the words of a man telling you to kill, think instead of the words of God. Thou shalt not kill! No soldier is obliged to obey an order contrary to the Law of God. In His Name and in the name of our tormented people who have suffered so much, and whose laments cry out to heaven: I implore you! I beg you! I order you! Stop the repression!*

Father Roy was at Fort Benning because graduates of the School included the men found responsible for crimes in El Salvador: the murders of six Jesuit priests, their housekeeper and her daughter, three American nuns and a lay missionary, as well as the massacre of 900 civilians in the village of El Mozote, and the assassination of Archbishop Romero himself, shot down in the very act of celebrating mass. Men guilty of atrocities all over Latin America have not only graduated from the School, but have been invited back as instructors. The leaders of the June 2009 military coup in Honduras were trained there.

Father Roy was arrested for his act of civil disobedience. Judge Robert Elliott (known for overturning the conviction of Lt. William Calley who was found guilty of the massacre of hundreds of women, children, babies, and elderly Vietnamese at My Lai), sent Father Roy to federal prison for fifteen months. Upon his release, Father Roy returned to Fort Benning and rented an apartment. In 1990, about a dozen people joined him for a vigil after he created School of the Americas Watch to educate the public and to lobby Congress to shut down the school under any name. He would go to prison again and again in his ongoing campaign.

Sixteen years after that first small vigil, Diane, Enzo, Carmen García, and I joined college students, parents with infants, a group called One Thousand Grandmothers, anarchists, nuns, puppeteers, percussionists, activists, and torture survivors—22,000 people in all—at Fort Benning, to demand the closure of the school. All week in Columbus, Georgia, we've taken over the Convention Center for speeches and discussions. Outdoors, at the fence that separates us from the army base, the wire is being covered and filled in with flowers, crosses, banners, and names of the dead. The Puppetistas—dozens of protestors who've created giant papier-mâché figures as well as cardboard bad guys mounted on sticks—are rehearsing. Dozens of newly minted percussionists are learning how to play samba-reggae rhythms on empty buckets and garbage pails. A group called "Living the Dream" in honor of Dr. Martin Luther King is here after a weeklong march from Selma, Alabama. In the center of the road, people create silent memorials with their bodies, more and more people lower themselves to the cold ground and lie motionless amid scattered clothing bearing the names of massacre victims. Inspired by the anonymous man in front of the White House, Diane, Enzo, and Carmen wear orange jumpsuits and black hoods, but are threatened with arrest unless the hoods come off. It's illegal here to mask in public, a law that was enacted to prevent the Ku Klux Klan from terrorizing people with impunity, but the police are ready to enforce it against protestors.

Near the fence, a loudspeaker repeats the warning: *If you enter this installation, you will be in violation of Title 18 United States code section 1382 and subject to fine and imprisonment.* A grandmother climbs over the fence and is charged with "unlawful entry." A college student, a sixty-nine-year-old pastor, an artist, a sixty-four-year-old homemaker, a stay-at-home mom, a retired school superintendant, a seventy-one-year-old nun: in all, sixteen people are taken into custody.

SUNDAY MORNING: THIS IS why people return to the Fort Benning vigil year after year, for a protest action that is also a profoundly spiritual experience.

I stand on the outdoor stage along with other survivors. We each give a brief testimony. There's Maria Guardado, who was a middle-aged woman in El Salvador, raising the children orphaned by her sister's death, and working with labor unions in support of striking teachers when she was abducted from an ice-cream parlor by fifteen men with machine guns. They stripped her naked and raped her. *Me tenían atada y bendada. Me quemaron que después de 26 años todavía tengo señas de las quemadas.* She tells of being burned, beaten, kicked about like a soccer ball, and jumped on until her bones broke. She's in her sixties now and frail, but I see Maria Guardado at every demonstration. One way or another, she manages to get there. She has told me her captors threw her from a car after Archbishop Romero, in a homily broadcast to the whole nation, denounced her disappearance.

Adriana Portillo Bartow tells how the Guatemalan security forces detained six members of her family. *That day they took my father, they took my stepmother, they took my little sister—my eighteen-months-old little sister, one of my sisters-in-law, and my two oldest daughters who were ten and nine at the moment of their disappearance. I never saw them or heard from them ever again.*

Patricia Isasa speaks. She was only sixteen when she was arrested in Argentina in 1976, imprisoned and tortured for two and a half years without ever being charged with a crime. Following her release, she sought justice. Now almost thirty years later, her torturers have been jailed.

After each survivor bears witness, thousands of voices rise in song: *No más. No more. We must stop the dirty war. Compañeros, compañeras we cry. No más. No more.*

When Carlos Mauricio speaks, I don't listen. Today, I can't afford to be thrown back into that dungeon. Instead, I think about how exactly one month ago former Salvadoran army officer Gonzalo Guevara Cerritos, one of those responsible for the Jesuit murders, was found living in LA under an assumed name. He was arrested and will finally face justice.

No más. No more. We must stop the dirty war. . . .

Of course the real problem is U.S. foreign policy, not merely the brutal techniques taught here. Our protest is symbolic, but it's a symbol with profound meaning. Those of us who escaped to the U.S., even while knowing this country was complicit in what we suffered, heal when we are among thousands of U.S. citizens standing and crying with us, in a single voice, *No más. No more.*

One long street has been closed to traffic to accommodate us. We stretch from a shopping mall with its parking lot, now overflowing with our vehicles, all the way to the triple-fenced-off base. Just as we've done every day, we commit ourselves to nonviolence. Then the solemn procession begins. From the stage, a voice sings out a requiem. *Oscar Romero.* His name floats out over the hush, over our pulses and our breathing, and 22,000 people raise crosses and flowers and respond that he is with us in spirit: *¡Presente!*

The names of the dead continue, along with the response. Some names are well known. Everyone recognizes them. We honor the murdered churchwomen: Maura Clark *¡Presente!* Jean Donovan. *¡Presente!* Ita Ford *¡Presente!* Dorothy Kazel *¡Presente!* The names of the hundreds massacred at El Mozote: *José Francisco Reyes Luna, cinco años de edad*, intones the singer. Five years old. *¡Presente!* Vicenta Márquez, eighty years old, widow. *¡Presente!*

We move slowly in procession. In the crowd, a sprinkling of Jewish stars among the sea of crosses, *presente* but hardly enough to recognize all the members of the Jewish community targeted by the military dictatorship of Argentina. Every death we know of is commemorated: María Isabel Amaya Claros, eight months old, daughter of Domingo Claros. *¡Presente!* And we commemorate those who died leaving bodies without a name: *Niño desconocido. ¡Presente!*

Luis Eduardo López. María Ramírez González. For more than two hours, the names are sung and we call them back, present and remembered.

Juan Fernando Aristizábal. *¡Presente!*

I'VE BEEN PART OF this ritual many times. I'm always moved, but each year I'm left with the feeling that the rite is incomplete. If we don't return to life after mourning, we betray the dead because only the living can remember them. I don't want the thousands of people who've stood together in friendship and solidarity to leave this place cast down by grief and guilt. We need to celebrate life, to remember why our lives and the lives of those we've lost truly matter. When I talk to Father Roy, he agrees. So I'm hoping I can make this year different.

The percussionists march and play a dirge. Shrouded mourners move forward, their faces painted an eerie white. The Puppetistas perform street theater. When they draw near the stage, I tell a story inspired by Apache tradition. I tell how long ago in the world, some people began falling sick. Some people began to get into trouble. So the One who created the world said, *Listen! The things of the world can make you sick, but they can also heal you.* But the people still didn't do anything because they didn't know what to do. Finally, it happened that, one day, one thousand grandmothers gathered at a place called Fort Benning. I tell how they built altars in the four directions and they began singing and drumming and dancing. And the one who created the world said, *Go to those that are sick. Go to those who have forgotten who they are. Go to those who feel that life is about destruction. Go to those and heal them with your dancing and your praying and your beauty and your creativity!* And then they sang: *¡Presente!*

Now I'm walking on stilts, playing my djembe drum. The Puppetistas return down the road, but this time they are dancing. The percussionists dance with their shakers and homemade drums as they bring the world alive with the samba-reggae beat, but I still don't know if what I've imagined will work.

Then high above the crowd on my stilts, I see it happen: a celebration of music and flowers, a return to life and renewal and hope. Twenty thousand people are dancing.

Acknowledgments

PROFOUND GRATITUDE TO MICHAEL Meade and to all the people whose experiences and whose contributions to us and to the world are mentioned in these pages.

Special thanks to:

Ramaa Bharadvaj, Brian Biery, Sarah Bloom, Patrick Bonner, Blase Bonpane, John Calvi, Lynn Clark, Ayelet Cohen, David Cohen, Jeannine Davies, Frank Dorrel, Jory Farr, Gerald Fitzgerald, Wendy Goldsmith, Ellen Kamelson, Mona LaVine, Eisha Mason, Deena Metzger and Michael Ortiz Hill, John Meyer, Cole Miller, Maziar Senehi, Teya Sepinuck, Cara Trezise, Hendrik Voss, John Wayne, Ph.D., and Jennie Webb.

Sy Safransky and Andrew Snee at *The Sun* for publishing, "The Blessing Is Next to the Wound: A Conversation with Hector Aristizábal on Torture and Transformation" and to Jacqueline Johnson who, after reading it, suggested we might have a book.

Nick T. Spark for his extraordinary photo collage. (See more of his work at www.eyeballoverload.com).

Michael Murphy and REDCAT for providing the initial support that got "Nightwind" off the ground.

Filmmakers Kathy Berger and Ines Sommer for *Beneath the Blindfold* (www.beneaththeblindfold.org), their documentary about life after torture.

Marc Pilisuk, Michael N. Nagler, and their entire team for including an excerpt in *Peace Movements Worldwide: History, Psychology, and Practices*, published by Greenwood/Praeger.

Jeremy Shiok and *Two Review* for publishing an excerpt.

Dick Price and Sharon Kyle of *LA Progressive* for publishing Diane's articles about some of the issues we raise in this book.

Robert Bly for "Throw Yourself Like Seed," his translation of Miguel de Unamuno's "¡Siémbrate!"

Gbanabom "Elvis" Hallowell for his lecture, *"The Claustrophobia of Exile: African Poets Writing in the 'Wasteland,'"* at Vermont College of Fine Arts, printed in *AWP Chronicle*.

Amos Oz for *How to Cure a Fanatic*, Princeton University Press.

Claude Anshin Thomas for *At Hell's Gate: A Soldier's Journey from War to Peace*, Shambhala Publications.

Most of all, Gene Gollogly, Kara Davis, and Martin Rowe at Lantern Books for believing in our work—on and off the page.

About the Authors

HECTOR ARISTIZÁBAL was born and raised in Medellín, Colombia when it was the most dangerous city in the world. One of his brothers was seduced by the power of crack cocaine and another by the promises of revolutionary armed struggle. Hector's path was different. He worked his way out of poverty to become a theatre artist and pioneering psychologist with a Masters degree from Antioquia University, then survived civil war, arrest, and torture at the hands of the US-supported military. In 1989, violence and death threats forced him to leave his homeland. Since arriving in the US, he has won acclaim and awards as an artist and also received a second Masters degree, in Marriage and Family Therapy from Pacific Oaks College, leading him to combine his training in psychology and the arts with lessons gained from life experience in his therapeutic work. As an activist, he uses theatrical performance as part of the movement to end torture and to change US policy in Latin America. His nonprofit organization, ImaginAction, taps the power of creativity in social justice programs throughout the US and around the world as far afield as Afghanistan, India, and Palestine for community building and reconciliation, strategizing, and individual healing and liberation.

DIANE LEFER is an author, playwright, and activist whose most recent short-story collection, *California Transit*, was awarded the Mary McCarthy Prize in Short Fiction and published by Sarabande Books. She is also the author of two other collections— *Very Much Like Desire* and *The Circles I Move In*, as well as the novel, *Radiant Hunger*. Her fiction has been recognized by the National Endowment for the Arts, the  New York Foundation for the Arts, the City of Los Angeles, and the Library of Congress. For 23 years she taught in the MFA in Writing Program at Vermont College of Fine Arts and has been a guest artist at colleges, writing conferences and festivals. She has facilitated creative workshops for high school students, adjudicated youth in lockup and on probation, and children in the foster-care system. Diane's ongoing collaboration with Hector Aristizábal includes work for the stage and for the page, and social-justice action workshops. She is a frequent contributor of articles to *LA Progressive*.